Designing the
Domestic Posthuman

Designing the Domestic Posthuman

Colbey Emmerson Reid and Dennis M. Weiss

BLOOMSBURY VISUAL ARTS

LONDON · NEW YORK · OXFORD · NEW DELHI · SYDNEY

BLOOMSBURY VISUAL ARTS
Bloomsbury Publishing Plc
50 Bedford Square, London, WC1B 3DP, UK
1385 Broadway, New York, NY 10018, USA
29 Earlsfort Terrace, Dublin 2, Ireland

BLOOMSBURY, BLOOMSBURY VISUAL ARTS and the Diana logo are trademarks of
Bloomsbury Publishing Plc

First published in Great Britain 2024

Copyright © Colbey Emmerson Reid and Dennis M. Weiss, 2024

Colbey Emmerson Reid and Dennis M. Weiss have asserted their right under the
Copyright, Designs and Patents Act, 1988, to be identified as Authors of this work.

For legal purposes the Acknowledgments on p. vii constitute an extension
of this copyright page.

Cover design by Louise Dugdale
Cover images: top, Olga Rai/Adobe Stock, bottom, artkozyr/Adobe Stock

All rights reserved. No part of this publication may be reproduced or transmitted
in any form or by any means, electronic or mechanical, including photocopying, recording,
or any information storage or retrieval system, without prior permission in writing
from the publishers.

Bloomsbury Publishing Plc does not have any control over, or responsibility for, any third-
party websites referred to or in this book. All internet addresses given in this book were
correct at the time of going to press. The author and publisher regret any inconvenience
caused if addresses have changed or sites have ceased to exist, but can accept
no responsibility for any such changes.

A catalogue record for this book is available from the British Library.

A catalog record for this book is available from the Library of Congress.

ISBN: HB: 978-1-3503-0120-7
ePDF: 978-1-3503-0122-1
eBook: 978-1-3503-0121-4

Typeset by Deanta Global Publishing Services, Chennai, India
Printed and bound in Great Britain

To find out more about our authors and books visit www.bloomsbury.com and
sign up for our newsletters.

Contents

List of Figures vi
Acknowledgments vii

Introduction: Designing the Domestic Posthuman 1

Part One Posthuman Persons

1 Posthuman Parturition: An Origin Story 19

2 Domestic Posthuman Second Persons 43

3 Myths of Domestic Posthuman Second Persons 71

Part Two Posthuman Artifacts

4 Softwear 93

5 (Un)homely *Techne* 119

6 Myths of Domestic Posthuman Artifacts 137

Conclusion: A Design Sampler for the Domestic
Posthuman 161

References 177
Index 189

Figures

1   Exterior view of *Eliza's Peculiar Cabinet of Curiosities* 12
2   Interior view of *Eliza's Peculiar Cabinet of Curiosities* 40
3   Boxing gloves, *Eliza's Peculiar Cabinet of Curiosities* 68
4   Botanicals, *Eliza's Peculiar Cabinet of Curiosities* 76
5   Princess Leia, *Eliza's Peculiar Cabinet of Curiosities* 88
6   Button, *Eliza's Peculiar Cabinet of Curiosities* 116
7   Dolls, *Eliza's Peculiar Cabinet of Curiosities* 134
8   Handwarmer, *Eliza's Peculiar Cabinet of Curiosities* 152
9   C-3PO, *Eliza's Peculiar Cabinet of Curiosities* 158
10 Quilt, *Eliza's Peculiar Cabinet of Curiosities* 174

Acknowledgments

Designing the Domestic Posthuman aims to articulate a new brand of posthuman assemblages defined by networks of care and connection. The book itself is a product of just such an assemblage, made possible by networks of care and connection enabled by a panoply of posthuman technologies, including FaceTime, Zoom, texting, email, Google Docs, and yes, even good old-fashioned conference travel. We're grateful for having shared adjoining offices for a too brief time more than fifteen years ago where we could connect over a shared love of television, including enthusiasm for a certain vampire slayer that began a winding series of collaborations that led to rethinking posthumanism from the vantage point of its neglected intersection with the home, homelike places, and home things. We're grateful, too, for having spouses that are generous in their attentive care and connection and who create homeplaces that are convivial and conducive for getting work done, among other things of course. We'd also like to recognize and thank artist and Afrofuturist creative designer Folayemi Wilson for being a generous spirit and sharing with us her thoughts and images from her project *Eliza's Peculiar Cabinet of Curiosities*, which serves as a throughline in this text for one variation on the domestic posthuman. We are both fortunate to work at institutions that continue to support scholarly projects and both of us have benefited from grants and release time as we labored on this project. We owe thanks to Columbia College Chicago and York College of Pennsylvania for their generous support. We'd also like to thank the supportive people at Bloomsbury Publishing, especially Olivia Davies and Hattie Morrison, for helping guide this project to fruition and three anonymous reviewers who helped us craft a richer account of domestic posthumans.

Introduction

Designing the Domestic Posthuman

This is the quantum leap of the radical feminist vision.

—ADRIENNE RICH

Home is the place where humans first cultivate our humanity in an extended embodied dialogue with our caretakers and personal belongings. Yet home and care have largely been passed over in discussions of human futures and the mediating technologies expected to catalyze them. When we look to the artifacts that will bring about our "quantum leap" into the next evolutionary incarnation of the human we tend to look to silicon, chemicals, and algorithms as the tools of our transformation: computer hardware and software to alter and expand us, pharmacological innovations that heal us, algorithmic intelligence to accelerate and replicate us. These are made and used in labs and institutions by programmers and engineers employing scientific methods and mathematical formulae. The "leaps" that they engender happen in an instant with the push of a button or swallowing of a pill. The sites of investigation are rarely domestic ones. And the future humans in question usually are or imitate Enlightenment-inspired fantasies of rational, white, Western masculinity. While they are occasionally women and sometimes culturally diverse, they are almost never mothers, infants, children, disabled, or old.

The digital technologies flourishing in laboratories, offices, cities, and marketplaces have commanded the primary attention of philosophers and scientists of technology since the 1990s. The heretofore barely imagined prospects and alien possibilities suggested by these ever-emerging tools are, as many have acknowledged, exhilarating to contemplate. They suggest that infinite strangeness and a version of being human that now looks completely outside the box await us in the not-so-distant future, and the philosophers and practitioners of this domain are already eager to get to know this heroically bold and dramatic version of the future. But a range of domestic materials and practices are equally rich in opportunities for exploring human hybridizations and augmentations, and the grand futures forecast by labs are frequently already being embodied, albeit more humbly, at home. Perhaps we tend to miss them because they're in the "wrong" place, are soft to the touch, engage our emotions, live among a cacophony of contexts and relationships, and are—until we look more closely— cozy and familiar, and cluttered with networks less resembling of wires and code than relationships, feelings, and stories. Tapestries, for instance, have decorated the globe-wide homes of ancients and were used for everything from teaching to entertaining, warming the young and enshrouding the dead, telling a story, and ensconcing the teller in the act of telling it. They were made using needlepoint or looms and primarily by women, encouraged the form of discourse that women exchange when their hands are busy, could be passed among generations and through dowries between households, and so knit families, communities, and generations together both through the embodied practices of making, giving, wearing, and displaying them as well as through the mythical function of the religious and cultural stories told within humans threads. They are soft, silicon-free, and sentiment-full. But as tools for human networking that surpass human-to-human relationships and aim to depict humans interweaving with objects, nature, animals, and even the gods in everyday living, tapestries are *techne* of the extra-human, meaning "more than," but also "very," in ways that circumvent and deprioritize conventional constructions of the term.

"Posthuman" has become a common way of designating nascent hybridized or entirely digitally generated human-machine amalgams that may also be the destiny of the human as it evolves in the era of the technological mediation of almost everything. Posthumans entwine their native organic components with biotechnical materials and cybernetic processes—or are entirely biotechnically or cybernetically generated. The term captures the sense of something external to us that also is the future and destiny of us and so might be at the same time intrinsic to us, and its designated subjectivities and embodiments have excited scholars and scientists who find evidence of an ontological strangeness that might also be our future in contemporary technologies like video games, smart devices, traffic algorithms, pharmaceuticals, electricity, trash, and a host of new media forms. It's alluring to think of "getting out of some of the old boxes and opening up new ways of thinking about what being human means" (Hayles, 1999: 285), and these eerie and alien forms offer the refreshment of an escape from what can be the crushing burden of our seemingly endless and endlessly frail humanity. The idea of a domestic posthuman grates against the escapist pleasure of the posthuman, by setting up so banal a space as the home as the habitat of a new humanity. Even the idea of giving the posthuman, so often configured as transcendent of place, something so primitive and ecological-sounding as a habitat rubs a little the wrong way. Posthumanism is meant to overcome the backward-feeling and -sounding animal nature of the human by merging with the fresh promises embedded in emerging technology. A domestic posthuman looks at first, on the other hand, like something we have already known and experienced. It does not appear, initially, to offer the adventure of exploration or the disruption of innovation. It appears to be continuous with the same-old humanity we grew up with. Can continuity ever provide the exhilarating "quantum leap" inventors of the posthuman are looking for? We believe that it can. But if it is to do so, it will require rethinking what innovation looks like in order to find more mind- and world-altering creativity in connection-making, caretaking, and the act of mending than most Western myths have primed us to see.

Exploring the neglected intersection of the posthuman with the home invites us to pay attention to a range of critically overlooked mediated materialisms and embodiments affiliated with home, an aboriginal human space and one in which there may be more estranged ontologies to get to know than acknowledged by posthumanism, which throughout this text is broadly defined as the postmodern philosophical strain in which conversations about humans' using and fusing with technology primarily take place. In doing so, one must confront the question of whether the real peculiarity of humanity has been sufficiently considered or experienced to be discarded yet. Might there be a quality of the posthuman already within the human, an as-yet-unknown embedded homunculus, whom we can get to know now with the help of ways of thinking and seeing that posthumanism lends us? In this project, we try to get to know the peculiarity embedded in the domestic posthuman, through what Lorraine Code calls a "dialogue with a residual humanistic subjectivity . . . that would be largely unrecognizable to its humanist ancestors" (1991: 82). What, we want to know, are the properties and propensities of this unrecognizable humanistic subjectivity? Is subjectivity as the term has conventionally been treated the right word for it? What aspects of the human have scholars and researchers forgotten to look more deeply into before deciding it was already time to discard them? In this book, what we see when we look at the human with posthuman eyes is something cyborg-strange but also family-familiar. To paraphrase the riddle: if the domestic posthuman is talking to you while sitting in an armchair in your living room and you don't hear it because you can't see it, was it really there? And when its algorithm-engineered double turns up later to finish the conversation, is it just another knockoff or another entity entirely than its humbler, more homespun twin?

In addition to recovering the "subjectivities" (we give them another name, discussed later) and objects affiliated with the overlooked and understudied entity of the domestic posthuman, we also want to understand why they first went missing. What are the reasons and ramifications of the dismissal of domestic subjects and objects among philosophers of technology? How would their inclusion in discussions of technological mediations redefine key components and assumptions in posthumanism? And moreover, and most importantly, how will theorizing another kind of posthuman, a domestic posthuman, change the way we think about and practice posthuman design in the future? We consider "posthuman design" to be future-making that looks to technology as a key mediator and catalyst for what's next. And we find that the domestic posthuman of the future will be made much like the domestic posthumans of the past, which we do believe to exist, and so less by engineers, or engineers in isolation, than by engineers supported or even supplanted by storytellers, caretakers, mythmakers, and other practitioners of the imagination who understand *what it means to be human* not merely as a categorical, technocratic kind of question but rather as a matter of deciphering and experimenting with "the arts of personhood." This is Annette Baier's (1985: 84) evocative phrase for the twenty-year-long, error-ridden, excruciatingly laborious, mother- and teacher-led, care-full, sentiment-rich, hyper-networked, culture(s)-fluent, highly iterative process that it takes to make a half-way-decent, marginally useful person out of the bundle of human-classified organs, flesh, sinews and synapses that members of our species start out as.

Designing the Domestic Posthuman thus becomes not only an uncovering and recovery but a design logic for an alternate approach to questions that have dominated the sphere of technological conversations and discoveries in recent years, questions about how to design truly intelligent artificial intelligence; how to create, cure, and prolong life; how to coexist with other human and nonhuman entities in and outside our planetary and galactic contexts; how to get what we all need to live on out of the world without obliterating it. Rather than the usual answers centered on coding optimization, political and economic structures, or legislative reform we take a grassroots approach and look instead at specific care practices, relational strategies, interface organs, revisionist myths, and connection-affects as extraordinary *techne* of (both the past and) the future. At the center of this alternate approach, which assumes a relational self in dialogue with a host of human and nonhuman others, is a different cast of characters and typologies than the adult, able-bodied scientists, doctors, engineers, and coders that have been at the crux of the other version of the ultimately extractive, often annihilating, not infrequently military-industrially originated thing that has been passing so far for future-making. The domestic posthuman is embodied by grandmothers, infants, children, and pets; cared, imagined, and iterated into maturity; is as likely to materialize in the kitchen, around the hearth, or in a closet or *chiffonier* as a computer or hospital laboratory. Achille Mbembe refers to these alternatives to globalization, neoliberal capitalism, colonialism, and technological expansionism as the "micro-movements and micro-postures" (2019: 160) of vulnerability and hospitality in the relation of care. The new humanity built by them is, in Mbembe's account, "a primitive situation that every human has previously experienced: the return to a state of absolute vulnerability, the child-mother relationship, hygiene needs, the suckling infant, one's first words, first faces, first names, first steps, and first objects" (2019: 177). These are not held up as retreats from the future but as materials for building what Arturo Escobar, quoting Tony Fry, calls "a future with a future" (2018: 207).

Back in 1978 the poet Adrienne Rich, concerned with the prospectus of the imagination in creating a feminist society, asked a question aligned with Mbembe, Escobar, and Fry's ways of thinking: what it would be like to conceptually reposition mothers and mothering at the center of society instead of on its margins—an imaginative act already plausibly true from the experiential viewpoint of some humans (e.g., children). She called her thought experiment "the quantum leap of the radical feminist vision" (1979: 273), aligning futurity, innovation, electric transformation, and the crux of feminist thought with a relatively homely act and figure typically positioned as anathema to all these things: a mother. "Motherhood: The Contemporary Emergency and the Quantum Leap" was presented at the Women's Resource and Policy Development Center Conference on The Future of Mothering in Columbus, Ohio, in 1978, and remains timely for those of us living and writing and designing in the United States in 2023. Rich's "contemporary emergency" refers to an assault on women's bodies, limitations on women's access to abortion, punitive policing of gender roles, and the corporate exploitation of women in underdeveloped countries—all matters still roiling US society and global politics today. Her address also presciently decries the invisibility of women's work to the technocratic elite of the time. Rich argues that women's work in the home is largely invisible to "the statisticians, the political scientists, the economists, the image-makers of television and other advertising, the professionals, who depict the woman at home as 'not working,' as invisible, as an empty-headed consumer." Women's work has been dismissed as mere "decoration" or "craft" or "scribbling." And she adds:

> feminist artists, historians, anthropologists have been the first to show concern and respect for the crafts of the midwives and grandmothers, the anonymous work of women's hands, the oral culture of women sitting in kitchens, the traditional arts and remedies passed on from mother to daughter, the female culture never granted the reverence accorded to "high art."

Rich asks us to look with fresh eyes on all that has been trivialized, devalued, forbidden, or silenced in female history. Building on the lived experiences, situated knowledges, and embodied practices of diverse women, she calls for us to discover and create "conditions which would make life more livable for the living."

Designing the Domestic Posthuman takes up where Rich left off, by taking seriously the question of what we mean when we talk, in English, about the "mother of inventions" and wondering what has been and still can be cared into changing who and what it means to be human. Paradoxically, the end game of a domestic posthuman is to circumvent nativist, divisive constructions of the human to explore a planetary version of the species, one attained not through cosmopolitanism, a notion predicated on impersonal relations among non-citizens in public spaces, but hospitality, a relationality of protective intimacy extended even to strangers. The pursuit of a hospitably planetary humanity brings new caretaking figures into the foreground of posthumanity: mothers, certainly—though we turn primarily to the figure of a trans-grandmother; but also teachers, makers, and other kinds of healers.

With Rich, we revisit the traces and so the origins of an alternative future in figures associated with bygone cultural forms that were discarded by humanism too soon, before they could be fully explored for their own exhilarating, outside the box potential. In this book, we hope to make some room for it. This is work aligned with contemporary design discourse but with a difference. Indeed, Rich's imaginative vision predicated on the lives of diverse women and their experiences presciently anticipates Arturo Escobar's account of a pluriversal imagination in *Designs for the Pluriverse* and his championing of a matristic, convivial, futuring, relational vision (Escobar, 2018: 7). Rich, and our conceptual framework for the domestic posthuman, finds common ground in Escobar's point that "reimagining the human needs to go beyond the deconstruction of humanism (still the focus of most posthumanist thought) in order to contemplate effective possibilities for the human as a crucial political project for the present" (2018: 21). Where Escobar turns largely to indigenous communities of the Global South to contest mainstream Euro-Latin modern ontology, Rich and the domestic posthuman focus on the still invisible lives and practices of children, mothers and othermothers, alloparents, and the neglected arts of personhood taking place in the home.

While *Designing the Domestic Posthuman* is not a design manual or manifesto, we do see it as in dialogue with and consistent with recent efforts to reconceptualize the discipline of design and make visible what has been obscured (see, for instance, Fry, 2012; Escobar, 2018; Wakkary, 2021), though our efforts are guided by the need to think differently about human-material assemblages, consistent with Rich's qualitative leap of the imagination, asking just what humans we are referring to and what kind of materialities we ought to attend to. More significantly, we don't seek to decenter the human, as Ron Wakkary does,[1] nor to offer a grand theory of design in the vein of Escobar (2018: 138), Manzini (2015: 2), or Fry (2020:148), all of whom speak of designing for civilizational, paradigmatic, and epochal transition. The domestic posthuman takes inspiration from the motto of the Craftivist Collective: "changing our world one stitch at a time." Emphasizing the world of gentle protest, the Collective highlights the need for a diverse design toolkit: "If there's time for the loud, there's also time for the quiet. If there's time for the fast, there's also a need for the slow. In everyone's heart is a desire to change things for the better—it is essential that there is an activist toolkit that is as diverse as humanity" (Craftivist, n.d.).[2] The theme of a diverse design toolkit is carried throughout *Designing the Domestic Posthuman* as we seek to attend to and recenter design on more capacious accounts of design practices (including crafting practices, which often receive little attention in design theories), humans (including babies and infants, disabled, and elderly people, still largely marginalized in accounts of design), and material culture (including what we later refer to as the softwear that is still often overlooked in design theories that highlight large-scale public hardware and infrastructure at the expense of domestic soft materialities).

Designing the Domestic Posthuman is divided into two parts that mirror the focus on human-material relations central to discussions of posthumanism and design. Part One is concerned with expanding the notion of the human with a more capacious account of domestic posthuman second persons, while Part Two expands notions of the kinds of artifacts and relations that are central to defining the domestic posthuman. We bring these two conceptual sides of human-technology relations together in our conclusion, where we articulate guidelines for a design practice oriented toward domestic posthuman second persons. A key assertion of this project is the need for alternative readings of the posthuman that complicate its origin stories and emphasize different standpoints from which to assess people, places, and products in a posthuman design framework. While we engage with many theorists and philosophers, we intend *Designing the Domestic Posthuman* to be ecumenical in its own theoretical and philosophical orientations, and—to employ a term we return regularly to—messy in its entanglements with diverse disciplinary interests. Thus we move back and forth between the high theory of malestream posthumanism (with its regular evocations of Derrida, Deleuze, Latour—as well as parallel invocations in the world of design theory to Fry, Escobar, Wakkary) to the low theory of television, toilets, and the cats and baby bumps of Instagram. As Margaret Gibson observes in introducing the anthology *Queering Motherhood: Narrative and Theoretical Perspectives*, motherhood and, we would add, the entire domestic realm, flies below the radar of academic and theoretical seriousness. "In taking motherhood seriously, scholars of mothering and motherhood have already challenged the very divisions between 'high theory,' 'low theory,' and real life" (2014: 9). She notes as well that scholars of mothering have drawn upon the popular, the silly, the mundane, even the stupid, as well as stretched what constitutes academic writing (2014: 10). We intend to do the same.[3]

Part One of *Designing the Domestic Posthuman* opens with a critical overview of the posthuman, identifying significant lacunae in how it is often theorized and tracing these lacunae back to its origin story. While there are a variety of posthumanisms, those of all stripes often begin in relation to several key assumptions, including a reaction to Cartesian liberal humanism, the sense that human-technology relations are moving us into a distinct posthuman age, and a recognition of the foundational role of the technosciences in radically rewriting human ontology. While predicated on dismantling boundaries between the human and alien others (technology, animals, the material world), theorizing the posthuman has itself been implicated in a series of dichotomies between the human and the posthuman and between some presumed boundaries dividing "high" digital technologies from more "lowly" analogue technologies that have largely been sidelined in discussions of the posthuman. The origin story of the posthuman is too often steeped in the digital technologies and networked systems that have become a commonplace in twenty-first-century Western lives. Chapter 1, "Posthuman Parturition: An Origin Story," seeks to complicate this origin story, recognizing a need to bring women, children, and human life history into the story of the posthuman.

Chapter 2, "Domestic Posthuman Second Persons," begins the work of revising the posthuman narrative and developing an account of posthuman second persons as a necessary supplement to critical posthumanism, moving it out of the labs and technoscientific domains it has haunted and into the domestic spaces where human persons are fostered and where care, connection, and community are central. In developing an account of domestic posthuman second persons, we emphasize personhood as an ongoing achievement executed in the company of other persons; recognize specific elements of human life history, including infancy and the extended period of vulnerability and dependency throughout childhood; attend to the evolution of extended networks of carers, including grandmothers and alloparents; and highlight the significance of home as a site of subversion and resistance. Exploring the fertile intersection of posthumanism and design from a feminist, care-oriented perspective, this chapter seeks to highlight and address a series of questions important to developing a domestic posthuman framework for design.

In Chapter 3, as well as Chapter 6, we turn more explicitly to mythmaking and often in language that is more personal and subjective than analytical and objective, critically examining some of the dominant myths that surround the posthuman and its artifacts, and proposing a set of new myths and dramatic pictures. These are offered in the spirit of what Lauren Berlant (2022) has called an "assay": modular clusters of reflections gathered around a specific object, scene, or case. Our assays are not comprehensive lists or exhaustive readings; they are example-based resources for designing a domestic posthuman less captive to the omnipresent machine myth, to give an idea of what technology with other mythical infrastructures might look like and hopefully immediately begin to call others to the reader's mind that could be enacted in their same style. We draw in this idea on the work of philosopher Mary Midgley to bring "the myths we live by" into more conscious awareness, and her insistence that "our actions are not primarily ruled by evidence but much more by our imagery, our world-pictures, the myths that we have grown up accepting" (2018: 207). Throughout *Designing the Domestic Posthuman*, we explore the various myths and imagery central to the posthuman and propose alternative dramatic pictures informed by our focus on different figurations of the human and the everyday, mundane, and soft objects that humans so often interact with. In Chapter 3 we begin that work by contesting popular myths of the posthuman (cyborg, designer baby, digital native, decentered self) and without necessarily rejecting these constructs articulate a core series of alternative mythic constructions that have differently directed our understanding of the posthuman (biosocial baby, playful child, grandmother).

Part Two turns more explicitly to the artifactual side of domestic posthuman-technology relations, examining what technological artifacts domestic posthuman second persons use to affect their self- and network-transformations. Recognizing that our mythical image of the posthuman and its technological instruments fetishize particular tools and technologies, Part Two aims to recover new myths and stories less encumbered by the hard surfaces of computational media and the splicing, quantifying, and dissolving of digital technologies. When we talk about the domestic, we use the term to refer to the home as well as the things home connotes. Through the connotations of the domestic, we generate a list of overlooked attributes of good self-extenders, self-transcenders, and self-modifiers. Chapter 4 begins this work by defining softwear, distinct from both software and hardware, as a key category of the domestic posthuman informed by alternative technomaterialities with very different attributes from those typically affiliated with technology and the future, and which include characteristics like feminine, embodied, material, intimate, emotional, relational, and storied. Objects that commonly possess these characteristics include clothing, accessories, domestic textiles, ceramics, furniture, wallpaper, and pets. Alternative *techne* suggests alternative attributes for technology and for the posthuman structures that are created when humans use and fuse with technology. When we can see technology as slow, soft, old, touched/smelled/tasted, ordinary, cozy, and material, alternative posthuman geographies, textures, and figures begin to move into the technological foreground.

In Chapter 5's exploration of "unhomely *techne*," we provide a theoretical framework for how to use posthuman thinking to simultaneously estrange the domestic space while familiarizing the process of technological assimilation. We endeavor to reveal the intrinsically unhomely, or in Freud's term *unheimlich*, quality of familiar spaces and objects through redescribing them as extra- (meaning simultaneously "very" and "more than") human. As opposed to the hard, fast, and digital, this chapter turns to a set of different attributes, including relationality (our tendency to connect intimately with things in ways that enliven them, or automatism and animism); storytelling (our tendency to seek meaning in the world, which the world seems to encourage, and support these meanings through the discovery of synchronicities, or repetition); and anthropomorphism (our tendency to interweave ourselves with otherness in order to mirror and then connect with it, or doubling).

Unhomely *techne* are older, less fashionable, fully domesticated mediation devices through which we seek connectivity, meaning, and relationality with the organic and inorganic environment. Specifically, unhomely *techne* are conventionally nontechnical things doing profoundly posthuman work, like fashion, cosmetics, ornaments, cooking, children's stories, pets, trash, and brands; they are also old-fashioned and homebound technologies ignored in the conventional posthuman spaces of nanotechnology, biotechnology, information technology, and cognitive science, such as robots, televisions, toilets, movies, prosthetics, and clones. Chapter 6, exploring artifact myths in the style of the "assay" as in Chapter 3, uncovers the concealed and withheld component of certain domestic objects to make them unhomely in spite of their familiar banality. We turn to saris, Chinese toilets, cats, televisions, and the kitchen table to evoke an alternative set of artifacts currently populating domestic posthuman environments and that seed ideas about what future such designed artifacts might be like.

In concluding *Designing the Domestic Posthuman*, we offer up the "four *bubbes* of the domestic posthuman" as an alternative to Rosi Braidotti's four horsemen of the posthuman apocalypse (2013: 59). Braidotti observes that the posthuman is an "opportunity to empower the pursuit of alternative schemes of thought, knowledge and self-representation. The posthuman condition urges us to think critically and creatively about who and what we are actually in the process of becoming" (2013: 12). But from where are we to draw these contestatory visions of a future humanity? What alternative schemes of thought are we to pursue? For inspiration, we turn to the image of the Jewish grandmother, or *bubbe* in Yiddish, and suggest that the four *bubbes* expand and shift human-technology networks to include an assemblage comprised of caregivers, skin, soft objects, myths, stories, homemaking, and home places and we conclude *Designing the Domestic Posthuman* with a domestic posthuman design sampler—a term drawn from the domestic art of embroidery rather than the historically martial language and connotations more typical of a design manifesto.

Eschewing purity tests and drawing on diverse threads while playing in domestic spaces, *Designing the Domestic Posthuman* champions a form of posthumanism that is, for all its evocation of children and grandmothers, quite promiscuous, maybe even a little dirty, and certainly as messy as a lived-in home in exploring entanglements that have been ignored or sidelined in other accounts of posthumanism, steeped as they still are in the figure of *homo faber* and his machine models. Given the complex and messy entanglements of human beings and artifacts, we shouldn't expect posthumanism to be overly tidy and clean, or particularly chaste. We accept, and even try to cultivate, some clutter. And while we are emphatically not anti-technology and are not saying "No" to conventionally digital, silicon, or pharmacological technologies, we do recognize that semiconductor cleanrooms and their suburban smart home analogs are not the kinds of places where we expect to find domestic posthumans. They are not conducive to the convivial modes of living characteristic of domestic posthuman second persons, who are created and thrive in more hospitable kinds of places.

Notes

1 Ron Wakkary notes in *Things We Could Design* that he "will deemphasize the role humans play to shed light on and to assert the role that things, as I see them, play and could play in design" (2021: 9). Rethinking design in light of humanism's shortcomings, he seeks to design for less human-centered worlds (2021: 3).

2 In *Design Justice* Sasha Costanza-Chock addresses a long-standing conversation about the relationship between local communities and technology development and points to small, local economies powered by place-appropriate technology that emphasizes small, local interventions (2002). As she notes in a conversation with the podcast *Radical A.I.*: "I think that sometimes it's about just developing small, local and highly customized solutions. . . . And if that means, you know, designing things for just one person, well, sometimes that's fine" ("Design Justice 101 with Sasha Costanza-Chock"). For more on small-scale design from a contemporary design perspective emphasizing local communities, see Enzio Manzini, *Design When Everybody Designs* (2015: 23).

3 We say "we" and "I" in the tradition of feminist academic writing, use contractions and the idioms of speech, and we're okay with metaphors and a little hyperbole and other folk patterns. In her anthropological work, Polly Wiessner (2014) notes the difference between "daytime talk," mostly about work, and "nighttime talk," mostly about stories and mostly told around fires where young and old gather together. A lot of *Designing the Domestic Posthuman* was "written" first in conversations imitative of nighttime talk facilitated by Zoom, FaceTime, text messaging, email, and the occasional conference-aided bar or restaurant.

Figure 1 Exterior view of *Eliza's Peculiar Cabinet of Curiosities*, Folayemi Wilson.

The question of what constitutes a "smart home" is at the forefront of conversations about the interface of technology with the home, preoccupying architects and engineers in search of the next disruptive innovation with equal urgency. Their forays lead us into the worlds of app design and the Internet of Things, where cooling and heating systems are controlled from afar, cameras surveil the nanny, voices sound the alarm when a fridge door is open, and appointments can be scheduled by speaking into thin air. Depictions of smart homes usually keep their infrastructures invisible so that their style can be sleek, clean, and spare. Think modernist architecture, lots of windows, neutral color schemes, very little furniture, flat reflective surfaces, and a Marie Kondo vibe. The Greystone Mansion in the SciFi Channel's "Caprica" (2009–10) embodies each of these features.

Folayemi Wilson's 2016 installation *Eliza's Peculiar Cabinet of Curiosities*, a full-scale nineteenth-century slave cabin that is home to a fictional woman of African descent named Eliza, dramatically shifts the context in which we might investigate the question of what constitutes a smart home. In the first place, Wilson conjures a home that is not a contemporary upper-middle-class domicile but a humble cabin, and specifically one associated with one of the more shameful chapters in America's architectural history. She designs a kind of cabin that is a home but could also easily be construed within the system of slavery as a prison, evoking "the peculiar institution" that has been slavery's euphemism. But Wilson transforms both, domesticating a potential prison, changing a cabin into a cabinet, and using the euphemism of slavery, peculiar, to evoke the mental attitude of curiosity. An instrument of enslavement, the stripped-down cabin built not so much for living as for storing human chattel, becomes in Wilson's exploration an essential site for the enactment of the varied arts of personhood which range, according to the echoes of objects assembled within the cabin(et), from self-care to childcare, contemplation to representation, creation to recreation. That a slave cabin should be transformed from an instrument of imprisonment into such a cozy and generative home suggests the deep connection of the human species with homemaking as a profound but usually overlooked biomedical and cognitive technology.

But what makes this peculiar cabin(et) so smart? Wilson shows us Eliza—who shares her name with ELIZA, the first natural language processing computer programs developed at MIT by Joseph Weizenbaum in the 1960s—as a kind of scientist, a person who scours her surroundings and gathers specimens to bring and keep back home. As a fictional entity characterized by her keen mind, Eliza offers an alternative picture of Artificial Intelligence to that exemplified by ELIZA. Though we never see or meet Eliza, her palpable consciousness is embedded not in software or hardware but in the things she decides to keep in her cabin(et), which themselves become the signs of her curiosity—which is to say that the objects are the assembled fragments of her mental life and emotional inspirations as well as the kind of character she might possess. Eliza's collection consists of signposts to the way she practices her personhood, their peculiarity only amping up our sense of her particularity. Thus this smart home—as far in style from the mansion in "Caprica" as you can get—embodies another way of thinking not only about artificial intelligence but how a home comes to be smart, here in the sense of having or showing quick-witted intelligence, and suggests another template for what such a smart space might look like and feel like to live in.[1]

Importantly, Eliza's smart home isn't constituted by network connectivity or the architectural equivalent of the other denotation of smart that often seems inextricable from configurations of smart homes: a sharp and tidy briskness. On the contrary, it is teeming with things and thus by implication it is dense with the habits, reflections, and queries of its inhabitant. Eliza's aliveness is constituted by its fullness. This is a smart home that resonates as a place where a person unacknowledged as a person in the public sphere might go to reconstitute herself in privacy among carefully curated curious possessions, each reendowing her with something of the vital consciousness for which its fullness and presence stands in effigy. This version of a smart home may be more in tune with how many people the world over regularly use their homes, which are less about task instrumentalization than soothing, affirming, and reviving ourselves. We need a whole network of objects and other humans to do so. They might, or might not, be digital objects or virtual humans. Eliza's cabinet, which contains several anachronistic digital and virtual curios, accommodates both.

Throughout this book, we will return to a selection of objects Wilson has described as those that "a 19th-century woman of African descent might have collected in her own unique *Wunderkammer*."[2] We do so at the designer's prompting of viewers to consider the objects as windows to the past in a way that can illuminate aspects of the present and construct the future. In October of 2016, a group of scholars and artists "trekked to the cabin where they poked and pried Eliza's curiosities, each selecting an object or two that anchored their comprehension and experienced. Discussed in an open forum, these objects retained a certain intimacy: at once Eliza's, but then ours" (McGee 2016). Like these prior scholars, we have poked and pried Eliza's *Wunderkammer* in the same way we imagine she would have poked and pried her world to create it, treating Eliza's belongings as illustrations in the project of designing the domestic posthuman. Alongside the myths of posthuman second persons and domestic posthuman artifacts that we develop in Chapters 3 and 6, we hope they round out our conceptual framework to provide designers with a range of inspiring examples.

Notes

1 For more on the smart home from the perspective of the domestic postman see Reid and Weiss (2024), "Alternative Domiciles for the Domestic Posthuman," Architectural Digest.

2 See https://www.fowilson.com/ (Accessed April 30, 2023).

PART ONE

Posthuman Persons

Chapter 1

Posthuman Parturition

An Origin Story

Posthuman Technogenesis

When was the posthuman born? What were the conditions of the birth of posthumanism? Complicated questions with complex answers, no doubt. Some might look to 1966 and the publication of Michel Foucault's *The Order of Things*, in which he announces man's erasure, "like a face drawn in sand at the edge of the sea" (1973: 386–7). Or perhaps it was 1968 when Jacques Derrida delivered his lecture "The Ends of Man" (1978), at a colloquium on philosophy and anthropology. Katherine Hayles, Cary Wolfe, and others locate the origin story of the posthuman in 1945 and the Macy Conferences on Cybernetics. Competing narratives and conflicting visions of the posthuman. To gain a little genealogical perspective, we might turn to three seminal texts that introduced the debate over the posthuman and posthumanism: Elaine Graham's *Representations of the Post/Human* (2002), Hayles' *How We Became Posthuman* (1999), and Wolfe's *What Is Posthumanism?* (2010).[1] Doing so, we see that while MAN was killed off, in its place a group of engineers and scientists built a posthuman that still bears the marks of his origins.

While Hayles helpfully tells us how we became posthuman, we might turn to Graham's *Representations of the Post/Human* for a clue as to when. It turns out the posthuman was born at eleven o'clock on the morning of June 21, 1948. That was, Graham reports, the date and time of the birth of Baby, the world's first successful electronic stored-program computing sequence on a machine (ix). The Manchester Small-Scale Experimental Machine was indeed the world's first stored-program computer and, yes, it was nicknamed "Baby." This was, to say the least, a unique birth. Baby came with its own specifications (32-bit word length, serial binary arithmetic, a computing speed of 1.2 milliseconds per instruction) and had three fathers (the Manchester Baby was built at the University of Manchester, UK, by Frederic C. Williams, Tom Kilburn, and Geoff Tootill) and no mothers. It was Baby's birth that was instrumental in attracting Alan Turing to Manchester University, where he wrote "Computing Machinery and Intelligence" and where he hoped to participate in the "education" of Baby (Sterrett, 2012). And while Baby's parts were soon repurposed for building the next-generation Manchester Mark 1 computer, Baby was actually rebuilt in 1998 to celebrate its (his?) fiftieth birthday. No doubt Baby's fathers were exceedingly proud of their progeny.

Graham notes that the birth of Baby and the later discovery of the structure of DNA "triggered a technological and cultural revolution" (2002: ix). Graham's Introduction to *Post/Human* opens with a nod to an essential humanist statement: "This is a book about what it means to be human." But she immediately shifts attention to the realm of technology: "Or, more precisely, it is an examination of the impact of twenty-first technologies — digital, cybernetic, and biomedical — upon our very understanding of what it means to be human" (2002: 1). Baby, it turns out, together with its various digital, cybernetic, and biomedical progeny discloses the constructed, artificial character of human nature. Graham notes that today our definitive and authoritative representations of being human are found in Western technoscience and science fiction and that this has rendered more transparent that human nature is a matter of human artifice. The posthuman baby is a product of our converging digital, cybernetic, and biomedical technologies, developed and overseen by heroic inventors, tinkerers, technologists, and theorists who are predominantly Western and male.[2]

While Alan Turing wasn't present at Baby's birth, he did much to oversee its growth and maturity, so much so that Hayles' tale of how we became posthuman opens with what has become an inaugural moment of the computer age and a primal scene of the posthuman: sitting alone in a room with two computer terminals, engaged in an interrogation. It's the story of Turing, computing machinery, and intelligence. It's also the story of bringing up Baby. Once the computer was turned on at Manchester U, Turing was attracted to the university and began working on raising Baby as the Deputy Director of the Royal Society Computing Machine Laboratory. While Alan Hodges (2014) reports that Turing was put off by the construction of Baby, he still "could foster it, and there was the prospect of using it" (496).

How exactly does one foster such an unusual Baby? While "Computing Machinery and Intelligence" is often turned to for a discussion of Turing's account of the Imitation Game, the essay includes an equally fascinating account of educating Baby. Turing wonders how one is to try to imitate an adult human mind, the goal of the Imitation Game, and he observes, "Instead of trying to produce a programme to simulate the adult mind, why not rather try to produce one which simulates the child's?" Imitating an adult human mind involves, Turing suggests, a child-programme and an education process. What do we know about the child-brain? Turing hypothesizes,

> Presumably the child-brain is something like a note-book as one buys it from the stationers. Rather little mechanism, and lots of blank sheets. . . . Our hope is that there is so little mechanism in the child brain that something like it can be easily programmed. The amount of work in the education we can assume, as a first approximation, to be much the same as for the human child. (1950: 456)

The education process seemingly involves a few blows, as Turing further observes:

> We normally associate punishments and rewards with the teaching process. Some simple child-machines can be constructed or programmed on this sort of principle. The machine has to be so constructed that events which shortly preceded the occurrence of a punishment-signal are unlikely to be repeated, whereas a reward-signal increased the probability of repetition of the events which led up to it. (1950: 457)

Bringing up Baby, then, involves a blank slate being subjected to regular blows until it "learns."[3] What becomes of these child-machines? Here we're led to Hayles' second primal scene of the posthuman and the nightmare that gave birth to Hayles' book. While the Turing Test enacts the erasure of embodiment and the difference between human and machine, it is the apotheosis of that erasure that serves as the genesis of *How We Became Posthuman*. As Hayles notes, *Posthuman* was occasioned by her reading of another tale of technological patrimony, Hans Moravec's account of his, or at least someone's "mind children."

> This book began with a roboticist's dream that struck me as a nightmare. I was reading Hans Moravec's *Mind Children: The Future of Robot and Human Intelligence*, enjoying the ingenious variety of his robots, when I happened upon the passage where he argues it will soon be possible to download human consciousness into a computer. (1999: 1)

Moravec imagines a future in which it would be possible to liberate the mind from its biological substratum, transplanting it, layer by layer, into a computer. Moravec suggests that a person's identity would be preserved in such a process because the essence of a person, their self-identity, is the pattern and the process going on in one's head and not the machinery supporting that process. The final stage of this process comes when we move the mind into cyberspace itself, completely freed from any body image, achieving the ideal of a "truly bodiless mind" (Moravec, 2013: 180).

While Hayles focuses on Moravec's nightmare vision of disembodied mind, she has relatively little to say about those "mind children," Turing's babies, now grown up. Moravec imagines a scene not unlike Foucault's, in which human beings are swept away, erased not by ocean tides, but by a technological revolution in which human beings are usurped by their artificial progeny. Explicitly appropriating the language of paternity, Moravec muses:

> Today, our machines are still simple creations, requiring the parental care and hovering attention of any newborn, hardly worthy of the word "intelligent." But within the next century they will mature into entities as complex as ourselves, and eventually into something transcending everything we know—in whom we can take pride when they refer to themselves as our descendants. (1988: 1)

Freedom from biology applies not only to us but to our mind children, our intelligent robot creations who will be unleashed from the plodding pace of biological evolution giving rise to a population of "unfettered mind children," which we can take fatherly pride in, as opposed to our current newborns hardly worthy of the word "intelligent." Our post-biological future is driven by technological inventions, all of which converge on the intelligent robot. The posthuman is literally post human beings: "When that happens, our DNA will find itself out of a job, having lost the evolutionary race to a new kind of competition" (1988: 2).

Hayles finds Moravec's transhumanist dream of downloading to cyberspace a liberal humanist nightmare and *Posthuman* argues that this dominant image of the posthuman recuperates the worst aspects of liberal humanist subjectivity, especially the erasure of human embodiment. By separating information and materiality, marginalizing materiality, and making patterns of ones and zeros the essential characteristic of information processing devices, mechanical and human alike, the cybernetic view of the posthuman perpetuates a long tradition in Western thought of downplaying human embodiment. Nonetheless, Hayles does seemingly accept Moravec's account of our origins, the technogenesis of the human being. As Hayles has repeatedly noted in her accounts of human-technology assemblages, it is our nature to use technology. Human beings have coevolved with technology, and cultural and technological evolution have now so converged with biological evolution that they can no longer be meaningfully considered isolated processes (Hayles 2010). While she rejects Moravec's account of that coevolution as another variant on the liberal humanist subject, she seemingly agrees with the trajectory of his account. As she notes, "Whatever our future, it will almost certainly include human interventions in biological processes, which means that 'human nature' will at least in part be what humans decide it should be" (Hayles, 2005: 147–8).

Like Graham, Hayles sees these technological interventions in biological processes and the constructed nature of humans as central to how we became posthuman. A similar genealogical narrative unfolds in Wolfe's *Posthumanism*. While we have been exploring the when and the how of the posthuman, Wolfe is more interested in the what. What is posthumanism? Wolfe suggests that it would be an appropriate posthumanist gesture to begin his book with the results of a Google search. He observes that in the summer of 2008 if you Google "humanism," you'll be rewarded with 3,840,000 hits, while "posthumanism" yields a mere 60,200. As a sign of how much has changed and how much has not changed since 2008, the results are (as of the close of 2022):

Humanism About 135,000,000 results (0.55 seconds)

Posthumanism About 3,850,000 results (0.51 seconds)

The birth of the posthuman has been attendant to an explosion in posthumanist discourse. Wolfe chooses to introduce posthumanism with an "appropriately posthumanist gesture" and consults Google. But what makes this a posthumanist gesture? Presumably, posthumanism begins with technology, a search engine, which has replaced what might have previously been done by a human being, maybe a research librarian, opening a dictionary. Perhaps another thing that marks this as an appropriately posthumanist gesture is that the replacement of the human being with the Google search engine harkens back to another genealogical element of posthumanism: the death of Man. Wolfe informs us that we can trace posthumanism back to the "death of man" genre of pronouncements by figures such as Foucault and Derrida. This erasure of man finds its mirror in another "well-known genealogy" that Wolfe, like Hayles, finds in the Macy Conferences on Cybernetics, which "converged on a new theoretical model for biological, mechanical, and communicational processes that removed the human and Homo sapiens from any particularly privileged position in relation to matters of meaning, information, and cognition" (2010: xii).

Wolfe's genealogies of posthumanism highlight the death of Man, the removal of the human from any privileged position, and our reliance these days not on librarians but on search engines. And one might add a search engine that was invented and monetized by two men, Larry Page and Sergey Brin. Attendant to the birth of posthumanism then were death-of-man poststructuralists, early cyberneticists, and the inventors of Google. Altogether then, this genealogical account of the parturition of the posthuman was an entirely masculine affair.

Indeed, absent Wolfe's genealogical forays on Google are research librarians, 83 percent of which are women. Baby is all grown up and our mind children, having been properly educated and disciplined, seemingly have little use for women. Technogenesis is largely a male affair.

One might further assume that posthuman technogenesis belongs largely to Google, for Wolfe observes that his sense of posthumanism is a product of our congress with technology, including presumably that original impulse to go to Google when questioning, "what is posthumanism?" It is that congress with technology that makes posthumanism so easy to see and so impossible to ignore. As Wolfe notes,

> posthumanism names a historical moment in which the decentering of the human by its imbrication in technical, medical, informatic, and economic networks is increasingly impossible to ignore, a historical development that points toward the necessity of new theoretical paradigms (but also thrusts them on us), a new mode of thought that comes after the cultural repressions and fantasies, the philosophical protocols and evasions, of humanism as a historically specific phenomenon. (2010: xv–xvi)

Not simply a matter of our current situation, though, Wolfe reads our imbrication in networks back into the very birth of the human, for it turns out we have always been posthuman. As Wolfe notes, posthumanism

> names the embodiment and embeddedness of the human being in not just its biological but also its technological world, the prosthetic coevolution of the human animal with the technicity of tools and external archival mechanisms (such as language and culture) of which Bernard Stiegler probably remains our most compelling and ambitious theorist—and all of which comes before that historically specific thing called "the human" that Foucault's archaeology excavates. (2010: xv)

The human being is and always has been the prosthetic being and we can see this now as a result of our daily imbrication in technoscientific networks. Even before the death of Man announced by Foucault, we were already posthuman, our very birth as prosthetic beings a product of our tools and archival mechanisms. Posthumanism is all about confronting the decentering of the human in relation to either evolutionary, ecological, or technological coordinates (Wolfe, 2010: xvi). Our technical networks today have enabled us to see clearly what posthumanism is and how we posthumans emerged long ago in the imbrication of biology and technology. We can observe here the patriarchal patrimony of the posthuman in the technological networks shepherded into existence by the likes of Page, Brin, and Baby. It's the origin story of our technogenesis.

The Uncanny Absence of Mother

The when, how, and what of the posthuman tells an interesting origin story that on the surface appears to break with typical human origin stories in focusing not on the human but on its technogenesis. And yet, as this tale unfolds in the work of Graham, Hayles, and Wolfe, we see a strange parallel between the origin story of the posthuman and more typical origin stories in Western thought. In *Maternal Ethics and Other Slave Moralities*, Cynthia Willett recounts interpretations of human origins from the Judaic-Christian tradition, the liberal atomism prominent in Anglo-American culture, and European dialectic. She notes that "a peculiar absence marks the three classic narratives that enframe and validate mainstream Western cultures" (1995: 13). In Genesis, Hobbes, and Hegel, there is an uncanny absence.

> Nowhere to be found in these infantile fantasies, in the mythogenetic beginnings of history, is the first person in the life of the child, the mother. The three classic statements on the origins of the person betray the abstractions— if not sheer fabrications—of a father who in point of fact has all too often been absent from the family scene. (14)

Willett's observation seems especially apropos of the story of Baby, mind children, and the decentering of humans in information and media networks. The mythogenetic tale of the posthuman involves paternal figures drawn from the fields of mathematics, engineering, cybernetics, and European philosophy departments, giving birth to babies, children, and theories proclaiming the death of MAN or at least his erasure at the hands of his technological progeny. While suggestive of a break with the human and oft-told tales of Western liberal humanism, the posthuman and posthumanism's efforts to theorize its genesis participate in some of the same exclusions that have long characterized Western thought and its mythic origins. Despite all the talk about Baby, mind children, and child brains, these accounts of the posthuman have little to say about the role of mothers or any actual children.[4] It's as if the exemplary posthuman scene is an adult human being, probably male, surely Western, sitting in front of a terminal Googling or at least trying to engage a machine in conversation about intelligence.

The difficulty of a complete break with Western thought's origin stories is made nowhere clearer than in Neil Badmington's efforts to theorize posthumanism, which, like Wolfe, begins with a coterie of male poststructuralist theorists, including Derrida and Jean-Francois Lyotard. Badmington readily admits humanism's staying power and is reluctant to claim for posthumanism any kind of break with humanism. As he notes, "Apocalyptic accounts of the end of 'Man,' it seems to me, ignore humanism's capacity for regeneration and, quite literally recapitulation" (2003: 11).

Badmington finds in *Time* magazine's 1983 "Machine of the Year" cover an indication of humanism's staying power.[5] While celebrating the machine that's moving in, *Time* maintains the centrality of MAN on the cover, witnessing the machine's moving in. Anthropocentrism maintains its grip, even as the machine tries to muscle in. Referencing the "pathetic anthropomorphic figure that sat to the left of the computer," Badmington writes:

> If technology has truly sped "us" outside and beyond the space of humanism, why is "Man" still at "our" side? If "Man" is present at "his" own funeral, how can "he" possibly be dead? What looks on lives on. The end of "Man" was suddenly in doubt. I had come up against the problem of what to do with human remains. (2003: 13)

Badmington reads the cover of *Time* as indicative of the problem of human remains and the problem of humanist remains. Man, or "Man" lives on. But the figure of the human remains that he locates and denominates "Man" is only one figure on *Time*'s cover. Badmington completely overlooks the second figure hidden behind the fold of the cover, which unfolds to reveal a second "pathetic anthropomorphic figure" lying even further on the margins, and this figure appears to be a woman, and the differences between these two anthropomorphic figures are instructive.

The man, sitting to the left of a computer, could be working from home, perhaps a product of the Covid-19 shutdown. He's at a table, maybe a worktable, directly confronting the machine that moved in. Perhaps he's waiting on a Zoom call or, following Wolfe, simply Googling. He's that archetypal figure that opens Hayles' *Posthuman*, a lone maybe lonely man sitting in front of a flickering terminal. Except he's not alone. Completely escaping Badmington's efforts to theorize posthumanism is that woman. She's in an altogether different arrangement. She's sitting more casually with a cup in her hand, coffee perhaps or an afternoon cocktail. She appears barefoot, with one foot sitting comfortably on her wicker chair—no straight-back chair for her. And the computer is off to the side. She's not facing it, not confronting it. It's smaller, its screen plaintively looking up at her, perhaps, in a suitably different kind of posthumanist gesture, asking for attention, reaching out. Perhaps, as many mothers have done in policing their children's screen time, this woman has put the computer off to the side in a show of resistance.

This second figure, with an entirely different relationship to the machine that's moving in, completely escapes Badmington's attention. In theorizing humanism, he turns to the MAN, just as in theorizing posthumanism he turns to Derrida and Lyotard for clues as to the meaning of the staying power of humanism. Posthumanism is less about human-technology relations than about MAN's relation to certain forms of technology taken to be central to our posthuman experience. And yet that figure of the woman remains too. What's her story? What's her significance? How does she figure in human-technology relations?

Time's cover is notable because the machine of the year becomes the machine of the year when it moves into the home—into the domestic sphere, a sphere most often relegated to women and, again, a sphere largely missing from efforts to theorize posthumanism. The PC became "machine of the year" not with Baby or Eniac's powering up or following the Macy Conferences on Cybernetics, but at the point at which it moves into the home. In this domestic space of the home, *Time*'s cover replicates a common dichotomy that reemerges when (male) theorists turn to technology: the displacement of women and the home. On the actual cover itself we have a man sitting at his work table confronting the computer directly. The woman is relegated to the space beyond the cover fold.

Why turn to the inside fold? Perhaps because this woman seems more interesting. The man is rather stooped, tired from a long day of Zoom meetings. The woman on the other hand has relegated the PC to an appropriate place in the domestic sphere, off to the side. She's sitting comfortably, having a drink. She's figured out the place of the computer in her domestic environment. Maybe she's even domesticated it.

This might suggest that as the computer moves in, we're obligated to consider the implications of this not only for the computer, that machine of the year that has displaced MAN of the year, but also for the diverse human encounters that can be read into this moving in. As our computers and their digital progeny take up more and more time and space in our domestic environments, as they move in today even more assuredly than in 1983, and as we wrestle with questions about human-technology relations and what it means to be human or even posthuman, we ought to remember that humanity is a diverse lot and its ways of accommodating the tech that moves in are equally diverse.

Badmington's reading of this image reflects Hayles' account of the computational regime and its power to compute the human. In all these cases, our thinking about humans and posthumans takes place against the backdrop of the computer and its digital offspring. And to some extent this seems right—at least to those of us living in developed, industrialized societies. The warp and woof of our lives has certainly taken on a technological character. But in placing all this emphasis on the computer, what is obscured? Returning for a moment to the image from *Time*, we might wonder what's missing and what doesn't draw too much attention. Notice the absence of children—our two human beings, presumably a man and a woman, are childless. Also missing, at least in part, is the space into which the computer is moving. In the cover image it is represented in rather abstract terms—a window hanging against a black backdrop, looking out to more blackness. Furniture in primary colors. Wood floors. This house lacks any kind of ornament. Indeed, we might say that it lacks any kind of life. The computer is moving into a cold and lifeless space. It's not at all like the domestic spaces any real human beings live in nor the domestic spaces that are reimagined to accommodate our machines.

Posthuman Mythogenetics

Reviewing the birth of the posthuman in these seminal accounts reminds us that visions and images of the posthuman are powerful memes in the posthuman economy and in these influential tales of posthuman origins we see them converging on some similar themes, constructing a shared narrative about life in the twenty-first century lived amid our technological networks, the imaginative picture of the posthuman. Its primal scene takes place in appropriately posthumanist contexts, as Wolfe might observe, sitting in front of a computer and Googling. Its central element is the computer and the technoscientific networks it has made possible. It's a narrative in which the human being has been displaced and decentered and made aware of its constructed, artificial nature, perhaps soon to be replaced by our technological progeny. It's a picture of our prosthetic being, revealing of the evasions and inadequacies of the liberal humanist subject we once mistakenly took ourselves to be.

It's also a story that involves issues of genesis, babies, and children, told largely if not exclusively in terms defined by male theorists, engineers, inventors, and technologists and the tools they have built. Notable in this tale of the death of Man and the technogenesis of Baby is the absence of women and any actual infants or children. It is a story about the birth of a new mode of thinking about human beings, but one that features almost exclusively the men who have built the very information networks that give birth to both the posthuman and this new mode of thought. The posthuman is born almost exclusively in the context of Western technoscientific technogenesis overseen by its male progenitors. Perhaps posthumanism and its object of study, the posthuman, is not quite yet the radical rethinking of human ontology it is sometimes taken to be (Sharon, 2012: 8).

What we see in these accounts is an imaginative vision or dramatic picture, a myth in other words, of the human being shaped by the impact of converging technologies. In treating the birth of the posthuman as a myth we are drawing on the work of philosopher Mary Midgley who, in a series of books and essays addressing fundamental questions about what it means to be human, forcefully calls attention to the role of the imagination in shaping our thinking.[6] When dealing with issues about what we human beings are, what our place in the world is, where we come from, and where we might be going, these issues are seldom addressed as straightforward factual matters. Rather, they are tangled up with powerful folk tales and pictures and myths, dramatic stories of creation and descent, good and evil, freedom and alienation. Indeed, all human thought,

Midgley suggests, is animated by these basic patterns emanating not solely from reason but from our imagination. The kinds of fundamental existential questions we human beings often ask, Midgley observes, are addressed in terms of imaginative visions that help structure our thoughts and orient ourselves. She often refers to these imaginative visions as myths, but not myths in the sense of lies or metaphysical sketches that are wrong or false. As she notes,

> (E)very thought system has at its core a guiding myth—not a myth in the sense of a lie but of an imaginative vision, a picture which does indeed express its appeal to the deepest needs of our nature. . . . This is as true of world-views that are accepted as scientific as it is of other world-views. True beliefs need their imagery quite as much as false ones. (2001: 200)

A number of such myths have played a role in Western thinking about the human being (economic man, fallen man, the noble savage, the beast within, the automaton), nature (red in tooth and claw, the selfish gene, the clockwork universe), and technology (the engine of progress, Frankenstein, the computer age, the Faustian bargain). Midgley refers to such myths as dramatic pictures and the emphasis on drama is meant to bring out the way in which they organize our thoughts into a pattern of significance, helping to organize the myriad facts of the world into a coherent symbolic picture. They help direct us to what to attend to, what's significant. As she notes, "Facts will never appear to us as brute and meaningless; they will always organize themselves into some sort of story, some drama" (1985: 4). Often these imaginative visions draw on both science and imagination and serve as powerful folk tales we tell about human origins.

In calling attention to what she refers to as the "half-conscious apparatus of thought surrounding the official doctrines" (1992: 15), Midgley urges us to critically reflect on the role of these myths in shaping and sometimes determining thought, for good and for ill. We must, she says, subject these myths to scrutiny. As she explains, "We need to compare those visions, to articulate them more clearly, to be aware of changes in them, to think them through so as to see what they commit us to" (2001: 36). Midgley's work is focused on attacking dominant imaginative visions she thinks have outlived their usefulness or are now getting things wrong, and developing new images we might use as a corrective for inadequate ones. She rightly observes that while we don't have a choice of foregoing imaginative pictures, we do have a choice of what myths will help us understand our core existential questions (1992: 13).

Situating the posthuman in the context of Midgley's discussion of myth and imaginative visions enables us to see how this recent myth shares both some significant continuities with previous imaginative visions as well as some weaknesses. For all the emphasis on death, decentering, and the post of the posthuman, this imaginative vision shares deep continuities with earlier imaginative visions which call out for scrutiny and the need for, if not alternative then at least, different imaginative visions. The origin story of the posthuman is largely still caught within the orbit of traditional Western origin stories.

Let's examine several significant continuities that situate the posthuman myth in these broader concerns, beginning with Midgley's observation that these imaginative visions are powerful folktales about human origins that speak to fundamental human concerns about being human and our place in the world. They have what we might think of as a necessary cartographic function. In *Making Gender* Sherry Ortner argues that there are certain basic existential questions or structures, she also refers to them as riddles, which are apparent in all cultures, which humanity everywhere must cope with, and while the individual answers posed to these questions admit of great variability, the questions themselves have a certain constancy and regularity (1996 178–9). These are, Ortner suggests, "factors built into the structure of the most generalized situation in which all human beings, in whatever culture, find themselves" (1996: 25). One such question, Ortner suggests, is how to think about the confrontation between humanity and nature. As she notes, "the problem of the relationship between what humanity can do, and that which sets limits upon those possibilities, must be a universal problem—to which of course the solutions will vary enormously, both cross-culturally and historically" (1996: 179). As nature has increasingly been displaced by technology in our lives, especially in modern industrialized Western societies, the confrontation between humanity and technology has taken on the guise of a fundamental existential question, or perhaps riddle.

Approaching *the posthuman* and *posthumanism* as imaginative visions, then, underscores the observation that posthumanism is part of a long tradition addressing fundamental concerns. Whether human or posthuman, humanist or posthumanist, the motivation here is to address still other deeper questions. What does it mean to be a human being? What is our place in the world? How ought we to relate to other inhabitants of our world, whether natural or technological? What role does the material world play in shaping the human being? How do we orient ourselves in a world where we have powerful technologies that allow us to transform that world and us? Midgley suggests that our imaginative visions are responses to these fundamental questions, maps that help us to orient ourselves in the world, recognizing that in periods of rapid change, our myths change and patterns that were once useful prove to be sources of difficulty (2004: 4). The posthuman emerged during a time of rapid technological change, global environmental and climate crises, and challenges to the assumption of human distinctiveness and superiority. This is an insight that Rosi Braidotti shares, recognizing that the posthuman calls for new cartographies of the human:

> the posthuman as cartographic figuration is a branch of contemporary critical thought that allows us to think of what "we" are ceasing to be—for instance,

the Eurocentric category of universal "Man." It also sustains, however, the effort to account for what "we" are in the process of becoming—the multitude of ways in which the human is currently being recomposed. (2019: 37)

Hayles too regularly comes back to the notion that her work is devoted to "developing new frameworks with which to understand where we are and where we may be heading" (2005: 33).

But Midgley also cautions that such imaginative visions don't alter in brisk, wholesale ways. As she notes, "The belief in instant ideological change is itself a favourite myth of the recent epoch that we are now beginning to abuse as 'modern'" (2004: 4). And indeed, for all the emphasis in accounts of posthumanism on developing new theoretical paradigms and modes of thought and how the human being is "currently being recomposed," the myth of posthuman technogenesis has troubling continuities with earlier efforts to address these fundamental concerns.

Consider that for several hundred years in Western thought our imaginative visions, especially those responsive to questions about what it means to be human and how we understand our place in nature, were often addressed in terms borrowed from technology (Midgley 2018: 65). There's a long-standing continuity here in which we understand our nature and place in the world in terms of a defining technology, Jay David Bolter's phrase for those technologies that move out of the laboratory and forge relations with a culture's science, philosophy, and literature. "A defining technology defines or redefines man's role in relation to nature" (Bolter, 1984: 40). Such technologies come to serve as metaphors through which a culture can view both its physical and its metaphysical worlds. Bolter argues that the computer is the most recent example of a defining technology, contributing to a general redefinition of certain basic relationships, including "in the broadest sense, of mankind to the world of nature" (1984: 9). As Midgley points out, "throughout the history of modern science, machines have been the standard model for describing the natural order" (1994: 95).[7] We build our technologies and in turn our technologies shape our symbolism and thereby our metaphysics.

Such feedback loops were central to the story Hayles tells of how we became posthuman and are central to accounts of posthuman technogenesis. One of the earliest accounts of posthumanist culture, Ihab Hassan's article "Prometheus as the Performer: Toward a Posthumanist Culture? A University Masque in Five Scenes" (1977), identifies HAL and AI as the agents of a new posthumanism:

More soberly, more immediately perhaps, a posthuman philosophy must address the complex issue of artificial intelligence, which most of us know only by the familiar name of HAL. Will AI supersede the human brain, rectify it, or simply extend its powers? We do not know. But this we do know: AI . . .

32   Designing the Domestic Posthuman

> will help to transform the image of man, the concept of the human. They are agents of a new posthumanism, even if they do no more than the IBM 360-196. (1977: 845)

From the IBM 360-196 to Andrew Pickering's (2010) fascination with Hal Ashby's homeostat, Bruno Latour's fascination with computer chips and Monsanto (1993) and Aramis (1996), Mark Poster's (2006) embrace of network digital information humachines, and Mark Hansen's (2006) theory of media exteriorization, the posthuman emerges in the context of the developments of twenty-first-century technoscience. Braidotti's characterization of Donna Haraway's work is applicable more generally to the entire thrust of posthumanism: its conceptual universe is the high-technology world of informatics and telecommunications (2016: 680). Indeed, as Pramod Nayar observes, the philosophical foundations of critical posthumanism "are to be found in new developments in robotics and computer technology where new forms of the human, and the machine, emerge, and in the biological sciences where new theories of the emergence and evolution of life circulate" (2014: 45). The hybrids and networks that are the centerpiece of such analyses are products both of our increasing familiarity with networks of human beings and digital technologies and the products of such networks, including genetically engineered organisms, artificially intelligent computer systems, and cybernetic technologies.

The origin story of the birth of the posthuman is to be found in digital, cybernetic, and biotechnological revolutions that lead to the reconfiguration of human life.[8] Indeed the very birth of the human being is located in the technical register. The "birth of the posthuman" is, in turn, read back into the very origins of the human in the work of Bernard Stiegler and Hayles who espouse the theme of technogenesis.[9] Stiegler observes that "the human invents himself in the technical by inventing the tool—by becoming exteriorized techno-logically" (1998: 141). The human being is the prosthetic being par excellence. So not only do we become aware of our current condition as posthuman, we recognize that we have always been posthuman and that technology lies at the origin, the birth, of the (post)human. It seems that once Baby grew up, he (it? she?) forced us to come to terms with our own patrimony. Tools and technologies are presented as fundamental to the human—the human-computer relation becomes the defining and fundamental feature for understanding how we became not simply posthuman but human. The only game in town now is to "compute the human," to borrow a phrase from Hayles (2005a), who doesn't necessarily contest this as the only game in town. That game, though, is played largely in terms set by a technoscientific paradigm defined by a narrow class of technologies produced by a narrow class of tech designers. As Julia DeCook observes, "Epistemic sites of thought in the theorization of the transhuman, of the posthuman, of the cyborg all exist within the same epistemic paradigms upon which all science and technology are built—colonialist, Western, white—and thus are limited in fully conceptualizing a beyond" (2021: 1164).

Our current posthumanist imaginative vision then shares more than a little with earlier imaginative visions populating Western thought. We are still deriving our imaginative visions from technology and from a small circle of technologies reflective of the currently dominant interest in what has been called converging technologies: information technology, genetic technology, robotics, and the cognitive sciences (Roco and Bainbridge, 2002). Such machine metaphors and images have been used so extensively that they seem like literal descriptions and often in the context of posthumanism they are treated as literal. This also points to another idea that Midgley emphasizes. Such myths are not loose cargo and cannot be jettisoned promptly and replaced by new ones (2003: 152). Habits of thought that express them are deeply woven into our lives. The posthuman and posthumanism haven't jettisoned older myths that rely on technological visions of the world. They've merely updated them in terms of newer technologies. The computer has indeed moved in and we have become, borrowing the title of Bolter's book, *Turing's Man*. Baby has grown up and given birth to Turing's Man. As Bolter notes,

> We are all liable to become Turing's men, if our work with the computer is intimate and prolonged and we come to think and speak in terms suggested by the machine.
>
> Turing's man is the most complete integration of humanity and technology, of artificer and artifact, in the history of the Western cultures. (1984: 13)

Could it be that the exemplary posthuman figure, the imaginative vision of posthuman parturition, is Turing giving birth to MAN? We are all Turing's men now, except for those who are women and children and not quite men.[10]

This recognition of our technogenesis leads to a final revealing parallel between humanist and posthumanist origin tales and dramatic pictures: the absence of women and children. We witnessed the death of Man but apparently Man lives on. He lives on in the centrality given to technology, and to particular technologies, to the focus on stereotypically masculine affairs and places, and to the things that men do. It's not a matter of what things do, it's a matter of what things men do with the things they invent and build. We are overly preoccupied with the role our tools and technologies play in fashioning the posthuman and largely ignore what has been ignored throughout the history of Man: women, children, the work women do, the places where they do it, the becoming of personhood, and the relational and affective work that is central to that becoming. In tales of posthuman technogenesis, the only parties to the coevolution of humans and technology are men and their intelligent machines. As Hayles notes in a rather striking way, "No longer the measure of all things, man (and woman) now forms a dyad with the intelligent machine such that human and machine are the measure of each other" (2005a: 148). Our dyad is human and machine and here human implies MAN, with woman relegated to the parenthetical, in a move not unlike Badmington's consigning of woman to the margins beyond the fold. Might it be time to exorcize the ghost of Turing from posthumanism?

Bernard Stiegler has critiqued Western philosophy for its evasion of the important role of technology in the invention of the human, and yet Western philosophy has long engaged in a deeper and more persistent evasion regarding the place of women and caregiving and the role of infantile experience. Jane Flax has observed that Western philosophy has often denied early infantile experience and women's activity in the house and failed to inquire into how subjectivity emerges and we become persons. She argues that the denial and repression of early infantile experience have had a deep and largely unexplored impact on philosophy. This repressed material shapes by its very absence in consciousness the way we look at and reflect upon the world. As she notes, "The possibility and plausibility of many theoretical claims and social practices rest in part on the evasion, denial, or repression of how important human attachment is in the constitution of the subject and cultures more generally" (1993: 118). Western philosophy, and more recently posthumanism, has ignored that subjects start out as infants and children, that their subjectivity is something of an achievement, often made in a domestic context in which they are still today largely cared for by women.

Badmington is certainly right to call for theorizing posthumanism. And he's not wrong to think that technology has moved into the space once largely occupied by human beings and we need to think about the implications of technology moving in. But if posthumanism is devoted to thinking through human-technology relations, then we equally well have to grapple with the actual human beings who are working and living with the technology, as well as the myriad spaces in which they are doing it, all of which posthumanism has paid insufficient attention to. The domestic posthuman seeks to investigate those matters that have been obscured by our focus on the computational regime and the computer as a defining technology. The domestic posthuman doesn't begin from Turing's Man, housed mostly in departments of computer science and robotics in advanced research labs and universities, but with the domestic spaces in which even posthumans still spend most of their time. It's time, perhaps, to gender the posthuman technological imagination and ask about that absence of women, children, and homeplaces.

A (More) Radical Leap

Our posthuman origin stories rely too heavily on a mythic tale of technogenesis shaped by narrow accounts of technoscience and held captive by a framework that may not be up to the task of understanding where we are and where we may be heading. Central to the argument of this book is that we need a more diverse range of myths, media, and metaphors for comprehending what posthumanism is and what its possibilities may be. What might posthumanism look like if the standpoint from which we begin our theorizing is not the masculine parturition of machine babies but the maternal and domestic sphere in which most human beings begin life and develop? The domestic posthuman critically interrogates the master narrative of the posthuman and begins with the recognition of an absence in the dominant narratives, myths, and images of the posthuman. It is the absence of women and children and narratives of growth and development, of non-Western and trans voices, of technologies fostered and practiced in the home, of mundane and everyday objects entangled with humans and the spaces where you find them. If the posthuman is still centered on the figure of Western Man, perhaps it is time to decolonize the posthuman and explore alternative figurations less beholden to its Western parturition, centering designing the domestic posthuman not on men and their digital information machines but on women and children, on indigenous practices of making, on analog practices that stitch and weave soft objects.

Hayles' nightmare vision of the posthuman was occasioned by Moravec's mind children leaving their now proud father behind as they take up residence in cyberspace. She shouldn't have been surprised by this nightmare vision, though. After all, it's a vision that begins with the birth of Baby, who's then subjected to blows while being educated according to the worst traditions of the British schooling system, forced to undertake oral exams to establish her competency and make her father proud. Is it any wonder that when this artificial brain grows up to be a mind child, she sees no need to keep her fathers around and relegates them to the dustbin of evolutionary history? All of which begs the question, might this child-machine have been brought up differently? What might have happened to the course of the posthuman had our child-machine been of woman born and raised? What, in another phrasing, might have happened to Turing's child-machine had she been mothered? What might our posthuman child have looked like had she been born not in the lonely confrontation between an adult interrogator and a flickering terminal, all the while undertaking a Google search, but in a domestic environment characterized by a messy entanglement of parents, grandparents, and other caregivers, as well as pets, toys, and favorite outfits, all gathered around a warm and inviting kitchen table? Can we build an alternative narrative, a different dramatic picture, out of these more mundane and domestic objects and matters?[11]

If kitchen tables seem out of place in an account of the posthuman, we might recall the role of a kitchen table in Hayles' own tale of how we became posthuman, for it's around a kitchen table that we learn the story of another parenthetical woman. In a few fascinating pages at the end of her account of the Macy Conferences on Cybernetics (1999: 80–3), Hayles finds herself sitting at her kitchen table examining a photograph of the Macy Conferences' mostly male participants (the sole exception being Margaret Mead) in which there is a woman sitting with her back to the camera who is wrongly identified as Janet Freud. She is in fact Janet Freed, the secretarial assistant largely responsible for transcribing and thereby preserving the record of the conferences. Hayles intriguingly suggests that the misidentification and effacement of Janet Freed are indicative of the way domestic labor is often an afterthought to the important work of men. And yet, it's the domestic labor that makes that manly work possible. Domestic labor that often takes place around the gathering afforded by that lowly kitchen table where Hayles is herself working and gathering photos and transcripts.

The work of preservation that Janet Freed engaged in, and which in fact helped make possible the cybernetic posthuman, is often seen as women's work and is often devalued and marginalized. Iris Marion Young notes in "House and Home: Feminist Variations on a Theme" that preservation is a typically feminine activity that has often been devalued but which has significant human value. As she notes in a point crucial to our articulation of the domestic posthuman, "Preservation makes and remakes home as a support for personal identity without accumulation, certainty, or fixity" (2005: 124–5). In "Motherhood: The Contemporary Emergency and Quantum Leap," the poet and feminist Adrienne Rich begins an analysis of motherhood by explicitly disavowing statisticians, political scientists, economists, and image-makers of television who devalue women's work in the home, in favor of a more "homespun" metaphor drawn from textiles and weaving, as she seeks to understand the complexity of mothering:

> Let us try then to do justice to the complexity of this immense weaving, even as we single out particular strands or finger particular knots that seem to account for the whole. For motherhood is the great mesh in which all human relations are entangled, in which lurk our most elemental assumptions about love and power. (1979: 260)

Rich argues that the traditional work done by women has often been trivialized and devalued.[12] In the context of 1978, Rich argues that this gynophobia, now linked with a male-dominated technological establishment, has created a contemporary emergency for women calling for a quantum leap of the imagination. As she writes,

> the "quantum leap" implies that even as we try to deal with backlash and emergency, we are imagining the new: a future in which women are powerful, full of our own power, not the old patriarchal power-over but the power-to-create, power-to-think, power-to-articulate and concretize our visions and transform our lives and those of our children. (1979: 272)

Already in 1978, Rich is concerned with accelerating technological change, the rapidly increasing complexity of systems, and the training of elite males who decide how and for what technology is to be used (1979: 264). Nicholas Gane suggests that the value of the concept of the posthuman lies "in the possibility of rethinking what we call human values, human rights and human dignity against the backdrop of fast-developing bio-technologies that open both the idea and the body of the human to reinvention and potential redesign" (2006a: 434). Rich reminds us that this fast-developing backdrop has never been neutral and has often marginalized and excluded all but elite males and that we ought to be wary of imaginative visions in which those men reinvent and redesign human beings. We need to reimagine the posthuman from a different place. As she notes, "nothing less than the most radical imagination will carry us beyond this place."

Returning one last time to the image of the kitchen table, we may recall Badmington's analysis of that pathetic (and white[13]) anthropomorphic figure sitting at the table in front of that computer that had moved in. In theorizing posthumanism, Badmington is worried about those human remains, suggesting perhaps that that man sitting at that table is better off dead. But what if we were to begin with a different image of a table, a kitchen table, around which we are not focused on human remains but the messy entanglements so characteristic of kitchen tables. The Black feminist scholar and activist Barbara Smith named her press run by and for women of color "Kitchen Table: Women of Color Press," recognizing the important role of the kitchen table in women's activism and work of resistance. As she notes, "We chose our name because the kitchen is the center of the home, the place where women in particular work and communicate with each other" (1989: 1).

The place and significance of the kitchen table as a site far different than that imagined on the cover of *Time* magazine is amply demonstrated in the artist Carrie Mae Weems' photographic series "The Kitchen Table Series," appearing seven years after *Time*'s cover story of the machine of the year.[14] Weems' images of life lived around a kitchen table show little evidence of that PC that moved in. The figures are not white, anthropomorphic figures, mere stand-ins for human beings. Their lives aren't defined by work. Rather, these are women and children involved in the reproduction of everyday life, caring for the body, its maintenance and preservation, passing on rituals of beauty. What does the posthuman look like when we begin from these other imaginative pictures? It is to this question that *Designing the Domestic Posthuman* turns.

Notes

1 While Donna Haraway's work will remain productive for us throughout this text and her "Manifesto for Cyborgs" is one of the most influential essays in discussions of posthumanism, Haraway herself has a complicated relationship to the term, telling Nicholas Gane in an interview, "I've stopped using it. I did use it for a while, including in the 'Manifesto'. I think it's a bit impossible not to use it sometimes, but I'm trying not to use it . . . human/posthuman is much too easily appropriated by the blissed-out, 'Let's all be posthumanists and find our next teleological evolutionary stage in some kind of transhumanist technoenhancement.' Posthumanism is too easily appropriated to those kinds of projects for my taste. Lots of people doing posthumanist thinking, though, don't do it that way. The reason I go to companion species is to get away from posthumanism" (Gane, 2006b: 140).

2   To the extent that posthumanism draws on standard accounts of converging technologies for its vision of posthuman personhood, it risks deploying constraining accounts of personhood defined by the interests of a narrowly circumscribed group of tech designers and innovators, a problem that persists well past 1948 and the birth of Baby. As Sasha Costanza-Chock observes in *Design Justice*, "Designers tend to unconsciously default to imagined users whose experiences are similar to their own. This means that users are most often assumed to be members of the dominant, and hence 'unmarked' group: in the United States, this means (cis)male, white, heterosexual, 'able-bodied,' literate, college educated, not a young child and not elderly, with broadband internet access, with a smartphone, and so on" (2020: 77).

3   For an alternative non-punitive account of the relationship of artificial intelligence and childhood, see Alison Gopnik (2020a; 2017) and Matthew Hutson (2018).

4   Sadie Plant (1997) observes that the prototypical history of computation in the West actively writes out of that account the role of women, including Ada Lovelace's role in the development of Charles Babbage's Analytical Engine and the contributions of women who worked in computing during the Second World War. In *Zeroes and Ones*, Plant traces an alternative genealogy of the computer, focusing on the women crucial to the development of modern computing, who have been largely erased from history.

5   The full image can be seen here: http://images.google.com/hosted/life /63d2387cee2b0935.html (Accessed April 23, 2023).

6   In attending to imagery and the work of the imagination, we situate our argument in a long line of work often associated with but not exclusive to feminist interventions in philosophy and technology. Drawing on Michele Le Doeuff's *The Philosophical Imaginary* (2002, 2003), Genevieve Lloyd (2000) argues that to take philosophical imagery seriously is to open out the reading of philosophical texts to their cultural contexts in ways that are often dismissed as irrelevant to the concerns of philosophy. Related discussions can be found in the work of Sheila Jasanoff (2015) on sociotechnical imaginaries and Anne Balsamo (2011) on the technological imagination.

7   See too the work of Andrés Vaccari, especially "Dissolving Nature: How Descartes Made Us Posthuman" (2012) and "What Is Technology? Unravelling a Great Idea," (2002), where he observes that technology and myth are deeply entwined.

8   Accounts of the posthuman that situate it firmly in converging technologies can be found in Sharon (2012), Soper (2012), and Miah (2008). Laura Forlano's "Posthumanism and Design" (2017) unites the discourses of design and posthumanism in terms of their treatment of complex sociotechnical systems.

9 Tony Fry's *Human by Design* (2012) draws extensively on Stiegler's account of anthropogenesis in his account of the technicity in ontological design. As in Stiegler, "the making of mankind" begins with stone tools: "Our story starts with accounts of two and a half million years ago, when our ancient hominoid ancestors first picked up stones and used them as tools."

10 In two insightful essays, Jean Lassègue (2009, 1996) engages in an exacting and illuminating reading of Turing's "Computing Machinery and Intelligence," noting that the Turing Test tells us more about Turing's psychological life than it does the science of the mind. As Lassègue notes, learning for Turing meant the repression of those things associated with the feminine: "In Turing's mind, the process of learning is therefore akin to a process of repressing feminine and childish bodily emotions" (1996: 10).

11 Writing in a similar vein, Alison Adams, in *Artificial Knowing: Gender and the Thinking Machine*, asks of Rodney Brooks' robot Cog, "Is Cog to be brought up as a boy or a girl? Will he or she see that mummies do all the nurturing work and hold the household together while daddies are absent, at work or elsewhere? Will Cog get a Barbie or an Action Man for Christmas? What happens when Cog's postgraduate student mother moves on and it gets a new one—will it pine for its first mother?" (1998: 149).

12 Not only have women largely been absent from the computational origin story of the posthuman, so is the craft work, such as weaving, that women have traditionally done. Sadie Plant observes that Ada Lovelace took inspiration for Charles Babbage's Analytical Engine from the punched cards used in the Jacquard loom, a point we shall return to. As Anne Mudde notes, the "the relational, embodied, and material knowledges that emerge from craft work are almost completely absent in philosophical practice" (2022: 67). We might add, a similar point about craft's elision is true of much contemporary design theory.

13 In "A (White) Cyborg's Manifesto: The Overwhelmingly Western Ideology Driving Technofeminist Theory," Julia R. DeCook questions the universality of the cyborg and the power structures reified by Western technoscience. Of Haraway's cyborg manifesto, she notes that despite Haraway's intentions, "In studying global digital cultures, Haraway's notion of the cyborg is deeply Western in its theorization, and leaves behind those who do not exist in Western conceptions of personhood" (2021: 1160).

14 "The Kitchen Table Series" is a collection of photographs by Carrie Mae Weems that explores the complex relationships and experiences of Black women. The series features Weems herself in various settings and poses around a kitchen table, accompanied by text panels that add context and commentary to the images. The full series of photographs can be accessed at https://carriemaeweems.net/galleries/kitchen-table.html.

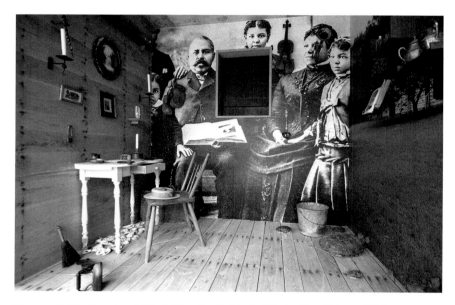

Figure 2 Interior view of *Eliza's Peculiar Cabinet of Curiosities*, Folayemi Wilson.

When confronted with *Eliza's Peculiar Cabinet of Curiosities*, sitting there, in the midst of a sculpture garden, one is immediately led to wonder: Who is this Eliza? What are we to make of her and her *Wunderkammer*? It's a confrontation that leads us to reflect on her peculiar personhood and her status as a mythic figure of the domestic posthuman second person. She's a person who was not recognized as such in her time. She's a descendant of persons who were treated as objects themselves and permitted few possessions of their own, a person whose story is told by a collection of objects. She's a second person who is storied into existence by things, and held in her identity by the personhood of the artist whose act of preservative love curates and tells her story.

In her account of second persons, Annette Baier argues that our personhood is called into full expression by other persons who treat us as one of them. Our personhood is responsive to the other persons around us. But it's hard to imagine Eliza being treated as a person by the persons around her. Instead, Eliza has her collections. Her personhood is called into being by the objects that adorn her cabinet walls and tell her story.

Too many accounts of personhood say too little about the things and places that hold us in our identity and are often a bulwark against fragmentation, against those things that threaten to fragment our sense of personhood. Eliza's possessions are not mere stuff. They are curated, displayed, important parts of her personhood. As Yi-Fu Tuan argues, "Our fragile sense of self needs support, and this we get by having and possessing things because, to a large degree, we are what we have and possess" (1980, p. 472). Eliza reclaims her personhood in a world that refuses to recognize the personhood of Black people by surrounding herself with cherished objects. We imagine the stories that these objects tell and how these objects help constitute and contribute to Eliza's story and thereby her personhood.

Eliza's personhood is also entangled in the personhood and storytelling of Folayemi Wilson, the artist whose work lovingly preserves Eliza and holds her in her identity. Both Eliza and Wilson are engaged in what Iris Young calls acts of preservative homemaking. "I define homemaking as the activities of endowing things with living meaning, arranging them in space in order materially to facilitate the projects of those to whom they belong, and activities of preserving these things, along with their meaning" (2005: 156). Young observes that it is traditionally women who preserve family history and Wilson's act of intergenerational storytelling holds Eliza in her personhood and fashions a timeless myth illuminating the many vicissitudes of personhood, past, present, and future.

Who is Eliza? An exemplary figure of the domestic posthuman.

Chapter 2

Domestic Posthuman Second Persons

The Case of Sophie

What happens when we invite the posthuman into our homes? To get a sense of this fraught terrain, we turn to the case of Sophie Hawkins, the youngest child of Joe and Laura Hawkins. Feeling overwhelmed by the absence of his wife, who is away from home while working, Joe decides somewhat impetuously to purchase one of a new line of synthetic human-like robots. As the salesperson describes his purchase: "Joe, this is the best thing you can do for your family. . . . Your brand-new synthetic. Unique styling, one of a kind Standard domestic profile installed. That'll cover all your basic housework." And so, Joe heads home with his female synth.

Sophie is taken by the pretty synth and soon enough has bonded indelibly with her (it?). Perhaps too indelibly, as she begins displaying signs of unconscious mirroring behavior.[1] As Joe observes to Laura: "She's just acting funny in a different way. Like she's trying to put up a wall or something. . . . I think we should get her checked out." Sophie is subsequently diagnosed with Juvenile Synthetic Overidentification Disorder (JSOD). As a family therapist explains to Joe and Laura, she longs for the perfection and emotional stability of synthetic life forms and is one of a growing number of human children who pretend to be synthetic.

Therapist: Basically, the patient identifies as Synthetic.

Joe: So she wants to be one of them?

Therapist: Perhaps she wants to be treated like one. We know Synths are incapable of conscious thought, but to a child, they're as real as you and I. Perfect, kind, gentle versions of all the adults around them. They never fight, they never get upset, they never worry or let you down. It's also possible that for Sophie, the boundaries between what is considered Synthetic and what is considered human have been blurred somehow.

The therapist counsels that the best thing now for Sophie is human contact. "No Synths, just her mum and dad, family and friends." When Sophie's brother Toby learns that their parents are thinking about medicating her, he appeals to his friend Renie who also identifies with the synths. Renie moves stiffly and mechanically, wears contact lenses to color her eyes a synth green, refers to "operating at full capacity," and accepts instructions from only her primary user. Toby appeals to Renie to speak to Sophie:

Toby: Sophie's still acting like a synth. Maybe you could talk to her. Help her out.

Renie: You assume she needs help.

Toby: Yeah, they're talking about medicating her. Look I get it. This is you. This is what you want. But she's just a little kid. She's confused.

Renie: Perhaps you're the one that's confused.

Toby: Tell me you're happy.

Renie: We do not feel happiness like you.

Toby: And that is not what I want for her.

Sophie and Renie are characters in the AMC drama *Humans*. *Humans* tells the story of a near future in which synthetic life forms, known as synths, have become common helpmates in all walks of life, and focuses on the domestic life of the Hawkins family and the consequences that result from Joe's decision to purchase a synth and bring it into his family home, including Sophie's diagnosis of JSOD. It is interesting for its focus on what happens when we introduce sociable robots into the sphere of the family where children are raised and nurtured and where they learn to be human.

Humans is a richly textured series that raises many questions central to posthumanism and our understanding of human-technology relations and invites us to think about a realm that is often missing in discussions of the posthuman: the realm of children, the domestic, the challenges of thinking about parenting amid, with, and sometimes against our technological tools. If we are designing a posthuman world, we might wonder what the implications are for thinking about parenting, raising children, and being children in such a world. Framing the question of the posthuman in terms of Sophie and Renie reframes the question of the human that has been central to critical posthumanism,[2] for it begins not from the standpoint of Descartes' liberal humanist subject (neither Sophie nor Renie finds much place in Western philosophy from Descartes to Kant and beyond) but from the standpoint of the not yet fully human, the individual still being shaped and shaping one's life. What happens when we refuse the paradigmatic adult human of the posthuman and substitute instead the developing human, the not yet fully formed human? In this chapter, we explore and synthesize the work of a number of figures whose thought begins with a recognition of the importance of natality and the distinctive life history of human beings, and we ask how beginning from this standpoint might inform a different perspective on the posthuman. Ultimately, we argue that it points to the need for a richer methodological framework than that provided by critical posthumanism.

How Ought We to Address the Case of Sophie?

Sophie's parents and her brother are troubled by her behavior and imitation of synth life. Should they be? When Toby implores Renie to intervene, she questions the assumption that Sophie needs help. Does she? While we have argued that dominant approaches to human-technology relations and critical posthumanism are largely silent on what we are calling the domestic posthuman, we can find some clues in that literature that suggest possible responses to these questions, in particular, in essays from two theorists who explore competing frameworks for evaluating the impact of technology on the kind of care that is at the heart of Sophie's parents' concerns for her well-being.

In "How I Learned to Love the Robot," Mark Coeckelbergh (2012) draws on Martha Nussbaum's capabilities approach to suggest that technologies are partly constitutive of the capabilities and that we should expect the meanings of health, affiliation, play, and other capabilities to change as technology changes. While the particulars of Nussbaum's capabilities approach are outside the scope of our concerns, Coeckelbergh's analysis of caregiving robots offers some intriguing clues as to one possible response to Sophie. Focusing on elder care, Coeckelbergh argues that we must avoid mere instrumental analyses of technology, determining instead whether the technology enhances the elderly's well-being and agency while recognizing that the technology itself will have an impact on how we define our goals and what we consider important. Employing a fictional scenario, Coeckelbergh imagines Grandpa happily spending time with his "intelligent and pleasant" robotic dog, who "helps with washing, plays a little bit with him, and then fetches breakfast for him" (2012: 83). Living with "FaceNet" and "TwitImage," Grandpa recognizes that he has lost physical contact with others and is more isolated, but he's virtually connected to the whole world. He enjoys spending time with his robot dog and he's better off than others in elder care, "where they had 'human contact' but where their minds and bodies were slowly withering away" (2012: 83).

While his scenario focuses on the elderly, Coeckelbergh's core point is that companionship, friendship, even love are co-shaped by technology and we must take into consideration how these capabilities will change in the light of future human-technology interactions. As he argues, "The meanings of health, affiliation, play, etc. . . . are not independent from information technologies but are partly constituted by these technologies. They change as technology changes" (2012: 82). Coeckelbergh recognizes that a younger generation who has grown up with technology will have a different understanding of the central capabilities. Noting that young people's conceptions of privacy, bodily integrity, and affiliation have changed because of their experience with mobile technologies, he notes, "Capabilities—and hence what humans are—are not fixed but change together with our technological and social context" (2011: 86). What we mean by friendship and love, Coeckelbergh asserts, is likely to change in the presence of synthetic robots such as those imagined in *Humans*.

Confronting the case of Sophie, Coeckelbergh might suggest that the therapist's advice to her parents to cut her off from her contact with the synthetic life forms and ensure contact solely with humans fails to first question whether, in the regular presence of synths, our very understanding of attachments and affiliations isn't changing. Perhaps Renie is right to question Toby's assumption that Sophie needs help. As human-synth relations become more pervasive, perhaps Renie is right to insist that to Toby, synthies "do not feel happiness like you." Sophie's parents, brother, and therapist are simply failing to understand the synthie lifestyle, judging it too harshly for not recognizing that in the presence of synths, evaluative standards are changing.

In a series of essays by Amelia DeFalco where she very explicitly seeks to interrogate the overlap in critical posthumanism and feminist philosophies of care, DeFalco reaches a similar conclusion. DeFalco examines the Swedish television program *Äkta Människor* (translated into English as *Real Humans*), which was the inspiration for *Humans*, and the film *Robot and Frank*, and asks a variant of our question, what happens when robots become increasingly integrated into everyday life? DeFalco's work focuses on the ethical and ontological implications of the increasingly blurred distinction between human and machine, especially in contexts of care, questioning the ontological assumptions underlying the understanding of care that equates real care with human care. She argues that the kind of caregiving robots explored in *Real Humans* and *Robot and Frank* have a potential transformative effect, liberating us from the contingencies of species-specific caregiving. Like Coeckelbergh, DeFalco suggests that our experiences with robot caregiving will alter our understanding of care and that we ought not to insist on anthropocentric visions of human care. While DeFalco is critical of

Domestic Posthuman Second Persons

the way in which *Real Humans* is insufficiently posthuman and reinscribes the "primacy of a narrowly conceived version of the human" (2020: 44) she writes approvingly of *Robot and Frank*'s portrayal of human-robot relations:

> Read against the grain, the film appears more nuanced in its treatment of posthuman possibilities. One can find critiques, albeit subtle and fleeting, of anthropocentrism in its portrayal of human inadequacy, of the fallibility of human care. As a result, I argue, the film offers an intriguing, if conflicted, vision of posthuman interdependency. (2018: 24)

DeFalco's argument is a rich and nuanced exploration of the intersections of philosophies of care, the nature of memory, and critical posthumanism in which she raises important questions about the meaning of care, who cares, and the labor of care. Central to her argument is the claim that critical posthumanism goes further than philosophies of care in recognizing that the human being is, as Pramod Nayar recognizes, a congeries (2014: 18). Critical posthumanists, writes DeFalco, "affirm the human animal system as a complex assemblage inextricably embedded in a dense network of intersecting organic and technological structures and systems" (2020: 40). The humanist framework that identifies real care as human care needs to be dismantled because it is a futile gesture in light of critical posthumanism's critique of efforts to insist on a separation of the human and the machine. Theorizing about care has been taken by care philosophers to be theorizing about the human and they have failed to grasp how questions about who counts as human have been transformed by the posthuman condition and how we ought to question species, ontologies, and relationality. "Caregiving robots," writes DeFalco, "have the potential to help usher in a posthumanist, postanthropocentric perspective that elides categorical distinctions between human and machine" (2018: 12). DeFalco observes that posthumanism seeks to dismantle the boundaries between human, animal, and machine, undermining the increasingly precarious liberal humanist subject. "Without clear boundaries between humans and their non-human others, whether they be animal, machine, viral, or some combination of the three, the exceptionality of the human crumbles" (2018: 15).

DeFalco might join Coeckelbergh in suggesting that Sophie's parents, therapist, and brother have been insufficiently attentive to the impact of posthuman technologies on our changing conceptions of human being. Drawing on DeFalco's critical posthumanist framework, we might be inclined to conclude that the therapist's advice for Sophie of "no Synths, just her mum and dad, family and friends" is the same liberal humanist paean to anthropocentrism and human exceptionalism that posthumanism seeks to dismantle. Critical posthumanists have observed that technoscientific developments are in the process of rewriting human ontology, fundamentally changing what it means to be human, and *Humans* reinscribes humanist elements in insisting on a human-machine boundary.

Coeckelbergh and DeFalco's analyses break with the Cartesian liberal subject and embrace a more decentered ontology in which the nonhuman participates in the technogenesis of the human being. And yet, these analyses paradoxically remain firmly situated in a Cartesian world that marginalizes if not completely ignores questions about natality, human life history from infancy through adolescence and on to maturity and old age, and growth and development within the family.[3] The methodological and theoretical perspectives currently dominant in critical posthumanism are inadequate for addressing the challenges of our technoscientific culture, in part because they have ignored and downplayed significant aspects of our being human and in so doing they have robbed us of significant normative elements that we need in order to address the challenges we face.

While there has been a lot of attention in posthumanism paid to the impact of, for example, robotic care of the elderly and more generally technology's impact on end-of-life issues, there has been relatively little attention given to the impact of these technological developments on life's beginnings and its early stages in infancy, childhood, and adolescence. *Humans* and Sophie resituate the posthuman in the realm of family, the domestic, caregiving, and developing personhood. Where critical posthumanism begins from the standpoint of emerging technologies and technogenesis, *Humans* begins in the messy, entangled world of the Hawkins' household and their struggle with Sophie's emerging personhood. From this very different starting point emerges a different conception of the posthuman, a domestic posthuman.

We read *Humans* and the case of Sophie and her friend Renie as suggestive of an alternative account of the genesis of the posthuman that while not ignoring technology and material culture, situates the posthuman more squarely in a domestic environment, an alternative to technogenesis in which a certain breed of technology isn't the only and always the central drama to our status. In drawing on the case of Sophie, Renie, and JSOD as the starting point for our imaginative vision, we seek to address what this case makes visible that has largely been concealed or marginalized in most other discussions of the posthuman.

Natality and the Posthuman Condition

We start this account of the domestic posthuman at the beginning so to speak with a kind of exegesis regarding starting points, birth, natality, and a reminder that still, today, posthumans are born. Drawing on the work of Adriana Cavarero, Alison Stone asks us to imagine a culture that saw birth and being born—not death—as the central feature of human life, and she wonders what it would mean to have a birth-centered culture. She poses a couple of relatively simple questions: How are our lives shaped by our being born? How does being born shape our existence? To address these questions, we draw on a group of thinkers who place natality, growth, and development at the center of understanding the human being, including Marjorie Grene, Mary Midgley, Alison Stone, Jane Flax, Cynthia Willett, Virginia Held, and Annette Baier. In their thought, there is an implicit, and in the case of Willett fairly explicit, effort to develop a "more powerful philosophical anthropology" (Willett, 2001: 34) by taking seriously that human beings start with being born and that mediation begins not through technology but the maternal body.

In *Understanding Nature* Marjorie Grene turns to the work of the ethologist Adolf Portmann (1990) to argue that the pattern of human development, our human life history, is unique among mammals in that we have become secondary nestlings, born helpless but with our eyes and ears wide open. The ontogenesis of the human infant has been completely rewritten, Portmann argues, to emphasize our premature birth and our social gestation in the first years of life. As Grene observes,

> the whole biological development of a typical mammal has been rewritten in our case in a new key: the whole structure of the embryo, the whole rhythm of growth, is directed, from first to last, to the emergence of a culture-dwelling animal . . . in its very tissues and organs and aptitudes, born to be open to its world, to be able to accept responsibility, to make its own the traditions of a historical past and to remake them into an unforeseeable future. (1974: 288)

On this account, human beings are a part of nature, born premature as vulnerable and dependent animals, who achieve personhood in a world that is deeply social and cultural. Reminding ourselves of our kinship with animals also serves to remind us that human beings are characterized by some of the same drives, capacities, and needs of all animals. As Grene observes, "Curiosity, exploration, pride, shame, jealousy all seem to be observable in other animals as well as in ourselves" (Grene and Eldridge, 1992: 171). Flax and Midgley, too, emphasize that the human person is characterized by complex and sometimes contradictory drives and motivations, owing to our animal nature.

We are animals, then, but as Grene often notes, we are rather odd animals with a peculiar human form of animality dependent on culture. Human beings are odd animals in that our growth and development have been retarded. Our premature birth and long period of development before achieving maturity remind us that we human beings are born needy and dependent. To meet those needs, human beings depend on caregivers to provide affection, support, and interdependence. Those caregivers are still largely women, and primarily mothers, though birth itself must be understood socially in the case of human beings, in that women are often attended by other women who assist in birthing. Anthropologist Wenda Trevathan (2011) argues that the unique nature of human birth gave rise to "obligate midwifery" and the norm of having others present during what could be a traumatic event. In *Our Babies, Ourselves* (1998), anthropologist Meredith Small notes the significance of this development: "And so our birthing is not just a biological event, but a social event as well. It relies on the help of family and friends, and emphasizes how important interpersonal interaction is to the human species, even when one of us first appears" (1998: 14). The matrix of dependency and care into which babies are born is also being expanded by transmothers, gay fathers who act as mothers, or even straight male fathers who adopt a more mothering role. Alison Gopnik (2016) notes that babies can become attached to many different people, not just their mothers, and that what is important is that they can rely on the love of the people who care for them. Willett (1995) cites Patricia Hill Collins (1991) in recognizing that human tactile sociality attunes infants to othermothers as well as bloodmothers.

Being born immature and vulnerable, then, marks human beings as inherently relational and dependent upon others for our very survival. As Baier observes, we have a relatively long gestational period and a relatively long youth humans requires the care and protection of adults. Personhood is an achievement requiring successive periods of infancy, childhood, and youth, during which humans develop as persons. "In virtue of our long and helpless infancy, persons, who all begin as small persons, are necessarily social beings, who first learn from older persons, by play, by imitation, by correction" (1991: 10). But more than survival, this long period of social development is marked, as Jane Flax observes, by both emotional dependency and our rapidly developing consciousness of social relations. Feminist anthropologists Nancy Makepeace Tanner and Adrienne Zihlman observe that another unique feature of hominids is the emergence of childhood as a new stage of life.[4] As Zihlman and Deborah Bolter observe in "Mammalian and Primate Roots of Human Sociality,"

> This lifestage shift compared to all other primates may lie at the root of the human-unique adaptation as it opens up socialization beyond the mother-infant dyad. This wider social learning and communication during development may account for the more intense variation in human social structure and organization cross-culturally than seen among the primates. (2004: 41)

Cynthia Willett argues that if we ignore this social genealogy of the person in the matrix of the family, we miss much about what it means to be human. Willett emphasizes several elements of this matrix that are noteworthy, foremost among them the "sociality of the flesh." Our first relationship is mediated by the maternal body. Touch and skin, reminders of our being embodied animals, are central to the bonds formed between infant and adult. As Willett comments, "the child that is not touched does not thrive" (2001: 25–6). Willett characterizes these early socio-affective relations as biosocial eros and argues that the preverbal bonds forged during this period are central to the development of the self and carried forward into adulthood, pointing to the central importance of sustained, intimate relations with other persons in the constitution, structure, and ongoing experience of a self. Alison Stone (2019) concurs, suggesting that having been born helpless, infants heavily depend on their caregivers, that their attachment to their caregivers becomes immensely affectively charged, and that these early relations with primary caregivers constitute a person's basic sense of self and are carried through to their adult lives. As she observes, "we all begin life as children and we never entirely leave our childhood behind—it continues to shape us, even when we cannot remember it" (2019: 14).

Significantly, Willett's genealogy of the person finds confirmation in feminist anthropologies that challenge the traditional and almost exclusive focus on tool use as the foundation for being human and look instead to sociality, tactile communication, intense affective ties, and long-term interaction between child and mother as equally, if not more, significant. Tanner's *On Becoming Human* (1981) and Zihlman and Bolter's account of the mammalian and primate roots of human sociality don't deny the place of tool use in our evolutionary history, but rather than emphasize the hand that grasps the tool, they focus on how the hand contributes to social life through enhanced tactile communication in infant clinging, mutual grooming, and other physical contact. As Willett notes in emphasizing that sociality begins in the caress: "The hand that is not wrapped around the tool, the noninstrumental expression of the hand opened in the caress, resists the logic of predation and traces an alternative dynamic of the social process" (1995: 39).

Human persons develop and have a history in which they are recognized and responded to as persons. It is our social nature, the fact of mutual recognition and answerability and our responsiveness to other persons, that shapes and makes possible our growth and development. Baier puts this point in terms of our learning the arts of personhood. "The more refined arts of personhood are learned as the personal pronouns are learned. . . . We come to recognize ourselves and others in mirrors, to refer to ourselves and to others" (1991: 13). It is in the learning from others that we acquire a sense of our place in a series of persons, to some of whom we have special responsibilities. To be a person is to be a history, as Baier notes: "We acquire a sense of ourselves as occupying a place in an historical and social order of persons, each of whom has a personal history interwoven with the history of a community" (1985: 90). Stone makes a similar point:

We do not spring into existence as full-fledged adults but enter into shared ways of life through a temporal and developmental process. Through this process we receive and inherit from others, and learn to participate with others in, a pre-existing communal spirit, or set of production relations, or network of shared involvements—or something of all these. (2019: 99)

In beginning from the standpoint of natality and growth and development and our entry into shared ways of life, rather than a standpoint that begins with technology, as does much critical posthumanism, emphasis is placed foremost on social relations and dependency. We are social animals and the natural habitat of persons is with other persons. It is with this standpoint in mind that Willett criticizes the metaphor of man the machine as a fantasy of being "hard, detached, in control, and certainly not dependent upon the mother or her sphere" (1995: 72).

The Domestic Posthuman

To develop an adequate posthuman figuration, we must attend to both the relations and connections to the nonhuman and simultaneously, engaging in what Donna Haraway has characterized as double vision (1991: 154), not lose sight of what is distinctive of the human being. Posthumanism too often sees only one thing as it focuses on the nonhuman, particularly info-, media-, and bio-technologies. The domestic posthuman, like much feminist thought, tries to see with double vision, bringing into focus figures of vulnerability and asking how as vulnerable and dependent beings we become persons. The domestic posthuman is not technophobic and does not reject technology, but it also doesn't begin from the standpoint of technological mediation and from the assumption that technological mediations have reconfigured human life. It recognizes that there are other sometimes countervailing elements of human life and alternative forms of technological mediation that are often marginalized if not completely ignored. In looking at the human being through the lens of digital and informational technological mediations and ignoring other aspects of human and nonhuman animal life that suggest elements of a different vision of the human-nonhuman "continuum," posthumanism is held captive by the most monstrous and alien or newest and shiniest examples of the posthuman. But there is no reason to turn there; we could also look to pets, children, sick people, the elderly, the disabled. In looking at these more everyday examples, we end up reflecting differently on the relationship between humans and technology.

Rather than invoking the logic of a paradigm shift, the domestic posthuman is anti-rupture, invoking a logic of evolution and future-building predicated on continuity, care, and stability—a sort of patient ushering of the present into the next thing, which often looks messy but is less deadly. While the domestic posthuman is in dialogue with a residual humanism, it is a humanism that would be largely unrecognizable to its humanist (Cartesian) ancestors. In this, we take inspiration from Lorraine Code's observation,

> My continued engagement with problems of moral philosophy in the rest of this chapter . . . locates my critique, albeit ambivalently, in dialogue with a residual humanistic subjectivity, yet a subjectivity that would be largely unrecognizable to its humanist ancestors. Its postessentialist cognizance of its specificity, its locatedness, make it impossible for it to take up a humanistic "view from nowhere". It is a situated, self-critical, socially produced subjectivity, yet one that can intervene in and be accountable for its positioning. (1991: 82)

In this respect, the domestic posthuman is more relentlessly nonessentialist than critical posthumanism as it seeks to avoid the essentialism implicated in discussions of THE HUMAN and THE POSTHUMAN, presuming that we can unequivocally define "the human." There's a general assumption in critical posthumanist discourse that tends to essentialize the liberal humanist subject as the sole stand-in for the human being, a point that Alexander Weheliye makes in the context of an examination of race, slavery, and animal studies:

> many invocations of posthumanism . . . reinscribe the humanist subject (Man) as the personification of the human by insisting that this is the category to be overcome, rarely considering cultural and political formations outside the world of Man that might offer alternative versions of humanity. Moreover, posthumanism and animal studies isomorphically yoke humanity to the limited possessive individualism of Man. (2015: 9–10)

Being born as we are born suggests that there are significant differences between children and adults and discussions of "the human" in human-machine relations elide these important differences.[5] By attending to the variety of human lives and life stages, from infants and children to the elderly, and by attending to the particularity of human lives and the different ways they are embodied and embedded, the domestic posthuman seeks to construct a broader, more capacious posthumanism. The domestic posthuman recognizes that within the context of the home, all life forms can't be treated symmetrically and that species-natures still count for something as we "domesticate" infants.

The human being we are defining is relational, decentered, with strong ties to animals and nature and, yes, material culture. We cannot go back to some naive view of the human being that understands human nature or being human in the absence of such relationality. We can only fully understand how we become human by thickening and deepening our understanding of the relationships between humans, animals, and objects/the material world. And thinking in terms of the posthuman reminds us that the nonhuman is always a part of the human and that we cannot understand the human other than by thinking through the nonhuman. But we have to take that nonhuman as something more than simply information and media technologies.

The domestic posthuman reminds us as well that the struggle over the meaning of the posthuman is taking place not only in high-tech military labs and think tanks but in family rooms and domestic spaces where we consume TV images of the posthuman and struggle over their meaning, including their meaning to childhood and adolescence. Situating our analysis on the home reminds us too that the home is not simply a consumptive sphere of mindless consuming but is a productive sphere—it is where life is reproduced. As Lynn Spigel perceptively notes: "The home is not simply a receptacle of cultural consumption, the domestic sphere has also been a site of cultural production. The home is a place of creative activity" (2001: 8). That creative activity often takes the form of play. Willett's descriptions of early child-caregiver relations revolve around music, dance, laughter, and play, including the playful encounters that happen between different creatures in the home, between child and cat, for instance. Willett notes that "playful encounters between creatures with different modes of self-awareness are a source for the codevelopment of a biosocial self" (2014: 28) and she as well as Midgley emphasize the evolutionary origins of ethics in social play.

In "House and Home: Feminist Variations on a Theme," Young recognizes that house and home are deeply ambivalent themes, especially perhaps for feminists. But she turns to home and homemaking as important sources of human values and as sites of critical liberating potential. Young's philosophical reflections on home suggest that we need to revalue home and see it as a source of crucial human values. Homemaking provides the material support for the creation of a human being who has the resources to venture out into the world. And it is home to which we often return, especially when in need of care and nurturance. Home in this sense is a basic support for personal identity, a material anchor for a sense of agency. Relating the story of her own mother's efforts, Young finds in the preservative value of homemaking an important source of meaning-making often overlooked by other philosophers. "Homemaking consists in the activities of endowing things with living meaning, arranging them in space in order to facilitate the life activities of those to whom they belong, and preserving them, along with their meaning" (2005: 142). Importantly, too, we can see in Young's account of preservative homemaking a link to Baier's account of the arts of personhood: "The work of preservation also importantly involves teaching the children the meanings of things among which one dwells, teaching the children the stories, practices, and celebrations that keep the particular meanings alive" (Young, 2005: 142).[6] For Young, home carries a core positive meaning as the material anchor for a sense of agency and a shifting and fluid identity (2005: 149).

bell hooks makes a similar observation in "Homeplace: A Site of Resistance," arguing that for African Americans, the homeplace is a site of resistance and liberation struggle in the context of an oppressive and devaluing social reality. As she evocatively writes,

> In our young minds houses belonged to women, were their special domain, not as property, but as places where all that truly mattered in life took place— the warmth and comfort of shelter, the feeding of our bodies, the nurturing of our souls. There we learned dignity, integrity of being; there we learned to have faith. The folks who made this life possible, who were our primary guides and teachers, were black women. (2014: 41)

Beginning from the home reminds us that at least in the West it's in the home where we fully come into our humanity. It also allows us to recognize the importance of domestic labor: the labor that produces and cares for human beings, other life forms, and potentially even new life forms. The domestic posthuman recognizes that persons aren't produced algorithmically but domestically, through long and often difficult domestic labor and the arts of personhood, broadly construed as the domestic labor of reproducing persons. Alison Gopnik (2016) argues that a model of parenting predicated upon techniques, what we might think of as algorithmic parenting, subverts the very evolutionary purpose of childhood, designed to be a period for exploration, learning, and innovation. Gopnik (2020b) argues that our exceptionally long and helpless human childhood is indicative of a unique and uniquely important stage in human life history and that it is a mistake to look at children as simply unfinished adults. Rather, children and adults are different forms of *Homo sapiens*, with different developmental and evolutionary agendas and different kinds of cognition, brains, and experiences of the world, even if, as we earlier noted, adults never entirely leave their childhood behind.[7] Gopnik interestingly ties together tradition and innovation, arguing that the human being's most distinctive capacity is the capacity to change, but that that capacity is itself made possible by intimate caregiving. Our capacity to learn is intertwined with our long period of dependency, a period in which infants and children can explore and interact with their environment and attachments to diverse adult caregivers. As Gopnik notes,

> From an evolutionary perspective, the relations between human children and the adults who care for them are crucially and profoundly important; indeed, they are a large part of what defines us as human beings. Our most distinctive and important human abilities—our capacities for learning, invention, and innovation; and for tradition, culture, and morality—are rooted in relations between parents and children. (2016: 22)

Rather than looking to the techniques of algorithms as a model for culture, perhaps we ought to consider the arts of raising children. All persons start out as children, born to earlier persons from whom they learn the arts of personhood. We are, Baier notes, second persons who acquire the arts of personhood from those on whom we are dependent (1985: 84). Persons require, according to Baier, successive periods of infancy, childhood, and youth, during which they develop as persons: "In virtue of our long and helpless infancy, persons, who all begin as small persons, are necessarily social beings, who first learn from older persons, by play, by imitation, by correction." Baier observes that gods, if they were denied childhood, couldn't be persons because "(p)ersons are essentially successors, heirs to other persons who formed and cared for them, and their personality is revealed both in their relations to others and in their response to their own recognized genesis" (1985: 85).

Common to these views of personhood we have been exploring from Baier, Willett, Gopnik, and others is an understanding of the human being as embodied, social, and relational. As Baier notes, "Our personhood is responsive and called into full expression by other persons who treat us as one of them" (1991: 5). This begins at birth with the tactile sociality characteristic of the infant-caregiver relationship, is sustained in intimate relations of care and dependency for the vulnerable, and flourishes by virtue of what Hilde Lindemann identifies as the social practices that hold us in our personhood. Personhood, in this view, isn't some kind of substantial or essential identity but a social practice and an ongoing achievement. Building on Baier's insights, Lindemann emphasizes the social nature of this practice in which narrative plays a crucial role, especially the stories that family members tell and retell that hold us in our personhood. In *Holding and Letting Go: The Social Practice of Personal Identities* (2014), Lindemann emphasizes the role of storytelling in the matrix of the family as an important practice of personhood often overlooked in Western philosophical accounts of personhood. Gopnik makes a similar point, expanding on the role of narrative in the arts of personhood. In a discussion of "learning by listening," she emphasizes the role of stories in children's lives as she recounts the work of Polly Wiessner and the contrast between daytime talk (mostly about work) and nighttime talk, which largely revolved around stories.

> When the sun went down and the men and women, both old and young, gathered around the fire, the talk transformed. Eighty-one percent of the time, people told stories—stories about people they knew, about past generations, about relatives in distant villages, about goings-on in the spirit world and even about those bizarre beings called anthropologists. This nighttime talk engaged some of our most distinctively human abilities: imagination, culture, spirituality, and "theory of mind." (Gopnik, 2016: 124)

This is a point that Katherine Hayles recognizes and for which she defaults to a decidedly domestic and maternal metaphor. Addressing in *How We Think* Lev Manovich's claim that the database may eclipse narrative, Hayles responds,

> narrative is essential to the human lifeworld. Jerome Bruner, in his book significantly entitled *Acts of Meaning: Four Lectures on Mind and Culture* (1992), cites studies indicating that mothers tell their children some form of narrative several times each hour to guide their actions and explain how the world works (81–84). We take narrative in with mother's milk and practice it many times every day of our lives. . . . Wherever one looks, narratives surface, as ubiquitous in everyday culture as dust mites. (2012: 181)

Hayles' reference to mother's milk reminds us that the stories caregivers tell infants and children are never simply narratives but are always entangled with the sounds, smells, and faces of those very caregivers, as well as the rhythms and movements of their bodies. As Willett observes, the self begins in the subjectless sociality and affect attunement of infant and caregiver in which the infant seeks the voice, smell, and touch of the caregiver, often the mother. Willett's observations serve to remind us that we shouldn't lose sight of the tactile in this discussion of narrative. "In the beginning is not the word; it is the touch" (1995: 47). She emphasizes the nonverbal interaction between nurturer and child. "This liminal mode of social interaction brings the child into being as a person" (1995: 56). There's a form of tactile recognition that is important to the preverbal social bond between infant and adult and through which the child acquires a social presence of its own (2001: 216).

If there is a weakness in these accounts of narrative, the arts of personhood, and subjectless sociality, it's in the general neglect of the role of material culture in shaping and holding on to personhood, a point that often drives posthumanism. It may be a short step, though, to recognizing the way in which tactile sociality and stories are entangled with material culture. Staying with that literal mother's milk, Deborah Lupton (2013) observes that the infant's sense of self emerges out of the intercorporeality of the caregiver-infant relationship and that material objects play a role in the formation of the infant's self. Noting the importance of "skinship," Lupton suggests that this can extend to material objects as well. "Just as intercorporeality may occur between infants and their carers, in which a kind of affectively-charged space exists between them as part of skinship, so too, there may be a similar relationship of infants with the material objects that routinely touch their bodies"[8] (2013: 8).

Sounding a theme common to our critique of posthumanism, Lupton argues that too little attention has been paid to the material culture and agency of infants, arguing that "material objects . . . can be extremely important for infants and very young children. They comprise an integral dimension of their affective and spatial relationship with other people and material and non-material elements of their world" (2013: 3). Bodies and selves, Lupton notes, are entangled with physical objects and in the case of infants "soft objects" often stand in for the softness and security of a parent or caregiver. These soft objects—a teddy bear, blanket, clothing items—become imbued with the scents and traces of both the infant's and the caregiver's bodies: "The infant's soft bedding, comfort blanket or a sling in which it is carried, may provide this connection, again taking on the smell or marks from the baby's body (traces of dribble, milky leakages or tears, for example) if they are used over a period of time before being washed" (2013: 8).

Where machines and monsters are born of networks and assemblages, posthuman persons are born of messy entanglements fostered in HOMES. Posthuman persons begin as vulnerable and dependent infants, cared for and held in their personhood by a variety of bloodmothers and othermothers, situated in the home as a site of messy entanglements, a network distinct from the information networks so often highlighted in critical posthumanism, but equally a site of unruly activity in which there is a mess of practices, kids, caregivers, animals, things (lots of things sometimes) and in which a lot of learning (apprenticeship) happens. Simultaneously, though, it would be a mistake to think that the caregivers can't distinguish between the parts of this messy entanglement that need to have their diapers changed or be cared for in times of crisis or be shepherded into adolescent and even adult life. Posthumanism often celebrates transgressing boundaries and disrupting stabilities, embracing fragmentation and the power of networks or assemblages to be undone and redone. A deeper or thicker account of the human being might question these simple dichotomies where transgression = liberation, and stability = oppression. The domestic posthuman rejects this often-unquestioned assumption that transgressing boundaries is necessarily liberatory or pleasurable and that all forms of stability are oppressive, recognizing that human beings, like perhaps most social animals, have some need for, as Lena Gunnarsson notes, "stable social arrangements that predictably ensure that people's needs are met, while unpredictable ruptures of this pattern might prove destructive" (2013: 10).

Sophie, Renie, and JSOD

We opened this chapter by asking what happens when we invite the posthuman into our homes. For Sophie, bringing a synth into the home offers the possibility of some comfort as she embraces what we might characterize as a posthuman performance, embracing the disappearing boundary between human and machine. As she explains to Renie:

> Synths are perfect and clean. They don't make mistakes. That's what life should be like. . . . And you don't have to feel anything anymore. You don't have to worry about stuff, like your family. And you don't have to miss people. And you don't have to be sad. It's really hard to stop all those feelings, but then I see you. I'm going to be just like you.

Domestic Posthuman Second Persons

But Sophie's behavior continues to grate on her parents, especially Laura, who feels that Sophie's behavior continues to call into question her own capabilities as a mother. One night, seated around the dining table, Laura asks Sophie to pass her the salt. Sophie picks it up and hands it robotically to Laura, who in turns asks her to pass the salt "normally." Sophie responds, "Of course Laura." Enraged, Laura shouts, "Mum, call me mum. Stop acting like this. Stop it." It's at this moment that Joe gets up from the table and asks Sophie to come with him. He takes her into the kitchen and begins to drop eggs on the floor while laughing. As Laura and Toby question his odd behavior, he begins to make a mess, tossing eggs and flour and soda, and starting a food fight with the family. Sophie squeals with delight and comes alive as she tosses food at her brother and parents. Willett has observed that the home is often a site of playful eros and that play and laughter itself can disrupt borders and lower defenses, as Joe implicitly recognizes by encouraging his family to laugh and play, breaking down boundaries while breaking a few eggs.

In the movement from a perfect and clean life in which you don't have to feel anything to a family food fight we witness the full drama of human life, from worries about one's family to troubling feelings, including anger and frustration, to the sheer eruption of play and transgressive behavior when one's parent starts throwing eggs. In turning to Sophie and the predicament that she and her family face that comes from bringing technology into their home and their lives, we see dimensions of the posthuman that have been missing from most discussions of posthumanism, including especially the need to attend to the impact of those technologies on infants, children, and adolescents and the domestic spaces in which they are living with others and still negotiating their developing personhood.

This perhaps is the suggestion behind labeling Sophie's and Renie's overidentification with synth life a disorder, driven by Joe and Laura's concerns that Sophie for one is seeking escape from the messy entanglements suggested by the formative influence of the social presence of others, the importance of caregiver-child relations, and the matrix of the family as the source of identity. As befits a television show geared toward family viewing, *Humans* seems especially aware of the complicated nature of family dynamics and the way in which introducing new technologies can impact that dynamic. Laura in fact is concerned that Sophie has pulled away from her as Laura's life is increasingly consumed by work and her relationship with Joe breaks down. Sophie and her adolescent friend Renie seek acknowledgment and response, and not finding it, they mirror the one steadfast relationship in their lives, the synths. If Stone is right that "our natality means that our earliest relationships have special and unrivaled power to mould our emerging selves" (2019: 98), then surely Sophie's parents are right to at least question the impact of placing a synth at the center of that early relationship. In seeking escape from the contingencies and drama of human life and looking for refuge in mirroring the techniques of synth life, in "becoming-machine" (2013: 91) as Rosi Braidotti suggests, Sophie and Renie are unsettling to others, including their family members, in their performance of posthuman synth life. Sophie and Renie are running from aspects of their embodiment and the complexity of being human: roiled emotions, jealousy, family rivalries, and budding sexuality, seeking to flee from embodiment and the arts of personhood into dissociation and the techne of synth life. In centering its narrative of human-machine relations on children and adolescents, *Humans* suggests that any conclusions we draw about the transformative power of caregiving robots be informed by our understanding of all the stages of our life history.

By situating the story of sociable robots in a domestic context and focusing on the possible impacts on the lives of children and adolescents, *Humans* underscores that the introduction of technology into the home will likely have complex repercussions, reminding us that humanity is an ongoing process of growth and development that takes place in the home and can take complex, sometimes discomfiting forms. We can't get at the complexities of sociability until we think about it as situated in the proper context for studying it: in the home, with parents who sometimes fail us, siblings with whom we experience jealousy and competition, all the while experiencing emotions and desires that we sometimes find troubling. We become second persons in and through relations with others forged over long years during which we are vulnerable and dependent, often characterized by care and nurturance, but sometimes by aggression and hostility.

Such an understanding is largely missing from Coeckelbergh's and DeFalco's analyses of the impact of technology on human care.[9] *Humans* challenges the almost singular focus in critical posthumanism on recent technological developments and technogenesis—the technological genesis of the posthuman. Much of that discussion ignores anything else that might be going on around human-technology relations and focuses almost exclusively on the technology and its role in shaping the human being. But neither human beings nor technologies exist in a vacuum and the case of Sophie reorients our thinking about the posthuman by starting from a domestic standpoint that focuses on home, caregiving, and developing personhood.

Much discussion in critical posthumanism of the human being, embodiment, relationality, and subjectivity takes place at a highly generalized and abstract level that fails to question whether we need to distinguish situations where fully formed adults confront technology from situations involving infants and children, who may be entirely differently situated from the liberal humanist subject that is so often the target of posthuman critique. Interestingly, DeFalco is aware of the gendered and racialized representations of robots, but she doesn't attend at all to situations where robots are involved in the care of children and the implications of this care. The representations she examines from *Real Humans* and *Robot and Frank* focus exclusively on elder recipients of care and she implicitly assumes that all human beings are similarly situated to the elder recipients of care she examines. Coeckelbergh's analysis also deals exclusively with elder care. But Sophie is not similarly situated as Frank (from *Robot and Frank*) or Coeckelbergh's Grandpa, and to ignore the differences in their situations is to fail to understand the nature and importance of childhood. Being born implies growth and development, a body that changes and ages and is embedded in a particular historical, social, and cultural context and that has implications for thinking about species-specific kinds that critical posthumanism often obscures.

This is nowhere clearer than in DeFalco's discussion of touch in a pivotal scene from *Robot and Frank* in which she argues that the haptic communication between Robot and Frank is indicative of a sensual engagement and intimacy that undermines oppositions between human and machine, real and artificial, embodied and virtual. Robot is embodied and he is able to touch, DeFalco argues, suggesting that the haptic intimacy between human and machine exposes the vulnerability of embodiment. DeFalco's analysis treats embodiment and touch at a very general and abstract level. Missing in these explorations of human-machine explorations of touch is a deeper understanding of touch as involving skin-on-skin, the kind of touch that is central to the development of the person. As Willett observes,

> The deprivation of touch, perhaps more so than the other forms of sensory engagement, hinders the libidinal development of the person. The infant who is deprived of touch can become excessively withdrawn or even violent, and incapable of sustaining social bonds in later life. The erotic pleasure the infant takes in the inviting smells and in the warm taste of the mother's milky flesh does not only serve to stimulate and nourish the appetite of a biological organism. What the child finds pleasant in the mother's flesh welcomes the child into the world. (2001: 216)

While Willett focuses on the touch between infant and caregiver, it's equally clear that in the elderly as well, touch is central to well-being. As Ashley Montagu notes, "Tactile needs do not seem to change with aging—if anything, they seem to increase" (quoted in Field, 2014: 30). In an overview of Willett's work, Megan Craig recognizes the centrality of play, laughter, and love to Willett's biosocial eros ethics and points to the implications for a digital culture in which touch is increasingly and exclusively mediated by technology:

> The lack of contact endemic in modern society is exacerbated by a digital culture in which everyone can be connected all the time without having to touch or smell or feel another body, a culture in which surveillance replaces sensitized response. Therefore, in addition to the geographical challenges to finding a place to be with nonhuman persons, we are faced with the digital

challenges of losing touch with one another, as expanding networks of "friends" reflect increasingly self-replicating and insulated lives. (2015: 65)

Competing representations of the posthuman condition raise important questions about the kind of future we are looking forward to. Coeckelbergh and DeFalco imagine a future in which hybridity and human-technology relations transform our understanding of the human condition. As DeFalco writes,

> one can imagine a future of care that is both posthuman and posthumanist, in which life is marked by hybridity and it is increasingly difficult, even impossible, to distinguish where technology ends and human begins. In such a future, assistive technology would not be limited to caregiving robots, though certainly such artificial life forms are likely to become inevitable, familiar companions. Rather, the human would be eclipsed by the posthuman, by the cyborg, by the splice. (2018: 28)

Humans complicates our understanding of human-technology relations and should give us pause before we fully embrace the posthuman eclipse of the human. Writing in a different context, Kate Soper suggests that at times we must recognize "a species-specific and exclusive need for us to police divisions (between life and death, children and adults, nourishment and excretion, humans and animals) whose maintenance is seen as a condition of the possibility of any human community" (2009: 229). Flax (1993) too suggests that certain forms of life may preclude the possibility of enduring attachments or responsibilities to another in which the other can rely on one's stability and continuity of being. None of which disqualifies replicant and synth personhood nor suggests that human persons are somehow superior to replicants or synths. Nor should it be taken to suggest an anthropocentric view predicated on human exceptionality as defined by our being rational, autonomous, disembodied. In fact, beginning with natality and emphasizing our life history underscores some of the same points most central to critical posthumanism: interdependence, relationality, embodiment, being situated. But it is to suggest that efforts to elide the distinction between human and machine pay too little attention to the different stages of growth and development that human beings go through and the significance of birth, infancy, and childhood for becoming the persons we are. We never leave our childhood behind.

A Qualitative Leap

And yet we cannot simply ignore the technological developments that have been central to the posthuman dramatic picture of technogenesis. Joe and Laura Hawkins are advised that the best thing for Sophie is human contact.

"No Synths, just her mum and dad, family and friends." In fact, though, the advice from the therapist turns out to be futile, for the lives of all the members of the Hawkins family are increasingly intertwined with the synths. *Humans* reminds us that the path forward is not backward and that being human is a messy business and introducing sociable robots into the home is going to be complicated precisely because human life is messy. We see that ambivalence reflected in Joe and Laura Hawkins' responses to the growing presence of synths in their lives. Having divorced, partly owing to Joe's sexual relations with the synth he purchased and brought into the home, Joe moves to a small town that has banned synths and opens a small grocery store selling organic food. And yet, when a new class of synth children are discovered, Joe takes one of them, Sam, under his wings and introduces him to Sophie. Laura meanwhile becomes a leading advocate for synth rights. Indeed, precisely at the time that Laura is navigating Sophie's JSOD, she is working to establish that the synths are conscious and deserving of equal treatment. When Sophie learns that Sam is a synth, she chooses to take on the task of caring for Sam and helping him to develop a deeper understanding of human sociability, including learning how to play.

> Sophie: Sam, when I'm sad, I like to do something fun to take my mind off it. What do you like to do for fun?
>
> Sam: I don't know what I like to do for fun.
>
> Sophie: Well, why don't we carry on with your training. I think I know the perfect place to begin. (She leads Sam into her bedroom where she has built a fort out of blankets and chairs.)
>
> Sam: Children gain enjoyment from building things?
>
> Sophie: Yeah, it's fun, come on.
>
> Sam: What else do kids like to do for fun?
>
> Sophie: Sam, let me tell you about a little thing called a sleepover.
>
> Sam: Sleepover? What's a sleepover?
>
> Sophie: It's where kids stay the night at each other's houses and eat junk food at strange hours and watch bad films and play games like hide and seek or truth or dare.

Humans doesn't demonize technology but shows us the complex and sometimes unexpected ways in which humans and technologies interact. It's interesting to note that the central characters in Coeckelbergh's and DeFalco's dramas of posthuman care are elderly men. Coeckelbergh's Grandpa accommodates himself to a life of social isolation mediated by his technological tools, including FaceNet, TwitImage, and his robotic dog. Frank, an elderly man estranged from his family, reaches out for the cold hard touch of Robot, the only consistent presence in his life. Sophie, on the other hand, invites the synthetic child Sam into her bedroom fort to play games and eat junk food, socializing Sam into her world, rather than any longer accommodating herself to the synth's world. *Humans* reminds us that we human beings are intertwined with the material world of artifacts and how we think about what it means to be human is going to be impacted by our interactions with those artifacts. Sophie and Sam learn to play with one another as they work through new forms of human-machine relationships, suggesting that perhaps in the end it will turn out that the kids are alright.

Sophie's very capacity to navigate these new and complicated relationships may itself be a product of her natality and extended period of growth and development in childhood. Critical posthumanists, as we saw in Chapter 1, are motivated by an interest in reimagining what it might mean to be human, given our increasing imbrication with technology. We argued, though, that with their focus on technology, machine models, and the myth of technogenesis, the posthuman imaginative vision has yet to take a quantum leap of the radical imagination as suggested by Adrienne Rich. In her essay on motherhood and the contemporary emergency, Rich is critical of "the statisticians, the political scientists, the economists, the image-makers of television and other advertising, the professionals" (1979: 262), for denying the value and dignity of traditional women's work in the home.

> The feminist movement has from the first demanded choice as each woman's right, respect for each woman's being; feminist artists, historians, anthropologists have been the first to show concern and respect for the crafts of the midwives and grandmothers, the anonymous work of women's hands, the oral culture of women sitting in kitchens, the traditional arts and remedies passed on from mother to daughter, the female culture never granted the reverence accorded to "high art." (1979: 262)

Rich's quantum leap of the imagination is a radical feminist vision that seeks to design a culture predicated on the power of feminist mothering, what Rich also called outlaw mothering. Eschewing an account of mothering that ties it to essential accounts of female nature, the domestic posthuman advocates an imaginative vision for human-technology relations that takes seriously the work of outlaw mothering that takes place in the domestic spaces so often occupied by mothers, grandmothers, othermothers, and even outlaw mothers. It recognizes that change itself and the birth of new imaginative visions begins in natality. As Grace Jantzen observes, natality allows for hope: "(W)ith each new infant, new possibilities are born, new freedom and creativity, the potential that this child will help make the world better. Freedom, creativity, and the potential for a fresh start are central to every human life and are ours in virtue of the fact that we are natals" (2004: 38).

Alison Gopnik argues that childhood is the crucible of change, noting that "the evolutionary purpose of childhood is to provide a protected period in which variation and innovation can thrive. Play is the most striking manifestation of that strategy. Play is precisely an activity with no apparent goal or purpose or outcome" (2016: 101). In their play, children and adolescents, as *Humans* suggests, are often at the leading edge of technological and cultural change. Childhood and adolescence are evolutionarily designed, Gopnik argues, to give rise to innovation and new ways of thinking. One might suggest that it's our extended childhood and our periods of play and exploration that make possible the innovative images and dramatic pictures that critical posthumanists are looking for. As Gopnik points out, "This extended childhood that we have . . . gives human beings a chance to explore, develop new ways of being in the world, find new social relationships, and figure out new technologies. It's the protection and love of the parents that let the children do unexpected things" (quoted in Lewis, 2016).

Posthumanism is about imagining future ways of being human, of designing a posthuman that escapes from the logic of anthropocentrism and human exceptionalism and takes note of our significant relationship to tools and technologies and material culture. But it is clear that in designing a posthuman culture we can't lose sight of significant aspects of the variety of human beings meant to populate that culture. The domestic posthuman reminds us of the centrality of biosocial eros; of the importance of tactile sociality and the multimodal nature of touch involving warmth, smells, musicality, movement; and of the necessary stages of growth and development that human life history moves through. It's only on a foundation that includes these elements that we will be able to design a domestic posthuman.

Sophie and Renie might be at the foreground of creating a new way of being human and synthie culture might ultimately catch on with the kids, but if it does, it's only because those kids have benefited from the kind of nurturance that sends them out in the world to explore alternative spaces and ways of being. The radical qualitative leap that Adrienne Rich imagines is only made possible by mothers, othermothers, allomothers, and a rich and complex domestic and social life.

Notes

1 Writing in 1983, the philosopher of technology Jacques Ellul was already worried about the phenomena of mirroring behavior, observing that human beings were

encouraged by technical culture to mirror and adapt to machines and technique: "At the same time, one should not forget the fact that human beings are themselves already modified by the technical phenomenon. . . . Their whole education is oriented toward adaptation to the conditions of technique (learning how to cross streets at traffic lights) and their instruction is destined to prepare them for entrance into some technical employment. . . . In other words, it must not be forgotten that it is this very humanity which has been pre-adapted to and modified by technique that is supposed to master and reorient technique. It is obvious that this will not be able to be done with any independence." *Humans*, we might think, is in a contemporary vein posing the question of the extent to which we are designing a culture in which human beings are encouraged to mirror their machines.

2   As many authors have observed (see, for instance, Tamar Sharon, 2012 and Francesca Ferrando, 2019), "posthumanism" is a capacious term that encompasses a variety of approaches and methodological commitments. We're interested in that variety of posthumanism that involves "a radical rethinking of human ontology in light of emerging biotechnologies" (Sharon, 2012: 8) and is most often associated with the work of, among others, Badmington, Wolfe, Hayles, Graham, and Haraway. While Sharon labels this variety "radical posthumanism," "critical posthumanism is used more often in the texts we reference and that is the term we employ.

3   For more on the inadequacies of contemporary accounts of technological mediation for addressing matters related to subjectivity and natality, see Dennis Weiss "On the Subject of Technology" (2019) and "Natality and the Posthuman Condition" (2023).

4   There is a long history on the culture and meaning of childhood, much of which began with the 1960 publication of Philippe Ariès' *Centuries of Childhood: A Social History of Family Life*. We focus less on the historical and cultural meaning of childhood than on the significance of childhood as an extended period of growth and development in human life history. For more on childhood and human life history, see Hawkes and Paine (2006), *The Evolution of Human Life History*, especially Chapter 7: "Modern Human Life History: The Evolution of Human Childhood and Fertility," by Barry Bogin; and the 2020 Theme Issue of the Philosophical Transactions of the Royal Society, "Life history and learning: how childhood, caregiving and old age shape cognition and culture in humans and other animals" compiled and edited by Alison Gopnik, Willem E. Frankenhuis, and Michael Tomasello 2020.

5   Much contemporary design discourse evinces a similar weakness. Tony Fry's *Human by Design* (2012) and Ron Wakkary's *Things We Could Design* (2021) are replete with references to "the human."

6   Significantly, the role of homemaking is often overlooked in contemporary design's discussion of the home. Consider, for instance, Arturo Escobar's equation of the suburban home with a "world of decommunalized individuals." Drawing on the work of Juhani Pallasmaa, Escobar suggests that buildings possess a "tectonic language" and that architecture's growing instrumentalization and aestheticization alienates us from the "poetics of home" (Escobar, 2018: 39). Completely absent from his discussion of designing houses and homes is the kind of preservative homemaking central to Young's story of building and dwelling.

7   Jane Flax turns to the work of D. W. Winnicott and object relations theory precisely because it does not require a fixed or essentialist notion of human nature. As she notes, "The logic of object relations theory suggests that human nature may have many forms. As social relations and family structures change, so would human

nature. As the kinds of objects and relations between them a child internalizes change, so too would 'the child' and the nature of 'childhood' itself" (1990: 110).

8   Nick Lee (2008) makes a similar argument in "Awake, Asleep, Adult, Child: An A-Humanist Account of Persons," drawing on Winnicott's account of an infant's first transitional objects, which are almost always soft objects, to account for how the interrelations of infant, soft object, and caregiver foster the infant's "becoming person," in which agency is developed.

9   There are in fact interesting examples of caring mediated by technology that aren't predicated on decentering the human being and which actively foster human relations. Rosalind Picard, the founder and Director of the Affective Computing Group at MIT, helped found Empatica (their moto: "We create groundbreaking technology that is friendly, caring and more human" [Empatica]) and develop the EmbracePlus smartwatch, which alerts a loved one if it senses an imminent seizure in the wearer. Web services such as MealTrain.com and CaringBridge.org provide a technical interface for individuals interested in organizing food and caring for friends and family dealing with health issues.

Figure 3 Boxing gloves, *Eliza's Peculiar Cabinet of Curiosities*, Folayemi Wilson.

Do posthumans have families? How do they relate to one another? I wonder about these questions as I look at the back wall of Eliza's cabin with its enlarged photo of a historical Black family. Folayemi Wilson selected this photo because it represented a free family. The father came from Jamaica. He bought his wife's freedom. They married on Emancipation Day. Her name is Freedom. Hanging on the wall, near the father and son, are boxing gloves, perhaps suggestive of a father's and son's shared pastime, one of the rarely sanctioned masculine pastimes, mostly involving sports, in which men can freely reach out and touch one another. But equally suggestive of the struggle to hold one's family together in the face of powers—social, cultural, technological—that would sever families. It evokes questions. Do posthumans have families? How do they relate to one another?

Chapter 3
Myths of Domestic Posthuman Second Persons

In July of 2022 we had the pleasure of attending the third "Philosophy of Human Technology Relations Conference," held at Aalborg University in Copenhagen, during which we were able to participate in discussions of robots, cyborgs, artificial wombs, and the techno-Anthropocene. But it was outside the conference and university space that we encountered what we came to think of as the portraitist of the posthuman, at least the domestic posthuman. We happened upon the first large-scale retrospective in Scandinavia of the American photographer Diane Arbus. "Diane Arbus: Photographs, 1956–1971" featured 150 photographs, many of them featuring Arbus' fascination with, as the Louisiana Museum of Modern Art noted, the range of humanity. Noting that Arbus photographed babies, nudists, circus performers, cross-dressers, dwarves, and suburbanites, the Museum observed in its introduction to the retrospective, "Arbus aimed to describe, in vivid detail, a range of human difference, at a moment when visual culture strove instead to emphasize uniformity." They noted of Arbus' style, whether she was photographing mundane figures or their more alien counterparts, "The direct, even confrontational, gaze of the individuals in her photographs remains bracing to our eyes still today—provoking recognition, empathy and unease" ("Diane Arbus," n.d.).

In confronting Arbus' fascination with "the range of humanity," we began to think she complicated the simple formulation of human-technology relations that was central to both the conference and much of posthumanism. We found ourselves wondering, just who is that human so heavily featured in accounts of human-technology relations? While posthumanists may recognize that the human is a constructed and contested category, accounts of the posthuman trade freely in their reference to "the human." Consider, for instance, that Rosi Braidotti's *The Posthuman* (2013) includes hundreds of references to "the human," as does Pramod Nayar's *Posthumanism* (2014). Braidotti structures her account of the posthuman through the notions of "becoming machine," "becoming animal," and "becoming earth." (2013: 66). But she evinces little interest in "becoming human" and the variety of ways we become human or in the variety of human beings we become. Posthumanism has often allowed Cartesian Man to stand in for the figure of the human, reducing the variety and range of human beings to a single figure. But the category of not-man has always been something of a mongrel category. Judith Hughes notes that the great class of "not-men" has included women, animals, madmen, foreigners, slaves, patients and imbeciles, and children (Hughes, 1988: 72). In the previous chapter we advocated for a view of the human being that emphasized natality, life history, growth and development, and the emergence of second personhood, believing that such a view complicates our understanding of "the human." It is perhaps a similar motivation that led Haraway to embrace the notion of companion species. As she notes, "That is why I propose the term 'companion species' instead of human/nonhuman or humanism and its various prefixes. Queering has the job of undoing 'normal' categories, and none is more critical than the human/nonhuman sorting operation. That is crucial work and play" (2008b: xiv). Alexander Doty observes in *Making Things Perfectly Queer* that, "in any of its uses so far, queerness has been set up to challenge and break apart conventional categories" (1993: xv). Queering the human then is an opportunity to challenge and break apart a category which remains conventional even in posthumanism. But we might wonder if there are multiple ways to queer the human. Going the route of monsters or animals or companion species suggests some possibilities. But lingering with humans for a time may be another. And to too quickly label such attempts problematically humanist or anthropocentric seems essentializing. We suggest that there are many ways to queer the human, and one of them takes the route of emphasizing "becoming human" and what that entails. Lingering a bit on the human as a kinship term that brings together babies, children, adolescents, adults, as well as trans and queer individuals, disabled, and elderly may be a means to uncover aspects of posthuman second personhood that are often overlooked in posthumanism's too-quick turn to monsters, aliens, and cyborgs. Queering the human might allow us to develop a richer and more complete set of figures, a radical leap in imagining human becoming, that remains with the human while challenging the construction of the human. Arbus' attention to the range of humanity and its power to provoke both recognition and unease reminds us that sometimes those human beings closest to us can also be the most discomfiting.

To cultivate a different posthuman imagination, one that begins not from the ontology of the cyborg, monster, or alien but offers an alternative set of figurations from the perspective of the domestic posthuman, herein we offer a set of myths or images of the domestic posthuman second person, dramatic pictures for imagining the posthuman, recognizing that

- human beings are shaped not only by technogenesis but also by the distinctive pattern of human life history and processes of growth and development that run from birth to death, natality to mortality;
- personhood is not solely a matter of digital information networks but evolves and develops in rich networks of relationality and biosociality;
- vulnerability and dependency are characteristic of the entirety of the life history of human beings, rather than deformations of adult human autonomy and rationality;
- the self's decentered pleasures take place against a background of stability and centeredness;
- the very possibility of "opening up new ways of thinking about what being human means" (Hayles, 1999: 285) is fostered by early experiences of preservative care, love, and touch that center the human being.

Womb

Wombs have always been troubling and disruptive, especially in Western thought, beginning with the early ancient Greek notion of the wandering womb, running through more modern notions of female hysteria, and continuing on to contemporary visions of cybernetic wombs in films ranging from *Eve of Destruction* (she has a nuclear bomb in her uterus!), *The Matrix*, with its tagline "The Matrix Has You" featuring a blood-red, illuminated fetus hanging in a cybernetic biobag, to the more recent *Blade Runner 2049*, in which a replicant birth threatens, according to the film's chief of police, to tear down the wall separating kinds and bring on a slaughter. The troubling nature of wombs is always brought home when I teach feminist theory and have students read selections from Shulamith Firestone's *The Dialectic of Sex* (1970) and Jane Alpert's "Mother Right" (1973). Firestone's vision was posthuman long before posthumanism was a thing. Arguing that pregnancy is barbaric and a deformation of the body (childbirth, she reports, is "like shitting a pumpkin" [1970: 189]), Firestone advocates a feminist revolution spearheaded by a cybernetic approach to reproduction, including the development of an artificial womb. Alpert's "Mother Right" also speaks of revolution and a new feminist culture, but rather than turning to technology, Alpert turns to motherhood and its associated values of empathy and intuitiveness which, she suggests, is imprinted in the genes of every woman (1973: 8). It was surely this struggle over the meaning of wombs and reproduction that Haraway had in mind when she observed in one of the most oft-quoted lines in "A Cyborg Manifesto," "Though both are bound in the spiral dance, I would rather be a cyborg than a goddess" (1991: 181).

That spiral dance continues today. When my students confront Firestone and Alpert, they likely have in mind a whole different set of images than either Firestone or Alpert had in mind. They are likely thinking of Beyoncé, Rhianna, and Kim Kardashian and their Instagram photos of baby bumps. Hearkening back at least to *Vanity Fair*'s August 1991 cover featuring a naked and very visibly pregnant Demi Moore, the baby bump photo has become de rigeuer for today's celebrities and influencers. *US Weekly*'s "Baby Bump Hall of Fame" reports that in 2017 Beyoncé nearly broke the internet when she shared an image on Instagram showing her pregnant belly (Staff, *US Weekly*, 2022). Contemporaneous with these evocations of Alpert's "cult of motherhood" is the work of speculative designer Lisa Mandemaker, who designed an artificial womb for Dutch Design Week 2018 bearing an uncanny similarity to the Matrix's cybernetic womb. For Mandemaker, who collaborated with Maxima Medical Center, the artificial womb presents an opportunity to increase the chances of survival of extremely premature babies in the period of 24–28 weeks, when preterm infants are most at risk. Mandemaker employs speculative design to disrupt established thought patterns so people "can think with an open mind about where the world should be heading" (2022). It would seem that the choice between goddess or cyborg is as alive today as it was in feminist debates taking place in the 1970s and 1980s.

While the contrast between goddess and cyborg has received much attention, it's perhaps instructive to attend a bit more to the opening clause of Haraway's observation, "though both are bound in the spiral dance." It's the binding that it's the binding that is interesting here. What keeps these two figures bound in their spiral dance? What would it mean to unbind themselves from this spiral? Are there images of the womb that don't fit easily into this dance of goddess and cyborg? Excavating the space between goddess and cyborg, we might turn to Thomas Beattie, the "pregnant man." Beattie was assigned female at birth and came out as a trans man in 1997. He married and became pregnant in 2007 through artificial insemination and in 2008 published an article in *The Advocate* and appeared on *The Oprah Winfrey Show*. While Beattie's case is complex and generated much analysis about the media and its representation of Beattie's pregnant body, Beattie's own narrative focused on being the pregnant spouse of a happy couple. His essay for *The Advocate*, titled "Labor of Love" and suggestive of connections to Eva Kittay's feminist classic *Love's Labor*, opens with his ordinariness: "To our neighbors, my wife, Nancy, and I don't appear in the least unusual. To those in the quiet Oregon community where we live, we are viewed just as we are—a happy couple deeply in love. Our desire to work hard, buy our first home, and start a family was nothing out of the ordinary" (2008). Beattie's evocation of a happy couple living in a quiet Oregon community seems not to be part of the spiral dance in which goddess and cyborg are bound. Perhaps it's time to break that bind?

When held captive by competing images that no longer seem to work, Mary Midgley advocates turning to plumbing—a theme we also return to throughout this book. In "Philosophical Plumbing," Midgley argues that conceptual work is a lot like plumbing, it's complicated and messy, if not downright dirty. In doing the work that is necessary when the concepts we are living by work badly, Midgley cautions that we be wary of theories of everything or trying to find single patterns. Truth, she observes, is not monolithic. "The strong unifying tendency that is natural to our thought keeps making us hope that we have found a single pattern which is a Theory of Everything—a key to all the mysteries, the secret of the universe. . . . A long series of failures has shown that this can't work" (1996: 9). Rather than insisting on a theory of everything, we need to slowly and patiently correct one model against another. That's when "some sort of social life begins to look possible again" (1996: 8).

Goddess and cyborg myths alike are perhaps a little too constraining for domestic posthuman second persons. They suggest being bound to either the cult of motherhood and an attendant fear of technology or a potentially naive belief that technologies such as the artificial womb will prove socially disruptive and give birth to technogenesis. Rather than being bound in a spiral dance, maybe it would be better to let the womb in its wandering ways remind us that our entanglements are messy and sometimes dirty and always resist purity tests. Beattie writes that his "situation ultimately will ask everyone to embrace the gamut of human possibility and to define for themselves what is normal" (2008). It's that gamut of human possibility that the domestic posthuman looks forward to.

Figure 4 Botanicals, *Eliza's Peculiar Cabinet of Curiosities*, Folayemi Wilson.

> Domestic scientist. An oxymoron? Eliza's cabin suggests otherwise, for it's stuffed with herbs and botanicals and preserved animals and speaks to her being a food scholar familiar with indigenous foodways. Danielle Dreilinger's *The Secret History of Home Economics* (2021) tells the early history of women chemists, nutritionists, and homemakers, many of them Black women, who did pioneering work in the field of domestic science. The book's subtitle seems squarely at home with the domestic posthuman: "How Trailblazing Women Harnessed the Power of Home and Changed the Way We Live." Eliza and her botanicals speak to the power of home as a site of life-changing science and knowledge.

Baby

Whenever I return home for a visit, we invariably end up taking out family photos (or increasingly these days pulling them up on a tablet) and reliving moments in our family history. Visits home for many, no doubt, occasion the same practice. It's one of those preservative acts of family that hold us in our identity. My family delights in taking out a photo of me as a baby, lying on a bed naked, in the midst of a full-on wail. Yet I look at it and struggle to make a connection to that naked baby. That too strikes me as common. One of Arbus' most notable baby photos, simply titled "A very young baby, N.Y.C. 1968," was of a newly born Anderson Cooper, who reports in a reflection on the photo that "Diane latched onto me when she first arrived and became obsessed with photographing me." Noting that the photo is not cute and adding, "but Diane's work is not cute," Cooper comments, "I don't see myself in the picture, but a lot of my friends do. People say that I have the same mouth still" ("Anderson Cooper on Diane Arbus" 2015).

Baby complicates our picture of me and not me. We all start out as babies, and yet our lives as babies often remain a mystery. We see our baby pictures and think that's not us. We find stories about ourselves as babies fascinating but struggle to make them a part of our lives. That's not yet me, not yet the human I will become. Such thoughts aren't far afield from a common myth of babies as not yet fully human, the baby as *mängelwesen*. Western philosophy often treated babies as deficient, unfinished, not yet formed, and more recently with an incomplete brain not yet able to support the "higher" functions.[1] The philosopher Arnold Gehlen observes in *Man: His Nature and Place in the World* that the infant is a deficient being, a mängelwesen, quoting Herder: "Naked and bare, weak and in need, shy and unarmed, and—to make the sum of its misery complete—deprived of all guides of life" (1988: 74). It's presumably owing to our deprivations that we turn to tools and technology, including most recently genetic engineering and biotechnology. We're born deficient and detached and need to be completed, if not perfected, by our tools. It's a short step from the myth of the deficient baby to the embrace of the designer baby.

The baby as *mängelwesen* has remained remarkably persistent in Western thought as well as deeply problematic. David Chamberlain reports on a very long (and presumably painful) history of babies being pricked with pins, sometimes multiple times, in an effort to establish that babies didn't feel pain, despite their crying, facial expressions, body movement, and changes in their vital signs and hormones. Chamberlain concludes that the concept of the baby as a conscious, active agent simply didn't exist. "For centuries, babies have had a difficult time getting adults to accept them as real people with real feelings having real experiences. . . . Deep prejudices have shadowed them for centuries: babies were thought of as subhuman, prehuman, or, as sixteenth-century authority Luis de Granada put it, 'a lower animal in human form'" (1998: 168).

How different is Mary Midgley's account of "the importance of babies," in which she recognizes that babies are born with expressive capacities that foster engagement with others long before they are able to communicate, upsetting the facile distinction between speaking subject and mute object.[2] To the deficit model of infancy, we might counter the image of the baby as cunningly social, able to trap caregivers with smiles and gurgles into recognizing and responding to it. Work in evolutionary anthropology and child development presents a picture of babies as capable of, as Sarah Blaffer Hrdy puts it, exuding potent signals and captivating the susceptible (2011: 211). Human babies especially, given the significance of alloparenting in which individuals other than parents care for the infant, are already in the first year of life masters of teasing, joking, showing-off, or feeling shy, geared toward establishing a second-person relation between baby and caregiver. Deborah Lupton observes that infants are agential in forming attachments not only to caregivers but to material objects as well. As she notes, "Just as older individuals do, infants 'consume' objects by incorporating and domesticating them, bringing them into their everyday worlds, melding them to their bodies/selves and bestowing these objects with their own biographically-specific meanings" (2013: 5). Despite their lack of speech and "higher functions," babies surely are not mute—as any new parent will quickly confirm. Far from being helpless or subhuman or not me, a sociable, agential baby has all the tools it needs to begin to foster the recognition and relationality central to becoming a fully social human animal, a posthuman second person shaped by and shaping the arts of personhood. We just need to attend to them.

Child

Lingering for a moment longer on Diane Arbus' photos, we turn to "Child with Toy Hand Grenade, Central Park, NYC, 1962." Calling it one of the most significant

Myths of Domestic Posthuman Second Persons

photographic images in the history of fine art photography, Bree Hughes notes the tension in the photo: "Arbus captures a boy on the cusp of adolescence yet still playing with toys—but the object is a plastic grenade, an object of war" (Cascone, 2017). The photo evokes the innocence of playing in the park, as well as the park as a scene of potential primal violence.

Children and their toys have long provoked complex mythologies, especially when technology is involved, whether it be the technology of war (guns to grenades) or more recent digital technologies, from video games to social media. At the dawn of the Internet Age, there was already an intimation of violence regarding our children and their technologies. As John Perry Barlow observed in his "A Declaration of the Independence of Cyberspace," "You are terrified of your own children, since they are natives in a world where you will always be immigrants" (1996). Barlow's declaration was written in 1996 following the passage of the Telecommunications Act, which included the Communications Decency Act designed to protect minors from internet pornography. Barlow's image of natives versus immigrants was picked up by Marc Prensky in his characterization of digital natives as a generation that has "spent their entire lives surrounded by and using computers and videogames, digital music players, video cams, cell phones and all other toys and tools of the digital age" (2001: 1). As digital natives, our children are alien to us and ready to leave us behind.

Some twenty years later, though, that generation has children of its own and fears what screens are doing to them. In a 2018 series on children and screens, *The New York Times* reported that while large US tech companies design ever more distracting technologies, often selling them to schools, their employees are increasingly concerned about limiting their children's screen time and enforcing tech bans. Nellie Bowles reported, "A fleet of high-profile Silicon Valley defectors have been sounding alarms in increasingly dire terms about what these gadgets do to the human brain. Suddenly rank-and-file Silicon Valley workers are obsessed. No-tech homes are cropping up across the region. Nannies are being asked to sign no-phone contracts" (2018). As the subtitle avers, "the devil lives in our phones." Children, moral panics, and technology have been lashed together at least since the advent of the crystal radio,[3] and it would seem that our current fears revolve around screen time, from Jean Twenge's "Has the Smartphone Destroyed a Generation?," one of Atlantic Magazine's most read articles in 2017, to Facebook's 2021 revelation that Instagram was toxic to teen girls.

Whether thinking about what the kids are doing with these new tools or what these new tools are doing to them, much of the debate over children and technology has been occasioned by fearful images of children and their (our?) tech: fearing our children, those digital natives, and what they are doing with their new tech, or fearing for our children and what all that tech is doing to them. Perhaps we could benefit from an image of the child that isn't centered on tech but on play, innovation, and tradition, an image that begins with childhood as a distinctive stage in human developmental life history. This is precisely what Alison Gopnik does in her account of children and technology. Observing that plasticity and change are central elements of the human condition, Gopnik traces the human capacity for innovation back to the opportunities for play and exploration made possible by our extended childhoods. Children are exploratory learners, driven by neophilia or the love of the new, and most often they are learning from one another. As she notes, "childhood isn't really a period of innocence when children are protected from technological and cultural change—instead, childhood is the very crucible of such change. It is both the period when innovation becomes internalized and, especially in adolescence, the period in which innovation is often actually sparked" (2016: 216). Gopnik argues that the evolutionary purpose of childhood is to provide a protracted period of play and innovation, often in the company of other children. Where infants' and toddlers' attention is most often focused on adults, children's attention is more oriented toward peers (Hawkes, 2020: 5). In the messy, complicated, and unpredictable play of children, we should expect differences to arise, including in their play with technology.

All this time spent playing and innovating, though, does not come without risk, as many parents could no doubt attest. Gopnik importantly situates this extended period of childhood in an environment created by caregivers that fosters the opportunity to explore in a stable and safe context. "Our protracted immaturity is possible only because we can rely on the love of the people who take care of us" (Gopnik, 2011: 15). As Zihlman and Bolter observe, "Childhood could only have emerged within a social system friendly to children" (2004: 44). The other side of the life-history perspective is the caring and preservative love that creates an environment in which it is safe for children to explore and innovate. "Childhood and caregiving are two sides of the same coin; children can't exist without care. By giving an animal a protected early period, a period when its needs are met in a reliable, stable, and unconditional way, you can provide space for mess, variability, and exploration" (Gopnik, 2016: 31).

An image of the child steeped in play and innovation might also suggest that childhood is the very precondition of the posthuman, as Gopnik herself intimates: "Developing a new theory about the world allows us to imagine other ways the world might be. Understanding other people and ourselves lets us imagine new ways of being human" (2009: 8). Play, exploration, and innovation are intrinsic parts of childhood that allow us to imagine other ways of being. Children have the ability to conceive of change, but that ability must be shepherded, necessitating a connection to preservative love and care. From this perspective, we might think of children as neither just like adults (natives) nor completely foreign to adults (immigrants) nor in terms of moral panics occasioned by the latest technology, but as our kin in exploring and imagining new ways of being human. Picking up on Gopnik's metaphor of the garden, perhaps the blossoming of posthuman second persons is prepared in the soil of the human. Rather than digital native or moral panic, we have the image of the child as an explorer and innovator enabled by a network of caregivers.

Self

There's a certain image of the self that has taken root in accounts of posthuman persons: the self as inherently flexible, decentered, maybe even fragmented. The bad old Cartesian humanist self, unified and stable, has given way to the shifting, transgressive pleasures of the dispersed self. We're witnessing, as media theorist Mark Poster argues, a battleground over the nature of the human. Our experiences with electronic media, he suggests, may lead to the emergence of a global space of humachines fostering "the exploration of identity, the discovery of genders, ethnicities, sexual identities, personality types that may be enjoyed, experienced, and also transgressed" (2006: 230). Almost concurrently with the emergence of the internet and the World Wide Web, this image of the multiple and decentered self has come to dominate conceptions of the technologically mediated self or subject.[4]

While it would be a mistake to write off these shifting experiences of the self and the celebration of multiplicity and decenteredness that comes from our experiences with electronic media, in privileging the experiences of adult users of media technology, such a picture of the self says very little about the broader biocultural forces that shape both human beings and technology and pays too little attention to the human beings that are being constituted. Both the Cartesian humanist self and the posthumanist virtual self wandering cyberspace seem isolated from others, alone in their wanderings, with no roots in a homeplace or connection to other social practices. They also seem perpetually stuck between images of fixity and fragmentation. Here too we might benefit from shifting from an image of the self as a user of technology to an image of the self that is situated in human life history, recognizing that the pleasures of fragmentation and multiplicity take place against a host of competing and sometimes conflicting practices as we become domestic posthuman second persons.

Marjorie Grene argues that human persons cope with the complexity of the world, including a complex technological world, by acting out of a center. "To be a person, in the sense in which we human beings consider ourselves persons, is to be the center of actions, in such a way that we are accountable for what we do" (1995: 176). Being a center of action is in fact important for many life forms and operating under something like an ordering principle is probably essential to our human way of being. It's certainly essential to the process of raising children. As anyone who has observed either human beings or animals laboring under the burden of fragmentation can see, it is not a comfortable sight.

As Jane Flax observes, "Those who celebrate or call for a 'decentered' self seem self-deceptively naïve and unaware of the basic cohesion within themselves that makes the fragmentation of experiences something other than a terrifying slide into psychosis" (1990: 219).

But we need not think of those centers as fixed and singular essences. Human beings, we might think, are always in the process of becoming. Persons develop partially in and through powerful affective relationships with other persons as second persons. As Mary Midgley puts this point, we are not self-contained and self-sufficient, either as a species or as individuals, but live naturally in deep mutual dependence. In discussing the "importance of babies," Midgley observes, "we might do well to remember that this is a species whose members, as babies, communicate with other people long before they try to handle inanimate objects" (2001: 90). Rather than beginning with tools and technology, or even language, Midgley points to the significance of sociality, sympathy, and expressive behavior in the formation of human persons. We are social animals, and the natural habitat of persons is with other persons. As Hilde Lindemann notes in *Holding and Letting Go*, personhood is a practice in which we are made and maintained through the activity of other persons. Those other persons, together with the arts of personhood and the material culture of home, provide a context for the long and sometimes complicated process of becoming a person, including developing a center out of which to act.

Those practices involve the stories we tell, recall those family stories surrounding baby photos, but also adult practices that are often overlooked when thinking about technology and the self. Sarah Corbett, in *How to Be a Craftivist*, turns to crafts such as knitting, crocheting, and quilting for developing slow and gentle practices that foster mindfulness, including mindful activism addressing social justice. As she writes, "Our approach to craftivism focuses on handicrafts that use slow, repetitive hand actions so that we can also use the act of crafting to meditate and think critically about the social injustice we are tackling and the strategy we need to overcome it" (2017). In writing about crafting as a feminist and relational practice of care, Anne Mudde makes a similar point, observing that, "Craft is often deeply care-ful, attentive, and this is not of choice but of necessity; if you want your crafting to 'work', you have to pay attention" (2022: 70). Corbett quotes Rozsika Parker's observation in *The Subversive Stitch* that suggests that embroidery can have a transformative impact on the self, including the development of a sense of agency:

> The processes of creativity—the finding of form for thought—have a transformative impact on the sense of self. The embroiderer holds in her hands a coherent object which exists both outside in the world and inside her head. Winnicott's theory of mirroring helps us understand how the experience of embroidering affirms the self as a being with agency, acceptability and

potency. . . . The embroiderer sees a positive reflection of herself in her work and, importantly, in the reception of her work by others. (quoted in Corbett, 2017)

Significantly, neither Corbett nor Mudde is writing on behalf of a Cartesian self or a fragmented, disengaged self. Mudde emphasizes how craftwork involves not fragmented selves but bodyminds that privilege "the relational entanglements of human beings in the non-human or more-than-human world." Crafters, she writes, "are learners, parts of craft traditions, tied to place and materials. Other human beings and culture-ways infuse such practices, and critically, the non-human world shapes and allows (or refuses) craft, so that one comes to better know that world precisely through craft" (2022: 69). Corbett notes that craft can also be a tool to "unself—come out of yourself—and facilitate some worthwhile thoughts on our chosen issue to better our world and support vulnerable people in a thoughtful way" (2017). Corbett's self is embodied and embedded in a world shaped by communal crafting practices that have the potential to both center and unself the second person. Rather than Cartesian ego or decentered humachine, the self in both Corbett and Mudde is relational and emerges out of an assemblage of slow and repetitive practices that involve hands, handicrafts, and communities of others from whom they learn and for whom they stitch.[5]

Starting from the image of becoming persons as a process that takes place among other persons, often in domestic spaces in which parents and others care for and instruct children, worry about their development, and introduce them to a variety of sometimes conflicting practices, reminds us that persons and their selves take complex and sometimes discomfiting forms, even occasionally fragmented, multiplicitous forms. Those discomfiting forms, though, emerge from an equally important context that ought not to be elided in our discussion of domestic, posthuman-technology relations.

Grandmother

Returning to *Time* magazine's cover from 1983, "Machine of the Year," it pays to attend once more to the relegation of that woman to the inside fold of the cover, overlooked by Neil Badmington as he theorized posthumanism. She's in her bare feet, ignoring the computer beside her, a bit slouched over in her comfortable rattan chair, and has a patina of age. Yet she remains invisible to Badmington's theorizing posthumanism. This may not be surprising, as elderly women seem to be largely invisible to the posthuman imagination, typically showing up only in discussions of the ravages of Alzheimer's and as companions to Paro, the Japanese therapeutic robotic seal.[6] The posthuman body is often imagined to be ageless, endlessly upgraded, while postmenopausal women are out of date, past their prime, needing too much maintenance. Grandmothers have little place in a posthuman world.

How different is Marge Piercy's (1991) portrayal in her cyberpunk novel *He, She, and It* of Malkah Shipman, the lusty, cybernetically enhanced grandmother who helps create the cyborg Yod, sleeps with him to ensure that she has successfully designed and programmed his need for intimacy and connection, and then decamps with a Palestinian/Jewish cyborg to join a Middle Eastern matriarchal society. Piercy works within some of the standard tropes of cyberpunk, exploring the impact of technology on personhood and embracing a posthuman future and cyborg ontology, but she situates at the heart of her narrative a Jewish grandmother, a *bubbe*, who challenges our preconceived notions of cyborgs as well as postmenopausal women.

Piercy's *bubbe* reflects recent efforts to rethink and reimagine the role of grandmother, indeed the role of mothering, in the context of human life history. In *Mothers and Others* Sarah Blaffer Hrdy points out that while women past childbearing age were once deemed irrelevant and were often depicted in ethnographic descriptions as objects of ridicule, today grandmothers are hypothesized to be central to the emergence of modern humans (2009: 241). Challenging the man-the-hunter hypothesis, Kristen Hawkes argues that the longevity of postmenopausal women allowed them to contribute to the well-being of early human children. Hardworking grandmothers helped care for the multiple children of their daughters, taught those children how to forage and use tools to dig up hard-to-find buried tubers, and passed on rich troves of cultural knowledge. As Alison Gopnik points out, grandmothers and grandfathers "connect children to two generations' worth of experience and knowledge. Songs, stories, spells, recipes, even old wives' tales—we learn them all at the feet of our grandmothers" (2016: 74). Indeed, Malkah helps socialize the cyborg Yod by telling him bedtime stories.

Significantly, grandmothers—and their infant charges—were perhaps jointly responsible for the emergence of human biosociality and relationality. As grandmothers played a larger role in caring for infants, those infants came to find ways to engage their grandmother's attention. "Unlike other apes, human babies cannot count on their mothers' undivided commitment even though attention from their caregivers has life and death consequences for them. Thus, infants who are more successful at actively engaging their mothers and grandmothers have a strong selective advantage" (Hawkes and Coxworth 2013: 299). It was cooperative childrearing practices and the selection pressure it imposed on infants that Hrdy hypothesizes led to the evolution of social and emotional capacities and the emergence of alloparenting, in which caregiving moves beyond the mother to embrace larger social networks. Kristen Hawkes (2004) argues that grandmothering gives rise to cooperative childrearing and that in turn gives rise to the infant's drive for shared attention. The combination of grandmothers and infants in turn gave birth to alloparenting and the possibility of cooperative parenting.

Evolutionarily speaking, grandmothers are a recent invention. But given that evolution is a tinkerer and not an engineer (Jabob, 1977), grandmothers and the love and care they offer now take a variety of forms, blossoming into what Shelley Park refers to as the polymaternal family: "families created through adoption, lesbian parenting, divorce-extended and marriage-extended kinship networks, or some combination of these" (2013: 1). Recall Thomas Beatie's reflections on the construction of his family: "In a technical sense I see myself as my own surrogate, though my gender identity as male is constant. To Nancy, I am her husband carrying our child—I am so lucky to have such a loving, supportive wife. I will be my daughter's father, and Nancy will be her mother. We will be a family" (Beatie, 2008).

Hrdy notes that "flexibility was, and continues to be, the hallmark of the human family" (2011: 164). Recall that Gopnik too emphasizes that plasticity and change are central elements of the human condition. It's that flexibility and plasticity that allow us to queer the very notions of kin and family and no longer assume that grandmother is in fact a mother at all, or that straight guys or nonbinary persons can't play at being granny, or assume that a cis-female "naturally" wants to give birth or mother, or that every Jewish grandmother wants to be a *bubbe*. Man the hunter has been displaced by the infant-grandmother assemblage, an assemblage cobbled together on the basis of charm, care, stories, and tubers that gives birth to an ever-growing variety of kinship structures. Domestic posthuman second persons wouldn't have it any other way.

Disabled

Where ought we to look for fruitful encounters between posthumanism and disability studies? One might be forgiven for thinking that we should look to such exemplary figures as Aimee Mullins (2009) and Hugh Herr (2018), both of whom had their legs amputated below their knees, employ a variety of prosthetics, and have been popular TED speakers. Mullins' TED Talk, "My 12 pairs of legs," has close to five million views; Herr's talk, "How we'll become cyborgs and extend human potential," more than two million. Mullins and Herr exemplify the originary prostheticity (a key term in critical posthumanism, see Stiegler, 1998; Sharon, 2014; Lemmens, 2017) and technogenesis of the posthuman, in which we are all already cyborgs, whether we know it or not. As Hayles reminds us, "the posthuman view thinks of the body as the original prosthesis we all learn to manipulate, so that extending or replacing the body with other prostheses becomes a continuation of a process that began before we were born" (1999: 3).

But then I think of my brother, who is cognitively and physically impaired. My brother isn't very good at manipulating his body, which is always made clear to me when I take him tubing or kayaking, which he loves to do, but he invariably gets stuck on rocks or in tree limbs and I struggle to provide assistance. As visibly prosthetic beings, Mullins and Herr move through the world easily. Indeed, they sometimes suggest that they move through the world more easily given their prosthetics. My brother uses no prosthetics. He wouldn't be recognized as a cyborg. He doesn't move through the world easily and the more we engineer the technological environment to make it friction free, enabling fast and easy movement through it, the more he fails to fit. He is what Rosemarie Garland-Thomson calls a "misfit."

In "Misfits: A Feminist Materialist Disability Concept," Garland-Thomson (2011) proposes *misfit* as a new critical keyword for thinking through the lived identity and experience of disability. I'm drawn to the term for its many linkages with what we have been calling domestic posthuman second persons. Misfit, Garland-Thomson argues, focuses on the encounter between flesh and world, emphasizes the universal vulnerability and dependence of all human beings, and reminds us of the way we are all entangled in material-discursive becoming (2011: 592). I'm also drawn to the overtones of fit with clothing, soft objects, and fashion, themes we return to regularly in designing the domestic posthuman.

As a misfit, I'd like to think my brother is an exemplary domestic posthuman second person. He's a reminder that all human beings go through periods of vulnerability and dependence and that the person is intrinsically relational. For his family, he's a reminder that there are no persons without second persons. To be honest, until I encountered Eva Kittay's reflections on living with and learning from her disabled daughter, I never thought of my brother as disabled. He was just my brother, held in his identity by the kind of familial and intimate practices that Lindemann describes in drawing on her own experiences growing up with her disabled sister Carla: "We were holding her in personhood. Carla had a human life to lead, not only because of her human embodiment but also because she was born into the nexus of human relationships that made her one of us" (2014: 20). Chris was just one of us.

Where Lindemann emphasizes narrative identity, Garland-Thomson reminds us that fit is a matter of the material world as well. And here too my brother seems exemplary, even more so as we are reminded of the centrality of digital and information networks to posthuman lives. My brother's constant companions are his dogs and his television, not exactly avatars of our digital, prosthetic lives. He doesn't quite fit in the digital information structures we are increasingly immersed in and serves to remind us that as we design for the posthuman our assumptions shouldn't be driven exclusively by individuals who are able to navigate these informational structures. He also reminds us that for some, patterns of growth and development are slower and more diverse. While species have a life history, individuals live specific and particular lives.

We've said that our view of the domestic posthuman is ecumenical and perhaps nothing drives this in a future-forward way so much as recognizing that we cannot address cases like my brother without weaving together many threads in the hopes that we are stitching an account of posthuman persons that fits—fits not only those who have always been comfortable wearing the mantle of personhood but those who don't quite fit in our theories and for whom off-the-rack accounts of personhood simply don't fit. That's the challenge of articulating an account of domestic posthuman second persons, an account that recognizes misfit humanity, centers them in stories of recognition and relationality, and designs a material environment they can comfortably move through.

Notes

1   The deficit model is pervasive in the history of Western philosophy, as Judith Hughes helpfully catalogs: "What are the philosophers' children like? They have an 'immature' deliberative faculty (Aristotle), are not 'endued with Reason' (Hobbes), until roughly the age of 10 (Kant) and are 'incapable of being acted upon by rational consideration of distant motives' (Mill)" (Hughes, 1988: 76).

2   See, for instance, Ron Wakkary (2021: 25) who draws on the vital materialism of Jane Bennett (2010: 108).

3   In "Domesticating the Personal Computer," Lori Reed points to media use pathologies that were connected to the Ouija board, jazz music, the telegraph, and the PC (2000).

4   Similar claims can be found in Howard Rheingold (1993) *The Virtual Community*, Sherry Turkle (1995) *Life on the Screen*, Allucquere Rosanne Stone (1995) *The War of Desire and Technology at the Close of the Mechanical Age* and Bolter, Jay David Bolter (1996), "Virtual Reality and the Redefinition of Self.

5   An interesting parallel can be seen in Daniel Fallman's work on good design in human-computer interaction (HCI). Fallman proposes a holistic approach to design, which takes into account not only the usability but also the emotional and aesthetic aspects of the user experience. Writing in "A Different Way of Seeing," Fallman notes that good user experiences in HCI are "experiences that cultivate the value of individual patience; experiences that require substantial effort; experiences that require a great deal of skill on the part of the user; experiences that find a suitable balance between patience, skill, and effort" (2010: 59).

6   Women have long been invisible to the history of computing, beginning at least with Ada Lovelace's often overlooked contribution as "the mother of the computer" to Charles Babbage's Analytical Engine, and including the "human computers," almost exclusively women, who were responsible for much of the programming of early computers such as ENIAC. For more, see Plant (1997) and Schwartz (2019).

Figure 5 Princess Leia, *Eliza's Peculiar Cabinet of Curiosities*, Folayemi Wilson.

Wilson's cabin isn't just a reconstruction. It's a work of speculative fiction in a way that all smart homes—smart in the sense of quick homes, which is to say alive homes—are, if you think about it, works of speculative fiction. Princess Leia bookmarks the Afrofuturist element in the Cabinet of Curiosities; she must have been picked up in some journey to the future, where surely Eliza was interested to discover a Princess on American soil (even if she was White and a kind of sorceress, listening to unseen whispers of the world around her, which she, Eliza, does sometimes, too). But back in Eliza's cabinet, Leia isn't a future but a relic: a toy for playing with the future anterior tense. Other future options open up once they are held and known as past.

PART TWO

Posthuman Artifacts

Chapter 4
Softwear

Whereas the first section of this work investigated an alternative posthuman parturition in order to identify the posthuman second persons that can be discovered in human life stages, in the present section we return to the question of technology and examine what technological artifacts domestic posthuman second persons use to affect their self- and network-transformations. In this chapter, we note that the standard technological materials and objects—Rosi Braidotti's (2013) "four horsemen" of "posthuman apocalypse" (e.g., nanotechnology, biotechnology, information technology, and cognitive science)—are inadequate to reflect how a domestic posthuman second person functions and is formed. We propose an alternative technomateriality of the domestic posthuman grounded in skin and touch. Following the lead of the jewelry designer Ivy Ross, we call this alternative technomateriality "softwear." Softwear includes literally and metaphorically soft materials that activate embodied affect in users to network humans and objects and with other humans. Softwear activates what Pauline Brown (2019) has called "the other A.I: aesthetic intelligence." Aesthetic intelligence is a sensory system that uses ornament and style to perceive the myths embedded in objects. The technomateriality of the domestic posthuman invites us to reconsider and take seriously marginalized considerations in conventional technological realms, such as the physical textures and metaphorical "feel" of technological objects. Investigating domestic posthuman materials necessitates an unusual pathway in technical design, which is the consideration of questions of style and aesthetics, usually subordinated to function by software and hardware engineers. But the style of domestic posthuman technologies is important and is more prone to be soft, warm, textured, baroque, and emotionally resonant than modernist-influenced technological aesthetics that prioritize hard, smooth, sleek, deflective, and impersonal surfaces. The organ of the softwear interface is the skin and what Didier Anzieu (2016) calls the "skin ego," which allows for the transfer of skin functions onto the self and vice versa. In this chapter, we examine the role of the skin in softwear-mediated, touch-centric relations among humans and between humans and things, diverging dramatically from machine metaphors to explore skin-centric networking devices such as pélage, allogrooming, and vocal grooming; forms of social eros experienced through gossip and storytelling; and nonsymbolic, embodied communication formations like numinosity and myth.

Let's start with an *annuraaq:* an Inuit gutskin raincoat. Inuit raincoats are protective outerwear made of naturally waterproof whale and seal intestines. They look like semitransparent, crinkled ponchos made of cut and quilted stomach linings. An *annuraaq* is a variation on the skin clothing systems consisting of hide and fur that have long enabled Arctic-dwelling humans to inhabit damp and snowy regions prone to subzero temperatures. They facilitate their human wearers' transitions between land and water to hunt, fish, and travel. These richly textured skins invite rather than repelling or sloughing off, immersing the wearer in elements of the environment, integrating elements of the world with the self. Since they are used not only functionally, during rainfall and ocean travel, but ceremonially and as fancy dress, they are often decorated with brightly colored yarn, feathers, and other ornaments. The implications of living and embodying the mythical resonance of an Inuit raincoat include the creation of humans who relate intimately to the nonhuman environment and see themselves as part of it. Via ornamentation, this mythical resonance and its importance to other more pragmatic functions are called out.

The adaptive, cultural, and symbolic power of a waterproof gut skin coat is tremendous, and historians of dress have marveled at the engineering prowess exhibited by many multifunctional Inuit garments (Issenman, 1997). But Inuit designers are not often cited as technological masterminds in typical accounts on that topic, nor has northwestern Alaska yet to rival Silicon Valley as a recognized locus of technological renaissance.[1] Myths about technology, which according to Mary Midgely (2004) have tended to prioritize machines and their attributes since the seventeenth century, preempt both of these possibilities. Featuring native people as technology innovators, as Julia Watson does in her book on radical indigenous design (2020), would complicate the Primitivist designation of their way of life as an antidote to civilization (Lemke, 1998). Technology myths that prioritize synthetic, inorganic, and digital materials as the foundation of technological progress can struggle to assimilate objects that draw from and immerse users in the natural world.

In her book on "lo-tek," which Watson defines as a design catalog of technologies that rewrite the mythology of technology to foreground indigenous sophistication, Watson still tends to focus on native architectural, agricultural, and systems innovations around the globe. Even revisionist prevailing technology myths thus categorically tend to ignore developments in sewing, weaving, quilting, and embroidering. As the historian Kassia St. Clair observes, "this is inherently odd" (2018: 6). Weaving likely consumed more time than any other form of material production practiced by prehistoric humans (Barber, 1993), and the "industry of fabric is older than pottery or metallurgy and perhaps even than agriculture and stock-breeding" (St. Clair, 2018: 6). "Cloth," St. Clair points out, "is the original technology." It is also one of the most impactful, allowing humans to live and travel through regions physiologically prohibitive to them, creating trade networks that facilitate the very cross-cultural exchanges that drive historical change, playing a foundational role in the material histories of storytelling and the written word, and powering the Industrial Revolution (which began with the invention of the cotton gin).[2] But that cloth has been predominantly a female and feminine technological domain has made it symbolically negligible in considerations of the history, philosophy, and anthropology of technology. That it decays quickly has made it, compared to hard technologies, materially so. The simple act of repositioning textiles within both the history of technology and contemporary technology industries can fundamentally alter our understanding of the past, present, and future of that domain. The same could be said for materials like wood, glass, ceramics, herbs and botanicals, and more.

Technology histories, philosophies, and practices stack the deck against cloth through a broader systemic negligence and even antipathy toward attributes like slowness, smallness, softness, and the home. Contemporary technological paradigms prioritize fastness, bigness, hardness, and the public sphere. But not all "wicked problems" (Rittel and Webber, 1973) are hard. Difficulty and complexity are as likely to be porous, like cloth: something always sifting through to confound the container meant to hold the whole problem. And not all difficult problems benefit from big, fast solutions. Slower steps and longer scales of payoff may need to be considered. Small steps can sometimes allow for more adoption and the benefits of cumulative, communal responses. The locus of change must sometimes be at home, oriented toward and even initiated by children and the elderly.

Recuperating softness in technological spaces allows different objects, including but not limited to cloth, to attain status as technological materials. Sasha Costanza-Chock's (2020) reading of the Chinese night soil trade as worthy inspiration for contemporary waste management problem-solvers suggests what surprising upcyclings, recyclings, and anachronisms become resonant and relevant. New designers rise to prominence and attain status as technology innovators on the vanguard of soft problems. Costanza-Chock points out that users, user communities, and small organizations rooted in marginalized communities are often best positioned for innovation, "due both to the high amount of specialized domain knowledge they possess and to the low costs of testing possible solutions in the real-world 'laboratory' of daily life." Different places edge out labs, offices, cities, and institutions as the privileged loci of invention, replacing them with "microsites such as the home" (2020: 140). There, "constant, small-scale interactions within the space of the home, the family, kinship networks [and] communities" (2020: 141) carry out experimental and testing activities accountable for major technological gains in the modern era. Technological geographies can thus be relocated. Silicon Valley could be supplanted by the Arctic Circle.

We need to revisit the textures, geometries, chronologies, scales, and ecology of the posthuman and newly consider one made of soft stuff. For the Danish architect Juhani Pallasmaa, human experience must be grounded in all of the body's senses, which are themselves all "extensions of the tactile sense" and so "specializations of skin tissue" (Pallasmaa, 2007: 10). "The computer," Pallasmaa writes, "is usually seen as a solely beneficial invention" but "I wish to express my serious concern in this respect [as] computer imaging tends to flatten our magnificent, multi-sensory, simultaneous and synchronic capacities of imagination by turning [sensation] into a passive visual manipulation, a retinal journey" (12). In a revised paradigm for technological advancement through soft things, the linked history and future of posthuman persons is mediated by sensory experiences and bodily components tethered to touch, taste, sound, and smell and filtered through skin, muscle, ears, tongue, and nostrils as much as through our eyes and vision.

The emergence of a sophisticated domestic posthuman which can bend, perceive, change, grow, feel, influence, imagine, and connect makes contemporary algorithmically derived AI look like the true primitive in the room: some dumb machine, thinking with blinders on, missing its body, tragically tethered to silicon, metal, and other immutable things that just don't work that well for living. Hard to the touch, but soft-minded when it comes to deep thought and feeling. But a different posthuman, a domestic posthuman, its hour come round at last, is slouching toward Bethlehem to be born. This posthuman will need differently substanced tools, another kind of connectivity, and a new crop of myths about them for survival.

Softwear

The technomateriality of conventional posthumans is hardware and software, their fusions with humans most prominently figured as cyborgs and artificial intelligence. Hardware includes devices such as desk and laptop computers, tablets, and smartphones as well as accessories like cameras, microphones, and speakers. Chemical and mechanical prosthetics also count: pharmaceuticals, pacemakers, and the like. Software includes algorithm and code-based entities like apps, games, the internet, and operating systems. Both hardware and software have been treated extensively as central to the occurrence and design of the posthuman, which is primarily imagined in philosophy as a highly contemporary episode in digital technological development. The technomateriality of the domestic posthuman is something different. Let's call it softwear. Softwear includes materials that are soft, like textiles and skin, and fungible, like food and pheromones. It also includes forms that are superficially hard to the touch, like robots and televisions, but which signify culturally and mythically more akin to soft things, as caretakers, affect catalysts, and playfellows. At the same time, softwear excludes some things that may seem similar to textiles but actually function, both conceptually and literally, more similarly to categories designated as hard (e.g., some wearable technology, like Fitbits or Google Glasses). Softwear thus includes actually soft objects, like clothing and textiles, and also symbolically soft things, like jewelry, cosmetics, and decorative ornaments for the body and home as well as home-cooked meals, kitchen tables, pets, trash, perfume, toys, and a plethora of other items.

The neologism "softwear" was coined by Ivy Ross, a craft artist and jewelry designer whose work has been collected by global museums that include, according to Wikipedia, the Smithsonian in Washington, D.C., the Victoria and Albert Museum in London, the Schmuckmuseum in Pforzheim, Germany, the Cooper-Hewitt National Design Museum in New York City, and the Montreal Visual Arts Center in Canada. During her tenure at Mattel (the toy company), a team under Ross' leadership produced the award-winning Ello Creation System, a construction game for girls conceptualized as a cross between Lego and jewelry. Ross has also been a product developer or executive for a range of mass market and luxury fashion brands, ranging from Calvin Klein and Coach to Liz Claiborne, Avon, Swatch, and The Gap. She has described her design method as "design feeling," characterized by incorporating sound resonance into the ideation process by using felt sound frequencies to put designers in creativity-inducing states of mind. In an interview for the podcast *Time Sensitive* (Bailey, 2022) Ross attributed this method to an effort to reproduce the sound bath in which humans are bathed in the womb, and describes installing a sound studio in her Santa Fe home that uses reverberations to make you "[feel] like you're back in that place when we were all sound."

Ross also happens to be the current VP of hardware at Google, a role she has held since 2016. "Softwear" was the title of Ross-designed and Google-sponsored Milan Design Week installations in 2018 and 2019.[3] In the 2018 installation, Ross threw down a glove against the hardness of hardware with a depiction of its integration into soft things: upholstery, apparel, accessories. "Softwear" galleries were set up to look like a home, painted a cozy blue hue, and ensconced with potted plants and cultivated cottage-creepers. The interior galleries were designed to look like bedrooms, living rooms, kitchens; objects were artfully camouflaged as and among flannel shirts, plush hoodies, knitted blankets, comfy furniture, kitchen appliances. The implicit point was that the future of technology was going to look a lot less like a lab, hospital, or other public, institutional space than its consumers' own homes and closets, where the decorative and practical objects that populate the interior environment and users' bodies are increasingly networked and wired. Though some contemporary domiciles certainly embrace a sleek and modern look, the one that Ross chose to represent the future of Google specifically, and computer technology in general, looked like it could belong to a hobbit.

Some scholarship has acknowledged the relationship between what would become digital culture and weaving: "The computer emerges out of the history of weaving, the process so often said to be the quintessence of women's work. The loom is the vanguard site of software development" (Plant, 1997: 46). The connection is literal: the memory cards of Charles Babbage's analytical engine, an early computer, were modeled on those used in a Jacquard loom. "It was Jacquard's strings of punch cards"—the first to store their own information—"on which [Babbage] based his designs," which introduced the capacity to repeat information to the loom's pattern-storage system (Plant, 1997: 51–2). Textiles are as embedded in some versions of the future of human-technology relations, however, as they are in the past; engineers have been exploring the ability to weave wires into cloth-like wearable networks for more than a decade. This notion is the focus of the Internet of Soft Things, or Io(S)T, a project at Nottingham Trent University in the UK ("An Internet of Soft Things," n.d.). Like Google's "Softwear" project, a primary goal of the Nottingham Trent project is to challenge expectations about the look and feel of networking.

The Internet of (Soft)Things not only imagines new ways to integrate textiles into the IoT but also investigates how textiles can suggest new relational approaches for psychotherapy. They thus study how soft interfaces, independently of technological wiring, can impact thoughts and feelings. For the purposes of our study, this approach yields the more exciting development grounds. It also became the defining concept of Google's second Milan installation, this time designed in collaboration with Reddymade Architecture and Design Studio and the International Arts + Mind Lab, a neuroaesthetics institute at Johns Hopkins University. The Milan 2019 collaborators created roomscapes without modern technology in them, focusing exclusively on the interior finishes, decorative objects, and architectural millwork of conventional interior design. The technological hardware in this exhibit was worn by visitors: soft, stylish wristbands that monitored biofunctions (heart rate, breath rate, etc.) as they navigated the designed rooms. At the end of the experience visitors received a printout visualizing the progressions and transformations of their own bodily interiors as they moved through roomscapes. Using the burgeoning science of neuroaesthetics, which measures the biological, cognitive, and emotional impact of aesthetic experiences on humans, Ross and collaborators suggested that the conjunction of things like textiles, porcelains, lamplight, and windows needn't be "wired" in the clunky conventional sense to impact human users. This is a profoundly different approach, both in its reframing of soft objects as impactful technologies in their own right and also in its reframing of digital technology as a handmaid for measuring primary effects delivered through cloth, paint, and furniture.

The University of Toronto marketing professor Russell Belk makes an analogous point in his article "The Extended Self in a Digital World" (2013). Belk, who wrote a seminal essay on "Possessions and the Extended Self" (1988) to explain how much of the human ego is stored in the things with which we surround ourselves, writes in his more recent article:

> digital possessions as well as most digital devices lack the soft tactile characteristics of clothing and furniture that make it possible to almost literally embed our essence in such possessions (Belk, 2006). This essence is the characteristic that Benjamin (1936/1968) called "aura" and that Belk (1988) described as contamination (contagion)—the soul of the person rubbing off on or impregnating the object (Fernandez and Lastovicka, 2011). Furthermore, for virtual possessions that are endlessly replicable, it is difficult to regard them as perfectly unique, nonfungible, and singular, even if we have custom-crafted them or employed suitable possession rituals. Such assessments suggest that, while digital possessions can be objects of self extension, they may not be as effective as material possessions. (Belk, 2013: 480)

In Belk's reading, many digital and virtual objects and spaces possess physical characteristics that make them less suitable for things we want to do with them. Undergirding Belk's claim is the notion, unusual in engineering-oriented design frameworks, that there are human-centered characteristics and attributes that determine the feasibility of certain stylistic attributes in technological objects to perform as desired, intended, or even able the way they would be if operating in isolation. Midgely similarly observes that "when people who are worried about new technologies complain that they are unnatural, we should try to understand what they are objecting to. We might find something serious" (2004; 107). The serious thing we might discover arises because Midgely takes "the solidness of species" (2004; 109) seriously, meaning that creatures of a kind possess certain characteristics that are needed to fit them and their peculiar way of living and being in the world.[4] It is not only organic and inorganic materials that possess attribute-solidness, a thing well understood by product developers, but also prospective human users, a thing on which many have only a tenuous grasp. Both Belk and Midgely point to the extent to which humans, like all other animals, are also creatures of a certain kind whose soft, embodied nature can assimilate some kinds of tools more easily than others. This is not to deny the basic plasticity of human biology, which can morph, fuse, and appropriate in an astonishing array of ways. But it is to say that these morphologies and fusions are not infinite; are bound by material conditions that are real and deeply embedded in species (even our own); need to take certain properties, qualities, and conditions seriously; and work, often dazzlingly creatively, within the confines, call them the formal constraints, of matter. Our mythical image of the posthuman and its technological instruments often fetishize genres of tools that research suggests are equipped with properties that actively *inhibit* their capacity to do the things we expect them to for creatures of the kind that we are. Other tools, forgotten in these myths, are less encumbered.

Softwear, broadly defined, is a technomateriality whose tactile characteristics invite us to embed our essence in them and experience facets of ourselves and others through and with them. Softwear's technomateriality intervenes in narratives of technology as a liquidizer of the material world and renderer of all things into the virtual to create a disembodied, transitory future for humans (Bauman, 2000) by advancing the notion that soft solids have continued to exist and thrive in domestic settings and that they constitute a thriving nonliquifying relational space of experience-rich technological mediation and posthuman evolution. Absent in critical accounts of liquid modernity are a whole array of spaces, intersubjectivities, and engagements entangled with the soft materialities of the home in ways that our current term for technological solids, hardware, tends to exclude. These include but are not limited to sexuality and eroticism, parenting, aging, ailing, friendship, cooking, shopping, homemaking, grooming, teaching, introspection, feeling, reading, and care. The artifacts and devices to which humans become assembled through such networking mechanisms populate (indeed, often clutter) our homes, which are not sterile spaces but usually overflowing with the things we seem to believe we need, consciously or not, to execute our arts of personhood. We should not overlook the technologies we use to enact homely networks, nor should we essentialize technology by conflating it with its occasional formal attributes (as hard, fast, massive, laboratory-generated, and future-oriented—all discussed in detail in the final chapter of this book). Expand the formal range of technicity. eyond these sometimes-attributes and another kind of tech that is soft, slow small, homemade and quite familiar can emerge.

Skin Ego

An important consequence of the foregrounding of the domestic posthuman in softwear is the extent to which it relies heavily upon touch and felt embodiments, including movement, scent, taste, and sound (through vibrations) to construct its materiality, thinking, and relationship networks. Touch is the first sense to develop in utero and the most important sense for newborn interaction with the world. . . [S]kin is the most important organ of communication and contact. It is through the skin that the newborn learns where she begins and ends, where the boundaries of her self are. Here, she learns the first feelings of pleasure and displeasure. (DeFalco, 2018: 25)

While screen-based digital technologies can produce sharp images and resonant sound, they are still quite inept in their capacity to recreate touch beyond the tap. More robustly haptic and skin-mediated sensations, including those of touch, scent, sound, and taste, activate "the Other AI": aesthetic intelligence (Brown, 2019).

Aesthetic intelligence is not about rational consciousness or ocular beauty but a capacity to process (e.g., understand, articulate, recognize, seek out, and even create) and be impacted by vast nuances in physical and emotional sensations. Through aesthetic intelligence, we can retrace the evolutionary pathway of primal activities that we share with animals, like grooming, play, and care as well as embodied emotions like fear, awe, longing, loss, rage, and loneliness, as they all have evolved to forge higher-order cultural structures like art, myth, and religion (Asma and Gabriel, 2019). We can also begin to imagine a technological future made and inhabited by the Other AI, one made as much through methods honed in the arts as of science and yielding ever-more complexly feeling and intuiting beings becoming more sensorily and relationally alive.

The Other AI repositions the skin, and the suite of touch- and feeling-systems activated by and woven into it, as, respectively, the mother-organ and disbursed cultivator of embodied cognition, also called the cognitive nonconscious (Hayles, 2017), in a way that makes clear how important its capacities are to the development of aspects of the human associated with both individual and cultural refinement. In conventional AI, the skin is a bag of organs and bones, evoked dismissively by Andy Clark (2004) and positioned as a thing to shed if one desires "embodiment beyond the antique" (Ihde, 2003: 615). In the Other AI, the skin is an exquisite asset, emotionally intelligent, the progenitor and conduit of reflection, contemplation, imagination, eroticism, intimacy, taste, and a host of other sensation-based processes like rhythm, dance, and music, all reflective of highly evolved capacities in living organisms. Rather than seeing brain-mediated functions like cognition, consciousness, and symbolic language as the epitome of human sophistication, the Other AI sees these as blandly mechanical and primitive when divested of palpating, nonconscious, and embodied beingness to flesh them out (pun intended). The Other AI is developed through fundamental sensory capabilities grounded in touch but reaching beyond simple experience, satisfaction, or pleasure. They require a cultivated actual skin and projected skin, one that can mobilize the body toward complex emotional experiences that use rather than bypass the senses.

The Other AI was a term invented by Brown in the context of luxury brand marketing, where words like cultivation, sophistication, and refinement have class-oriented meanings. But luxury product development and marketing is not the foremost application of aesthetic intelligence or the foremost space of emergence of related experiences. We wish to reposition these experiences in the biological organism, where aesthetic intelligence is "first a mode of physically being in the world, the texture and surface displayed in clothes, carriage, voice, gesture: in presence, in sum." What Ross Posnock (2018) means by presence has been exhibited more exquisitely by Black civil rights protesters in the heat of their struggles than by the high fashion models, celebrities, or dot com billionaires more typically configured as the luxury consumer. The posthumans made out of the Other AI are "cultured," in both senses of the word, because of the advanced training of their skins, tongues, scents, sounds, and sight in all of the domestic arts of second personhood.

Didier Anzieu, the mid-twentieth-century French psychoanalyst, developed a theory of the Self and psyche grounded in touch, specifically via the organ of the skin, in a series of papers (and ultimately book) on "skin ego." We will turn to his writings, which have languished in philosophical and clinical obscurity since the 1970s, not so much for their psychoanalytic content or to provide a psychoanalytic theory of personhood but because Anzieu's work was prescient of contemporary developments in embodied and emotional cognition that increasingly foreground the body as important regions for the development of self and mind (Damasio, 1999; van der Kolk, 2015; Menakem, 2017). Anzieu argued that the skin is a powerful perceptive organ as much responsible for taking in, processing, integrating, and even transcending information about the environment as the brain, and he problematized any dialectical distinction between skin and mind by noting the formation of mind functions (like having a self) through skin functions; indeed, he pointed out that the skin and brain co-derive from the same embryonic structure, the ectoderm.

For Anzieu, the skin is a kind of screen that you can feel and, to date, it is the *only* screen that fully integrates tactile feelings into its processes and structures. He believed that all workings typically associated with the mental plane could be transposed into a bodily plane via the skin, and that ultimately the defining facets of mental planes only exist because the skin's bodily plane facilitated their growth and projection. He called this transposed and transposing organ the skin ego and identified a set of properties embodied by the skin but also necessary to proper holistic psychic functioning. These initially included the sense of envelopment and containment, for example, the sense that one is supported and held (the sack); the sense of having a protective barrier for the psyche, for example, the sense that one is differentiated from others (the screen, used in the 1970s by Anzieu in the sense of a visual blockade); the sense of possessing a filtering system allowing for the safe interchange of one's interior with the surrounding environment, for example, the sense that exchanges between one's self and one's environment are feasible without entirely diluting the one or the other (the sieve); and the sense of being a reflective surface, for example, the sense that one has the capacity to self-reflect upon occurrences that are happening to and within one (the mirror, which is actually more akin to how we think of screens in the present-day digital/computational era). Ultimately, Anzieu expanded these four gross functions of skin ego into nine more nuanced ones, whereby the organic skin and immaterial psyche corresponded through their mutual functions of holding, handling, protecting, individuating, interfacing, arousing, recharging, registering, and self-destroying (e.g., the psychic correlation of skin rashes). In Anzieu's model, skin creates an experiential plane that models the idea of a contained but environment-permeable organism as well as how to negotiate permeability with safety and even pleasure (while also acknowledging the existence of psychic allergies: the misrecognition of parts of the self as alien to it and needing to be attacked and destroyed). The experiential model lived out on the skin is then projected onto and adapted by the psyche—whose interior experiences in turn suggest co-evolutionary developments for the skin.

While a skin ego challenges constructions of mind grounded in scopic economies and focused primarily on cognitive functions (AKA "the disembodied computational paradigm" described by Asma and Gabriel in 2019: 4), it resonates deeply with more recent theories of the mind grounded in emotions, such as Stephen Asma and Rami Gabriel's account of *The Emotional Mind* (2019). These theories acknowledge the embodied nature of emotions, tracing ways in which psychological feelings are grounded in bodily sensations, and so ultimately giving credence to the notion of an embodied mind that uses skin and touch as a major perceptive and processing organ and function—and ultimately, then, as a feasible instrument through which to affect healing.

Anzieu's case analyses of treatments of patients examine how disorders of the psyche can be treated with ministrations to the skin. Specifically, he examines a practice called "the pack," a therapeutic technique in which a patient is wrapped in damp sheets.[5] The pack, or "damp packing," dates back to the nineteenth century and involves winding damp sheets around a patient who is naked or in underclothes:

They begin with his arms and legs, wrapping each separately, then they wrap up the whole body tightly, including the arms and legs, but excluding the head. Immediately afterwards, the patient is covered with a blanket so that he can get warm again fairly quickly. He remains lying down for three-quarters of an hour, free to verbalize his feelings or not, as he wishes (in any case, according to the medical staff who often undergo the pack treatment themselves, the sensations and emotions experienced at the time are so intense and extraordinary that words are hardly adequate to express them).

> The attendants touch the wrapped-up patient, communicate with him with their eyes or reply to what he has to say; they are eager and anxious to know what is going on inside him. (Anzieu, 2016: 492).

The pack therapy, Anzieu explains, is repeated three times a week to allow the patient to experience the phenomenon of a "double bodily envelope" (493), comprised, on the one hand, by the thermal envelope that alternates between the temperatures of cold and then warmth and, on the other, by the tactile envelope of the tight wet sheets that stick to the whole of the skin. During the process the patient experiences a sensation of "physical and psychical fullness," which Anzieu believes to derive from the construction of the Ego as both "separate from others and at the same time continuous with them, which is one of the topographical features of the Skin Ego."

Anzieu's treatment of psychological maladies through the skin resonates with conceptualizations of neuroses in Freud, Josef Breuer, and Carl Jung, who all note that psychic maladies can be played out upon the body in symbolic form. In Jung's words,

> a patient . . . who is confronted with an intolerable situation may develop a spasm whenever he tries to swallow: He "can't swallow it." Under similar conditions of psychological stress, another patient has an attack of asthma: He "can't breathe the atmosphere at home." A third suffers from a peculiar paralysis of the legs: He can't walk, i.e., "he can't go on any more." A fourth, who vomits when he eats, "cannot digest" some unpleasant fact. (Jung, 1964: 127)

A malady begun in the mind is expressed in the body; what is experienced on the body seeps through into one's interior life.

Though pack therapy may today resonate as a quirky byproduct of the 1970s therapeutic explorations now gone out of fashion, in fact it resonates strongly with the contemporary infant culture and psychology studies of social scientists like Deborah Lupton, Alison Gopnik (2011, 2016), Vasudevi Reddy (2008), and Alex Orrmalm (2020).[6] Babies are commonly swaddled in snugly wrapped blankets to make them feel comfortable and safe; Lupton also studies the blankets, sarongs, and swaddling clothes that bind babies to their mothers and become "superskins" uniting caretakers with their infants through the smells, substances, and textures that these soft structures can become imbibed with as they wrap around the codependent bodies of their wearers. Lupton points out that a kind of "skinship" develops between babies and their caretakers in this manner, allowing multiple organisms to bind together through the sensory experiences—primarily tactile, but encompassing, smell, taste, and sound as well—that are enmeshed in textiles. She cites the example of baby blankets that infants, toddlers, and children use as maternal substitutes until, in some cases, they literally dissolve and their swaddling, caring, and soothing functions become integrated into the child's own skin and self. Alex Orrmalm, a sociologist, sets out in one essay to study infants' interactions with iPads and becomes more interested in the way they interface with socks, which in the hands and mouths of babes become substitute skin egos that can be stretched, tasted, thrown, shaped, and filled to allow them to explore what a skin is and does and so, down the line, what a self can be and do in the world. Orrmalm's comparative research on the function of tablets versus socks in human cognitive and egoic development offers a paradigmatic example of the way that softwear versus hardware versus software can be reevaluated when we cease to presume that the evaluator is an adult and instead consider what another kind/stage of humans, babies, might think and (be) like. In the hands of these humans, iPads seem pointless; a sock, on the other hand, is divorced from its use-value and deconstructed into pure materiality, becoming therein a magnificent teacher of how to be, how to interface, how to become. All of this happens in the first year of life, a period that Alison Stone has observed is one that in other animals would be passed in a mother's womb, so that our final period of gestation as human beings, which takes place outside the womb and in the world, can incorporate cultural forces and material environmental elements into us while we are still being made (a process that will continue, if at a less intensive and accelerated rate, throughout our childhoods and even into adulthood). We learn what our skins are and then ultimately what we are from playing with and living among socks, blankets, saris, soft toys, and clothing. That babies have and express strong preferences among varieties of objects that they interact with—and even sway their caretakers' selections of them, all without words—is suggestive of the argument here advanced, that not all technomaterialities are created equal, and that adult Western users are not always best at distinguishing which are more adept. Still, whether we remember it or not (and thanks to what Alison Stone calls our infantile amnesia (2019: 157), more likely not), the fact that we finish our gestation in the presence of superskins and under the influence of skinship is both what allows us to be different from dumb machines, more supple and connected, and also from other animals, more culturally and environmentally attuned in the absence of their fully formed and robust instinct systems that predetermine how they will feed, migrate, mate, groom, and more already at their birth.[7]

The theory of the development of skin, skinship, and superskin into egoic functions and vice versa explains why our interface with softwear through clothing and accessories as well as many features of domestic interior décor (ranging among linens, wallpapers, paint, ornaments, curios, and upholstery) are so powerful. The skin-like properties of textiles, paper, and even ornamental design allow them to serve not merely as appendages and prostheses to our own forms and functions but also able to be integrated into our whole egoic structure; these also position textiles and decorative forms as optimal for egoic projections. Fashion and dress are often conceptualized as second skins, mediating between our bodily surface and the surrounding environment in order to acclimate or assimilate the one to the other. Even domestic structures like upholstery and blankets but also including walls, doors, windows, and ceilings can be seen as "extended skins," to paraphrase Belk, performing sack, screen, sieve, and mirror functions and explaining why clothing and home environments are so profoundly psychically, and not only physically, important. Other kinds of softwear, which we come to know not necessarily by wearing, swaddling, or living within but by cuddling and caressing, like pets, or by preparing and consuming, like food, or even by inhaling, as with scents, allow us to expand the skin ego's range as a mode of experiencing and communicating with the environment—in the one case reaching into the animal kingdom; in the other appropriating the organ of the tongue to perform skin functions of perception through intimate and even absorptive interface; in the third materially treating and knowing seemingly immaterial (nonvisible) entities (e.g., the way scent allows us to experience the tactile thereness of an invisible substance, like perfume or incense; discussed in Brown, 2009).

Pélage and Allogrooming

In softwear stories, the biosocial behaviors affiliated with grooming take center stage as core pathways not only to biological thriving but also to sociality, intelligence, imagination, spirituality, and culture (Asma and Gabriel, 2019). In grooming, animals communicate through chemical signals, touch, and sound. Grooming is part of biological organisms' inbuilt cleaning system, alongside microbiological and hydraulic evacuation and disgust triggers. Grooming appeals to organisms' pleasure centers, and the chemistry and neurology of attraction through which it operates are just as necessary to their vital cleansing instincts as fear, repulsion, and elimination (Smith, 2007). Feeding, nuzzling, handling, envelopment, and other kinds of sensual tactility are forms of parental grooming also allocated to sexual partners and mediated, in humans, by such objects as soaps, perfumes and oils, brushes, scissors and razors, fabrics, ornaments, makeup, creams, lotions, and salves. Grooming behaviors allow for soothing and rest during periods of de-arousal and so are typically dispersed between "energetic primary activities" (e.g., sex and feeding). They include the dry-grooming of the outer-hyde (called the *pélage*), allogrooming (social grooming that incorporates another organism), and vocal grooming (ranging from chirping, purring, grunting, cooing, spluttering, clicking, yapping, and tooth chomping in animals). These forms of grooming occur

> before or after social contact, sexual activity, or eating, after exploratory or defensive behavior or gaps in work, and before or after sleeping. During these resting periods peace is restored, and ruffled fur or feathers can be rearranged, repaired, and brought to their normal state of readiness. Grooming thus helps animals relieve stress: it is a useful way of going off duty, of taking a break. Grooming therefore does double work as work and play (and a surprising amount is play). (Smith 2007: 14)

Part of the touch-activated attraction system encompassed by grooming is smell, including the pheromonal sweat of other animals, a powerful trigger of endorphins and other pleasure hormones at the core of seeking, lust, and care emotional systems. In mammals, especially humans and primates, a "toothcomb" evolved in the mouth consisting of sensitive, pointed canine teeth to allow oral grooming actions and invite ancillary mouth and tongue activities like licking, spitting, sucking, nibbling, nipping, biting, and even eating. Combined, the reverberations of touch-smell-taste-sound centered behaviors characterized broadly as grooming facilitate domestic activities ranging among pair-bonding, alloparenting, and cultural transmission—the progenitors of all kinds of social and individuated attention and intelligence (Asma and Gabriel, 2019).

Care of bodily surfaces (COBS) studies is a zoological specialization that uses grooming behaviors to differentiate species; primates, for example, groom up to 20 percent of their time—an enormous expenditure unparalleled in other species and far in excess of what is required to control infestation or contamination. COBS thus presumes Anzieu's central point about skin ego: our surfaces have deep implications, and when we care for them we care for the most profound parts of ourselves and reveal something about our species-specific natures. COBS, however, exceeds autogrooming behaviors and includes allogrooming and its extension through vocal grooming, which occurs when the number of animals in a pack that must be groomed exceeds the number it is feasible to touch directly.

Virginia Smith (2007) has suggested that vocal grooming is the progenitor of gossip: a kind of free associative vocal session practiced in human grooming areas like bathhouses, barbershops, bedrooms, and bars and used to convey social power. Thus gossip, which appears at first to have nothing to do with the skin or skin ego, can be positioned as a kind of vocalized skin-cleansing behavior rooted in the tactile systems of *pélage*. Gossip is also suggestive of storytelling, which Smith positions as a derivative of gossip, as an extended *pélage*. Both singing and prayer can also be construed in this way, as forms of extended vocal pelage directed, in the latter example, even beyond other living humans (to ancestors, divinities, or nature). More, and more sophisticated, parts of us come back to our skins than you'd think, and the more parts of us that are skin the more we need(ed) softwear to become human, prehuman, posthuman, or anything on the primate spectrum at all. When posthuman philosophers acknowledge the importance of embodiment they often do so in the abstract, referring to the importance of "a body," much as the moniker "the human" in the work of theorists like Wolfe or Braidotti abstracts variations on the human (babies, children, teenagers, the elderly, disabled people, etc.) into the same category. Actual embodiment, however, can only be experienced through the sensations of specific bodily structures and their functions and shapes: not "my body" but "my skin," "my teeth," "my hair," "my tongue," "my fingers," "my back," "my blood," "my fat," "my sweat." These bodies are constantly changing within individual organisms. Too grotesque for most philosophers, even of embodiment, these site-specific domains remain un- or under-theorized and thought. The domestic posthuman, however, cannot avoid them: grooming takes them meticulously and categorically into contact with their own skin, hair, teeth each day and throughout the day; allogrooming directs the domestic posthuman to careful attention to the site-specific embodiments of second persons in their care; domestic posthumans also give these sites over to intimate knowing by the second persons who care for them.

Myth

Two masks: The first, an N95 mask, is the polypropylene air-filtering system worn tightly over the mouth and nose that became household medical equipment during the Covid-19 pandemic. N95s were one of the kinds of personal protective equipment (PPE) initially considered best at protecting healthcare professionals and the general population from the virus; very shortly later, they were catapulted to global fame by shortage. Long before Covid, PPE was mobilized as a technology for responding to the body's susceptibility to environmental contagions that circulate in hospitals and labs. On an ordinary basis, PPE marked the extent to which a person's separation from even invisible environmental conditions is illusory at best. An N95 mask is designed to accommodate a human bodily surface to atmospheric contexts to which it is permeable and which will, given the right conditions, invade and infect the body's interior. For a long time, this concern was primarily salient in units of hospitals dedicated to the care of very vulnerable people. The N95 mask was, and is, a functional accessory in the sense that all aspects of it serve its function. Though it is made to be worn, its makers are considered engineers and the mask itself is equipment or a tool.

In response to the N95 mask shortage, however, a second kind of mask rose to prominence. This kind of mask was handmade in the homes of quarantined people all over the world to use as protection while leaving the short supply of more sophisticated N95s and other PPE masks for frontline workers. At first, the handcrafted home masks were simple: old clothing was cut up and repurposed. These masks were primarily utilitarian, if less hyperfunctionally so, and worked much the same as traditional polypropene and paper equipment to limit the local exchange of air and so virus particles between people. The fact that they were built, of necessity, from recycled materials that quarantined people had in their homes, however, facilitated the introduction of some stylistic flourishes in the form of color, fabric, pattern, and shape. The development of fashion face masks shortly followed. Fashion face masks departed from the visual rhetoric of pure utility (while still referring to it, since most were made from deadstock fabrics held in-house by brands struggling to figure out how to exist in a world where interest in clothes had waned). In so doing, fashion face masks took on a bigger kind of environment than local air—not just the global atmospheric one implicated by a pandemic made of airborne viral transmissions but also the cultural environmental circumstances created by widespread human susceptibility to a novel coronavirus. *The New York Times* was already commenting on the mask as a fashion accessory on March 17, 2020—only four days after the declaration of a National Emergency that officially shut down most of the United States—and it continued to publish articles throughout the pandemic on such topics as which masks were most stylish, whether it was ethical to wear stylish masks, the affinity between masks and Muslim fashion, the case for buying a mask chain since the accessories were here to stay, and many more topics.

The brand Collina Strada's fashion face masks were one of the *Times'* featured masks among its coverage of the most stylish options; this mask was acknowledged in several such lists and commentaries. It was brightly citrus colored in deadstock custom-printed textiles: no two alike. Each was trimmed with elaborate bands and bows that could be tied in different shapes and combinations, transforming the elastic attachment mechanism sported by N95 masks and other face PPE into baroque ornaments and giving facemasks the look of elaborate millinery. Collina Strada's fashion face masks—especially the tendrilled, curling, excessive bows—marked the movement of PPE beyond a straightforwardly utilitarian function and into the realm of myth and imagination. A Collina Strada ornamental mask didn't just do the job, it *welcomed* antivirus safety onto the body's surface and integrated it subtly into mental concepts. In addition to offering protection to the wearers and to others with whom they may have come into contact, Collina Strada's fashion face masks also suggested the wholesale and even playful acceptance into everyday life of the mask and the attendant notion of protecting others from our own body's capacity to impact the environmental context of another human.

The stylish nature of fashion is not superfluous to the technological function of protecting the wearer from exposure to inhospitable temperatures, gazes, insects, and vegetation but a sign that (soft) technology is inseparable from the functions of myth with which it is often held in tension but which technology requires to function fully. Collina Strada masks, with their superfluity of imaginative flourishes, are an optimal example of what all fashion masks represent: they are slow (often handmade and if not trash then made of deadstock or leftover fabric), soft, felt on the skin, intimate, material, everyday, and accessible sophisticated technological devices. They do not shy away from or entirely eschew the elements of style but embrace style as an essential component of technology if it is to be fully adopted and assimilated into humans' bodies, cultures, exchanges, and interior lives.

Domestic posthuman technologies foreground style as an essential component of humans' using and fusing with things; it's how we absorb and connect to objects. Modernism's banishment of ornament in favor of smooth, bright, reflective, deflective surfaces as the visual signifier of the machine age and machines as the domineering symbols of post-seventeenth-century technological development fundamentally misunderstands how the human species uses touch to take our worlds in and convert them into tools or give them meaning. Contemporary design theory that engages with posthumanism by advocating to decenter the human (e.g., Escobar, Fry, and Wakkary) similarly unthinkingly embraces the machine myth in a banishment that could be read as embarrassment by ornament and decoration, the queer and feminine elements of the discipline. In doing so, posthumanism and design theory neglect, in their enthusiasm for decentering the human, one of the key ways one can do so, which is by recollecting the animal nature of *Homo sapiens* and acknowledging the serious centrality of grooming to all animals and of style, specifically, to human animals. Style isn't just a look but a feel, and the cultural fetishization of the Cartesian spectator and a narrow slice of visual processing, the focused gaze, has neglected and endeavored to banish the design of multisensory and haptic experiences with objects that invite touch through kinesthetic, textural, muscular, tactile, geometric, and dense shapes and forms or even peripheral, unfocused, vision. Technology, the architect Juhani Pallasmaa writes, "should not become transparent in its utilitarian and rational motives; it has to maintain its impenetrable secret and mystery in order to ignite our imagination and emotions" (2007: 62). It has, in another phrasing, to maintain its connection to style. The injunction is not moral but biological. Objects of a merely utilitarian, rational, representational nature simply falter when it comes to human use. Such objects ignite the focused gaze and imply an adoption story with a straightforward and results-driven beginning, development, and end. Other objects, and sometimes those same objects under different conditions, use style to shift into the peripheries of vision; maintain a sense of secrets and mystery; are plastic and intimate in their evocation and transmission of meaning; and are "known" and made near through the proxy of identification. They awaken the sense of touch and feeling and other specializations of the skin to facilitate becoming known in embodied ways that mobilize ritual through muscular, thematic, and sonic repetitions; they mobilize connoted and suggested meanings. In other words, more than simply being objects, they are myths.

Drucilla Cornell, Merlin Donald (2001), Mary Midgley, Ernst Cassirer, Carl Jung, Bruno Latour, and Marjorie Grene have all acknowledged in their various ways the pivotal role played by myth in human-technology relations. None treats myth as archaic and primitive in a chronological sense; all acknowledge that myth is an archaic and primitive system that, far from having been banished by science, remains vital and active in how and even whether we use its material and conceptual offspring. Myth is, at its essence, embodied communication that draws on the fullness of our capacities of imagination and feeling to function as a meaning system and transmits that meaning in ways designed to be consumed with the entire body as opposed to only the cognitive, discursive mind. Myth is a form of storytelling that departs from the notion of story as something told by the conscious mind, a sequence of events with a beginning, a development, and an end. Its meanings are implied, not conveyed. Its senses often are perceived intuitively and emotionally rather than because they have been explained or defined (there is heresy in its paraphrase, if also always a beckoning to paraphrase). Importance wells up in a myth, and it can contain multitudes, even contradictions. A myth is part story, part symbol, part song, and part prayer. It is known and transmitted ritualistically, through embodiments that activate habit, community, profundity, and transcendence.

Theorists of myth have conceived of the form as embodied storytelling. For Carl Jung (1964), for example, myth was more a constellation of highly "cathected," for example, emotion-laden, forms and their evoked sensations than a set of chronologically ordered narratives; these arraigned symbols, images, and sensations were stored in the body as epigenetically transmitted archetypes (to use a somewhat modernized paraphrase). The archetypes might come into consciousness in moments of rational mindlessness through dreams, the more affect-laden moments of literature and especially poetry, ritualized/ repetitive nonconscious actions and behavior patterns, and the shadowlands of erotic longing. Jung configured these embodied iterations as messages from the unconscious, itself formed through not only individual experience but also collective cultural and human evolutionary experiences—a notion that was banished from serious philosophical consideration as too esoteric and religious-sounding but which is supported by contemporary neuroscientific findings regarding the capacities of the nonconscious mind to know things that the conscious mind has yet to figure out. Jung's notion of a collective unconscious allowed for the capacity of this "unknown knowledge" to reside, latent in the body, for generations, acquiescing even to the ability of prehistoric ancestors to transmit their ways of thinking into the present. Jung's mode of articulating this notion maximized its affinity for spiritualization and mysticism, to be sure. Yet the contemporary scientific recovery of a skin-centric mind in which awareness of environments, selves, and relationships comes to humans through nonrational perceptions tethered to touch suggests that the mystical-seeming Jungian archetype can also be expressed scientifically, as epigenetically transmitted nonconscious, nonverbal learning.

Jung, like the mid-twentieth-century German Neo-Kantian philosopher Ernst Cassirer, worked from the Kantian Idealist premise that humans are "symbolizing creatures,"

> destined to come to a world through forms not entirely of our own making but which we, in turn, work with and ultimately develop and change as we struggle to come to terms with who we are and our place in the universe. Human beings . . . experience reality beyond mere receptor and effector systems in the biological sense and are imbued with the power of a third means that transforms the reality of human life through a symbolic system where "man lives not merely in a broader reality; he lives so to speak in a new *dimension* of reality." (Cornell and Panfilio, 2010: 4)

These dimensions and their symbols were not some sort of enumerated list of symbols to be conceived through an overarching system of reason but rather an endlessly shifting mixture of experiences and perceptions: "the varied threads which weave the symbolic net [are] the tangled web of human experience" (Cassirer, 1944: 25). For both Jung and Cassirer (and Clifford Geertz (1973), for whom Cassirer was a major influence), human beings live not in a supremely rational universe but rather one that is superlatively, richly symbolic.

Symbols are more than a straightforward definition or explanation but rather are images or other sensory impressions charged with intense emotions; symbolizing animals' capacity to do so is mediated through the skin and touch. This embodied history of the symbol is what allows some to "seem to hold a special spell" (Jung, 1964: 97, 120). The spell with which emotion can cast an image is what creates what Jung refers to as their numinosity (116). Numinosity is the emotional and vital importance that "later wells up" (118) as "a sort of afterthought" to meaning, perceived through a combination of "intuition" and "profound thought." The "dimensions in time and space" of such meanings are quite different from those of a traditional story, and more like a three-dimensional object that invites a symbolic fourth dimension: "to understand [a symbol] you must examine it from every aspect—just as you may take an unknown object in your hands and turn it over and over until you are very familiar with every detail of its shape." Numinosity, in other words, is meaning perceived through the body with the tools of haptics, skin, affect, and intuition, and not the conscious mind. Jung distinguishes this from most modes of symbolic knowing, mediated through language, practiced in modernity:

Today, for instance, we talk of "matter." We describe its physical properties. We conduct laboratory experiments to demonstrate some of its aspects. But the word "matter" remains a dry, inhuman, and purely intellectual concept, without any psychic significance for us. How different was the former image of matter—the Great Mother—that could encompass and express the profound emotional meaning of Mother Earth. In the same way, what was the spirit is now identified with intellect and thus ceases to be the Father of All. It has degenerated to the limited ego-thoughts of man; the immense emotional energy expressed in the image of "our Father" vanishes into the sand of an intellectual desert. (Jung, 1964: 117–18)

Numinosity, or what we might call the skin resonance of softwear, enables the extent to which individuals can perceive, listen to, and communicate with objects and images; it is what we use to make and remake the world, a preeminent tool. This tool, for Jung, is the opposite of those used in modernity to create and recreate the world, for example "the seizure of state power as the ultimate goal of revolution" (Cornell and Panfilio, 2010: 13). Nor was Cassirer's sense of a "new humanity" forged through what Jung called our fusing with "monstrous machines." Instead, numinosity allows humans to enlarge our mentality and enhance our humanity (Cornell and Panfilio, 2010: 12, 14). Cassirer calls this process "vivification" (Cornell and Panfilio, 2010: 26), allowing symbolic forms to give us "a tangled web of human experience, which can always be"—note the verb–"rewoven" (Cornell and Panfilio, 2010: 28).

Myth, the story form that activates nonverbal communication through felt meanings and communally transmitted experiences, consequently rises to the surface as a primary posthuman tool. Since myth is often associated with primitive cognitions and experiences, acknowledging its preeminent role in technological innovation, adoption, and experience complicates the chronological trajectory of the domestic posthuman, which may take its most sophisticated forms in *prehistory* when we are thinking in terms of our civilization, *childhood* when we are thinking in terms of an individual human lifespan, and in our vestigial and most primitive *animal* components when we are thinking in terms of the species.

The Proto-Technicity of Frivolous Bodily Decorators

The elision of the structures here associated with the domestic posthuman is not merely an oversight. Iris Marion Young writes:

> Misogynist mythology gloats in its portrayal of women as frivolous bodily decorators. Well-trained to meet the gaze that evaluates us for our finery, for how well we show him off, we are then condemned as sentimental, superficial, duplicitous, because we attend to and sometimes learn to love the glamorous arts. The male gazers paint us gazing at ourselves at our toilet, before the table they call a vanity. In their own image, the male mythmakers can imagine only narcissistic pleasures. (Young, 2005: 68–9)

In the case of fashion, the structure is actively shamed by misogynist mythology, which "gloats in its portrayal of women as frivolous bodily decorators." A person who engages with fashion is condemned as "sentimental, superficial, duplicitous" for attending to and learning to love "the glamorous arts." She is (they are?) rarely considered a pioneer of the posthuman. Consider the profound cultural distinction that operates to separate stylists from architects and engineers, or how accounts of the ways that design will change the world never include fashion design (Escobar, 2018; Fry, 2012; Mau, 2004). Yet, arguably, stylists do more work to mediate and integrate environments into human usability than either architects or engineers. They work with archetype, myth, and ornament in order to do it: three techniques are required, according to diffusion of innovation research, for artifacts to be accepted, adapted, and spread.

For Audre Lorde (1988), engaging in the narcissism, or self-care, that fashion demands is so forbidden to humans considered unworthy of preservation and care as to constitute an act of political warfare. For Rosalind Galt (2011), the author of *Pretty: Film and the Decorative Image*, modernism and postmodernism's aesthetics of fragmentation, rupture, and anti-ornament constitute acts of violence against prettiness, one of the aesthetics associated with fashion. "Slicing up eyeballs," Galt writes—the style associated with modernist and modernist-influenced filmmaking—"is necessary to guard against the aesthetic danger of women" and femmes (2011: 2).

There are, obviously, more ways to transform self and world than with style. But what does it mean when the idea of transformation through style seems trivial, or when "world changing" more immediately conjures an image of lab coats or automatic weapons than a soft pleated rectangle that you can, if you're inclined to, make in your home by hand? Claiming that fashion is a domestic posthuman form is not just about redirecting attention to wearable technology and smart textiles, though these represent an intriguing migration of computational hardware into softer spaces. It is about redirecting attention to the ways in which ornaments do something profound, beyond their function, by reaching into the spaces of imagination and myth in order to bring humans up close in relation to the other human and nonhuman components of the world in which we live. It is an example of a posthuman technology that has always known that sometimes the sign of this interaction cannot be seen but is felt and

Notes

1 Arnold Pacey's (1983) starting point in *The Culture of Technology* is also a facet of Inuit culture, but in that case he refers to the introduction of snowmobiles, which also transformed Inuit culture if in ways that were not always altogether beneficial. The raincoat is, arguably, a better example of Inuit technology but is overlooked because it doesn't conform to typical myths about what technology is supposed to be like.

2 The same is true of David Bolter's account of defining technologies, which include pottery, computers, and clocks. Lambros Malafouris, in *How Things Shape the Mind* (2016), does not discuss any fabrics or textiles; Bernard Stiegler (1998), in his analyses of *homo faber*, only discusses flint.

3 The 2018 exhibit was a collaboration with trendspotter Li Edelkoort ("Li Edelkoort and Google Explore How Digital Devices Can Be More Sensorial" 2018). The 2019 exhibit was a collaboration with Susan Magsamen of the Johns Hopkins University Mind Lab (Dickinson, 2019).

4 Kate Soper argues the same in her critique of posthumanism. Soper and Midgely's claims are not arguments for bioconservatism but rather for attentiveness to humans' embodied, material species-attributes.

5 The pack is reminiscent of Temple Grandin's squeeze machine (Guglielmo et al. 2018—and yes, we are intentionally citing an illustrated children's book). Grandin has been described as the woman who thinks like a cow and invented the squeeze machine used on cows to calm them when they get their veterinary shots. She also discovered that the squeeze machine, retooled as a hugging device, worked on her and other autistic people to calm them. Grandin's reconfiguration of touch as squeeze responds to myths about autistic people as intolerant of touch by nuancing the question around types and specificities of touch.

6 It also resonates with clinical practices in contemporary dance movement therapy, see Berrol (2006) and Homann (2010).

7 Things might go differently for autistic children; see *60 Minutes'* episode on "Apps for Autism" (2012).

Figure 6 Button, *Eliza's Peculiar Cabinet of Curiosities*, Folayemi Wilson.

It's a humble thing. A button. Next to Star Wars figurines, preserved botanicals, a child's dolls, a button seems, well . . .ordinary. But then we recall Eleanor Casella and Karina Croucher's excavations at a nineteenth-century British colonial prison in Tasmania, Australia, which turned up metal buttons that circulated within the convict black market and provided a means for convict women to sustain intimate relationships, a treasured material link to another person (2011). Entangling subjectivity and materiality, even a common domestic object like a button can tell a story about a lost loved one, a fondly remembered mended object, a relationship well preserved.

Chapter 5
(Un)homely *Techne*

What could be more familiar than family? Kinship is an anthropological tool so foundational as to seem, most of the time, invisible. You're either in the midst of experiencing yours, too caught up in it to see it, or you've moved out of your home and away from your family and haven't really been thinking about it. It's only when you return for a visit later in life, actually or in conversations with your therapist, that the infrastructure it made for you starts to come into focus as a thing that could have gone another way. You can see what kind of second person you are. At that point, things might get a little weird.

My family infrastructure unwinds from the spool of me to reveal two peripatetic generations of air force and army veterans and civil servants, with immigrants whose origins span Western, Northern, Southern, Central, and Eastern Europe populating the generations before that. I have never known how to answer the question: Where do you come from? And it only gets more complicated after that. My father divorced my mother and married a Lao woman, younger than both my little sister and me, whom he met while working in the Philippines; they have, in addition to my father's adult son with the German woman he met, married, and divorced during another overseas tour, four Lao-American children (including, I think but have not confirmed, a second half-brother). They all lived in Hawaii for a while, and when my father retired from the US Army Corps of Engineers they all moved to southern Alabama to start an organic *bok choi* farm. At one point, I was going to adopt their youngest daughter; my dad was almost seventy when she was born and was not her biological father. It didn't work out. My mother took a different tack: once divorced from my father, she moved to Florida with my sister and me and met and married an expat British Pentecostal minister. She'd converted to Pentecostalism from Catholicism while living in Hawaii in the 1970s, where her father was stationed and where she met my father, whose father was also stationed there, and none of whom were either Pentecostal or Catholic (if pressed, I'm pretty sure my dad would identify his religious affiliation as "surfer"). Mom's version of charismatic Christianity was filtered through the countercultural

Jesus Freak movement sparked on the West Coast and in Hawaii in the 1960s and 1970s; at first, everyone thought she was just another kind of hippie. The conversion went more or less well, until she had an affair with and married the English pastor of Suncoast Cathedral, a prominent Pentecostal church in St. Petersburg, Florida. That was not allowed; they converted to Methodism. I dated his son, my stepbrother, for a few months when we both were at the University of Florida in the early 1990s. Eventually, I moved to Seattle to get a PhD in English literature. He became a divorce lawyer in Clearwater. We never saw each other again. Much later, I married a Scotch-Irish punk rock drummer whom I met at the Mars Bar in Seattle. We moved to Chicago—our third landing place as a couple—and I'm typing this sentence on the porch of a rented beach house in Edisto, South Carolina, surrounded by four generations of my North and South Carolinian in-laws, including one Uncle Jerry, the retired Lebanese owner of the livestock feed store in Camden, who has seamlessly integrated *kibbe* into the family's southern culinary traditions.

My trans colleague, hearing a quarter of this story, which is, as you may imagine, itself only a quarter of the story, laughed gleefully: now I get why I get you—you're queer! I laughed too, with recognition. I mean, I hadn't really thought about it. But said aloud, the word rang true. I began to think about how wild it is to be the second person of so many humans. This is the wilderness of home, which intermingles strangeness with normalcy; metabolizes strangeness and strangers until both are alchemically transformed into another thing entirely that is colloquially called "family"; digests divergence using a combination of stories, habits, proximity, and time. You might, if you're so inclined (and very lucky), find ways to control yourself. But if you've ever tried to control your family, you've experienced the slippery impossibility of controlling your second self. You've experienced, this is to say, the essence of a posthuman personal infrastructure. I'm using the word "infrastructure" in Lauren Berlant's (2016; 2022) sense of the word, leveraged by her as an alternative to "institution" and a way of reclaiming the queerable capacities of anthropological structures like "marriage," here extended to include "home" and "family." Infrastructures are "not identical to system or structure . . . because infrastructure is defined by the movement or patterning of social form. [They are] the living mediation of what organizes life: the lifeworld of structure" (Berlant, 2016: 393). Objects have infrastructures, but so do humans. In this chapter, we want to lay bare certain "lifeworlds" implicit in the home and family to show how profoundly strange these familiar structures are, to surface the extraordinary work they do in manufacturing, with the applied arts of personhood, posthuman second persons.

A domestic posthuman second person prioritizes, as discussed in the previous chapter, different tools and users and thereby engenders an alternatively imaged and defined future. This future is built by familiar objects, fusions, and behaviors but that is not to say that it is conservative, nostalgic, or regressive. Our goal in this chapter is not only to discover the domesticity of posthuman genesis but also to recover the strangeness, and so the ecstatic quality—in Jung's words, the numinosity—of domestic *techne*. Freud has called this unfamiliar familiarity the *unheimlich*, which can be translated as, and also connotes in German, "unhomely." Most English translations and critical exegeses prefer to retain the German word, perhaps because of the *unheimlich* associations intellectuals often have with the home as an unserious, philosophically unworthy space. The notion of the unhomely, however, can call into question just how familiar, in the sense of simple and known, this oft-overlooked space is. Thus, what follows in this chapter reflects on the "unhomely *techne*" of the domestic posthuman. It calls into question the typical infrastructure of the posthuman, in which algorithms, silicon, pharmaceuticals, and code currently have a monopoly on posthuman apocalypse. In fact, it questions whether what posthumans offer is indeed apocalyptic, offers a more domestic and domesticated (normative) account of transformation and change, queers the fundamental structure of family, and shows ways in which the future might be productively—maybe even ecstatically—*homemade*.

Beyond Facts

In 1999, the filmmaker Werner Herzog gave a speech following a Milan screening of *Lessons of Darkness*. The film chronicles the ten-month burn of the oil field fires set by Saddam Hussein's forces as they withdrew from Kuwait in 1991. Herzog began his speech on the film by reading its epigraph, a line he attributed in the opening frame to the French mathematician Blaise Pascal. It said: "The collapse of the stellar universe will occur—like creation—in grandiose splendor." The line is startling in epigraph to a documentary about an act of war. But Herzog turns the screw in his commentary, announcing that the words he attributed to Pascal "are in fact by me."

Why lie? Herzog brushes the question aside: "To acknowledge a fake as fake contributes only to the triumph of accountants," and later, "if the factual were of significance, the truth at its most concentrated would reside in the telephone book." Let us put aside for a moment the question of whether facts matter as little as Herzog contends and try to understand his meaning. Herzog explains that he wants to question the extent to which the version of the truth that matters can be discovered in phone books and ledgers, both triumphs of facticity but often experienced as emblematically meaningless in an existential sense.[1] Sometimes the "falsified" is also "*not*-falsified," Herzog complains, in that it can help us to see something truer than facts—if we don't immediately discard it. "With this quotation as a prefix," he continues,

> I elevate the spectator, before he has even seen the first frame, to a high level, from which to enter the film. And I, the author of the film, do not let him descend from this height until it is over. Only in this state of sublimity does something deeper become possible, a kind of truth that is the enemy of the merely factual. (Herzog and Weigel, 2010: 1)

This "something deeper" Herzog calls "ecstatic truth," a concept whose operationalization can be witnessed across the filmmaker's canon in works that offer up images, stories, incidents, and emotions that sidle up to something more frequently associated with poetry and scripture than documentary film: revelation.

Ecstatic truth is neither about facts nor the interpretation of facts. It is a version of nonverbal, noncognitive knowing whose relationship to facts can reside only in those facts that "so exceed our expectations . . . that they seem unbelievable" (Herzog and Weigel, 2010: 9). Such facts are less relevant to literal (e.g., historical, scientific, or psychological) realism than to a palimpsest of messages and meanings that transcend the ordinary way in which things can be said to exist and be true and instead try to give us something beyond it; thus, a fact that seems impossible invites us to conjure meaning out of the space where incredulity resides in a way that a fact whose meaning is transparently obvious does not. The conjured meanings of extraordinary facts are apprehended not only cognitively, by the mind, but physically and emotionally, by the whole of the perceiving organism.

All of this is to say that ecstatic truth resides in the numinosity of objects and events: Carl Jung's (1964) term for their embodied, emotional resonance. Numinous also connotes mysteriousness and holiness, both derivatives of mythical meaning. Herzog's commitment to ecstatic truth stylizes him as a mythmaker and myth as a larger kind of truth-bearer, one more evocative of embodied emotional transformation in the organisms which encounter it than the kind of truth which reflects, in the sense of catalogs, something established and static. Myth cannot be cataloged: it enables the assimilation and integration of felt and thought realities into the self through a transformation of fact plus fact plus fact beyond sum and into a thing we call meaning. Meaning cannot be created merely rationally and additively (through the collection of sums of things) but must be generated emotionally and physiologically (e.g., known in the gut). To do so requires that supersensual state in which something is known in the sense of being not merely looked at, heard, or otherwise apprehended outside of the self but rather *seen*, *felt*, *listened to*, and otherwise *taken in*to the self. Myth is what enables this other kind of tingling, assimilative apprehension.[2] We don't keep myths in spreadsheets. Symbols and icons contain them. To retrieve them we have to encounter them, in the fullest sense of the word: subject ourselves to their slow unfurling.

Numinousness is not a rarified quality, though we live in a culture that has attempted to banish it as a relic of preindustrial society. And many technologies hailed, in Braidotti's terminology, as horsemen of the posthuman apocalypse—nanotechnologies, biotechnologies, information technologies, and cognitive science—are factually transformative but lack the deeper change mechanism of numinosity. They are in a position analogous to that of coffee in Japan in the 1970s when Nestle hired the international marketer Clotaire Rapaille to help them introduce that beverage into what they hoped would be the blue ocean space of a tea-drinking culture (Rapaille, 2007). Rapaille is a trained psychoanalyst who uses hypnotic and free-associative techniques to identify what he calls the "culture codes," or archetypes, that will allow him to create culturally meaningful frameworks for product messaging and design. Put differently, Rapaille studies the numinosity of objects to optimize design and messaging in ways that will signify profoundly in a nonverbal, nonconscious manner. In one anecdote, Rapaille recounts the story of Nestle's failed efforts to sell coffee in Tokyo, which led them to secure his consultancy to determine a Japanese "code" for coffee that would enable the brand to message their product to better effect. Rapaille's initial take on the problem was that it was doomed to failure, because Nestle had run up against the total absence of a culture code for coffee in a land traditionally devoted to tea. Likewise, many of the tools of the four horsemen of the posthuman apocalypse are as yet uncoded or barely coded; this is not to say that their codification is impossible, but that storytelling and mythmaking efforts must be amplified beyond the mere *ad hoc* creation of innovative objects to include their narrative and semiotic framing.[3]

Intriguingly, Rapaille's account of his work with Nestle includes the story of his successful effort to create a code for coffee in Japan. And it began with children. Rapaille's archetype-identification system involves taking adults into a meditative state so that they can relive their earliest memories, sense impressions, and emotional arcs regarding objects usually first encountered and encoded as children. Doing so is important because adult humans don't only sometimes *have* children, they also universally *were* all children and these children are carried beyond childhood into adulthood; this is the whole point behind the plethora of evocative objects that populate object relations theory. An object without an archetype is an object that never entered into the affective and cognitive domain of a child, and creating archetypes thus necessitates a metaphorical dialogue with the extant children stored in the furthest memory recesses of every adult.[4] In the case of coffee, a beverage for adults whose bitter flavor and caffeine content create conditions of taste that tend to obviate children's preferences entirely, there was nothing to dialogue with these vestigial "children" about. So Rapaille counseled Nestle to create sweet coffee-flavored desserts for children. Over time, these desserts consumed in childhood would accrue a cauldron of stories, experiences, memories—they would become enmythed and so become encodable. Coffee's archetype could be built on top of the remnant of coffee-flavored candies, shifted into the frame of adults on the basis of its experiential resonance with their child selves. The implication of Rapaille's method is that everything new, en route to assimilation, must wend its way through homes and children and the things that children do, see, keep, and collect in their home places. As Allison Gopnik acknowledges, children are the real innovators in human societies, responsible for exploration through play and the enacting of noncontinuous futures divergent from the ones their parents and grandparents set into motion. But they also are the ones who interact most vigorously with prelinguistic myth forms that determine whether artifacts are embedded and entrenched in human places like the home and psyche.

Objects generated in labs and relegated to institutions accrue specific use-values but have a thin mythical resonance at first. This is to say that they have functions and their form communicates a use-message but that these attributes are generally neutral, not numinous. In the absence of more ecstatic states of perception—a function dependent on mythical resonance through the accrual of feelings, stories, associations—they won't fully merge with their human users and become assimilated into the embodied cognitive field of the extended self (Belk, 2013). As such they are mere tools, awkward prosthetics in the sense of an adjoined mechanical appendage.[5] Alternatively, lab-born technologies do have a mythical resonance. Think of clone technology, which was born into a long history of science fiction-generated myths that preexisted actual technical capacity. These might be passed off as neutral in hopes of easing human assimilation. They might also be used to the product developer's advantage. In any case, both postures of neutrality and myth-building should always be studied and questioned.

A fuller fusing of human to environment, a broader and deeper acquisition, however, is possible. Certain technologies are so thoroughly juxtaposed with us as to become almost indistinguishable from us; at this point, we may even cease to consider them technologies.[6] Such an extension of self is posthuman, in the sense of indicating a category of technology-fused humans transformed in some manner by the fusion. But when the objects and events to which we fuse are construed more broadly than nanotechnology, reproductive technology, and information technology—which, Langdon Winner (1986) argues, are complex macrosystems of technologies that require huge bureaucracies to operate and should be distinguished from the microsystem of specific tools we invite into the home to interact with—we need another name for the kind of posthuman created by them. This kind of posthuman, we argue, is a domestic posthuman. The domestic posthuman is fully enmythed and is usually homemade.[7]

Humans first live with and toward enmythed technologies as children in their homes. The technologies in question are not computers and pills, though in a generation or two they might be since computers have taken forms that children can hold and play with and thanks to Westerners' unparalleled medication of children for diseases like diabetes, ADHD, depression, and anxiety. Computers and pills are like coffee: things adults use sweetened and so now passing through the hands, minds, and imaginations of children en route to acquiring numinosity. The question is not the essentializing "what is numinous?" (everything can be), but where the enmything happens and at whose hands and in what kind (developmental stage or existential state) of mind. The answer may lie embedded in a menagerie of posthumans, most of which are presently neither digital, surgical, nor pharmaceutical, but all of which can be exemplars of what a more homegrown approach to the posthuman looks like.

Numinosity Begins at Home

A body is made in utero, but humans begin in homes. Home is an aboriginal space, in the sense of being the place where we have our earliest beginnings and also in the sense of existing since the earliest times. Not the nuclear, middle-class, walled-in, geographically fixed kind of home upheld by "family values" that modern Western cultures commonly affiliate with home, but home in the archetypal senses of *hearth* and *kin*. Because of home's associations with developmental and prehistorical beginnings, it is often positioned in contemporaneity as the counterpoint to technology's orientation toward a cosmopolitan future. Its affiliated emotion is nostalgia, a backward longing, whereas the way we modern humans feel technology more often evokes excitement, a forward-leaning. The feelings and postures which now frame an understanding of home can seem deceptively Luddite, since home is where humans first encounter the objects, humans, and animals that they will intimately fuse with to become a self. Humans emerge as homemade second persons to caregivers, pets, friends, and neighbors as well as toys, furniture, spaces, and clothing. These latter entities are not just our instruments but our parts and makers. Our addition to existing accounts of second persons in the context of posthuman second personhood is to acknowledge the role of not only narrative but also material culture in creating posthuman assemblages that include not only other people but a mix of domestic objects which we want to reframe here as "technology."

If home is a posthuman workshop, it is not the kind to which adjectives like "exhilarating" frequently affix. Indeed, in the preponderance of myths of home and family, divergence is forbidden, the ultimate social and psychic taboo. Therein lies the trauma of the so-called vertical, or ancestor-divergent, identities discussed in Andrew Solomon's 2012 exploration of physical and emotional disabilities, *Far From the Tree: Parents, Children, and the Search for Identity*. Human beings don't tend to handle the intrusion of difference into domestic spaces and ancestry well. At the same time, our ability to craft and experience home as intrinsically our own and therefore as a space of metaphorical (if not actual) stability has also made it one where difference signifies with less disruption than difference does in public spaces. As bell hooks wrote in "The Role of the Homeplace in the Lives of Urban African American Women," home has both literally and symbolically been a place where Black women "could be affirmed in our minds and hearts despite poverty, hardship, and deprivation" and "restore to ourselves the dignity denied us on the outside in the public world" (hooks, 2014: 42). Iris Marion Young likewise affirms, in "House and Home: Feminist Variations on a Theme," the home as a preservative space in which we can locate values of safety, privacy, and individuation to address, recover from, and accommodate lived experiences of rootlessness and uprootedness as they transpire in our public lives. Whereas the marketplace, the street, and institutions—even those designed to provide care, like schools and hospitals and the government—may frequently destabilize, decenter, and dehumanize their users, the home is a place to go to be reassembled and rehumanized. Humans use home places to touch base with the people and activities we wish to own (acknowledge) as ours and us and to reject those imposed upon us by others; put differently, at home we reorient ourselves after othering and reconstitute subjectivity through contact with the people, pets, and environments constitutive of our particular humanity. Humans marginalized in public spaces (due to race, ethnicity, gender, sexuality, and more) can reposition ourselves as normative in home places where we and our ways of thinking and doing are not marginal but centered.[8]

Cosmopolitan homes, far from an oxymoron, are those characterized by international or other culturally nonconforming habits, languages, and sensibilities foregrounded as fully expressed centers of gravity versus the muted and diluted ways in which they circulate publicly in the city. Nowhere implicit in the notion of a homemade domestic posthuman is the conservative notion that home must be comprised of certain types or numbers or configurations of people, of particular values, or that mobility is forbidden (as it is to some categories of immigrants by nations whose borders are set up as untransgressable "homelands" within which certain individuals essentially belong and to which others are foundationally alien). On the contrary, home is the place where two fathers, transmothers, single parents, childless couples, an adult, and a (lot of) pet(s), a large extended family all living under one roof, polyamorous parents, a family of friends as we see among roommates as well as in communal housing, or a cluster of biologically related or unrelated humans uprooted from one place and rerooted into another are all experienced as normative, preservative, and safe.[9] Normative and preservative are not the same as conservative; many domestic arrangements experienced as the former are highly progressive, even divergent, compared to arrangements sanctioned in the culture at large. Also nowhere implicit in the notion of home as an essential space is any idea of all homes as invariably safe for all of the inhabitants who reside there. But the failure of some actual homes to be fully psychically and mythically functional is no reason to dismiss their value, and considering the rich psychic and mythical operations of home can provide an inclusive measure for evaluating behaviors and events that transpire in the home without relying on narrow constructions of what counts as a home or exclusionary configurations of people who can be construed as making a good home.

For all of the reasons detailed earlier—reasons in which home works as a counterforce to urban and global deracination and bears archetypal associations with preservation and safety—when modern humans are looking to get "outside the box" in our thinking we are more likely to look outside the home than within it. A home may literally be the "box" we want to get out of; at least, it is stereotypically identified as such in most Western philosophical accounts of maturity, where to be mature is to grow up and leave home (Willet, 2001). Offices, labs, factories, hospitals, institutions, cities—and the able-bodied 22–65-year-olds who run them—form a counterpoint to safety, privacy, and preservation where strangeness, excitement, newness, and change presumably await. At home, change is the opposite of disruptive. There, change means growing, as in growing up, which is incremental, slow, collaborative, sometimes playful, and often tedious. None of these qualities resonate with myths about technology as rational, disembodied, future-leaning, fast, disruptive, serious, and gratifyingly instantaneous. Contemporary technomythologies constitutively and preemptively forbid domestic mediation devices and experiences. A broader conceptualization of the pace, materiality, temporality, and affects associated with technological transformations of the human is needed. The domestic posthuman enables us to configure technological transformation in ways more consistent with growing (up), slowing down, scaling back, and mending things, as well as with the emotions associated with care, preservative love, and self-reassembly such as connection, stillness, and calm.

Central to home's capacity to function as a richly numinous space is the sheer density of storytelling and mythmaking that happens there (Gottschall, 2012). At home, caregivers tell us about our individual and ancestral origins, provide us with ways of thinking and behaving, give meaning to myriad objects and everyday rhythms and habits. Family and chosen-family photographs bring people who live outside the home into its sphere of interest; at the kitchen table, the household gathers at the bookends of the day to suture individualized happenings and events into a common tapestry of experiences and understanding. Family recipes—sometimes passed down orally, others in the careful handwriting of a grandparent with annotations by other relatives—can give home its flavors, transform it into physical nourishment, set the stage for bonding, and ultimately are passed down between generations to bind them together. Televisions import a chorus of narratives and storytelling voices; as Joshua Meyrowitz (1986) argues, they import us into the most private recesses of other homes and treat us like one of their intimate, knowing inhabitants. Phonographs, which became tapes which became CD- and then MP3-players, reenact the musical component of storytelling around the campfire, later the hearth, and eventually the living room, between close-knit members of a tribe.[10] Furniture, blankets, and bedding unfold their superskins around inhabitants and become so saturated with unspoken meaning that some children won't leave home without taking one of them as a token; even college students on their first forays into differentiated adulthood often bring their childhood blankets to school with them as a way to feel grounded in their homes away from home. Quilting, like that practiced by Rosie Lee Tompkins, is art forged by mothers' apprentices "in a kind of *atelier*: a small town full of female friends and relatives who [quilt], the older ones showing and telling the younger ones" how to suture together the fabrics of everyday life into polyglot skinship (Smith, 2020). These might include printed, panne, and crushed velvets as well as denim, faux furs, distressed T-shirts, fabrics printed with the faces of the Kennedy brothers, Martin Luther King Jr. and Magic Johnson, whole dish towels printed with folkloric scenes, parts of a feed sack, chunks of American flag, bits of embroidery, Mexican textiles, fabrics printed with flamenco dancers and racing cars, hot pink *batik*, and "a slightly cheesy manufactured tapestry of Jesus Christ" (Smith, 2020). Pets are distinguished from other animals because they allow us not simply to touch but cradle and caress them, listen to us, and are given voices by us and become integrated through cuddling and conversation into enmythed, numinous skinship with us. Home has a more condensed supply of softwear than any other human space. We are as human, and as posthuman, as we can get there. Like it says in the label copy of downtown Juneau's Walter Soboleff clan house, modeled on those of the Tlingit, Haida, and Tsimshian peoples that can be seen throughout southeast Alaska: "The house is everything."

Infantile Psychology and the Techno-sophistication of Children

Freud seemed to understand home's capacity to provide a rich space of human-technological fusion; we can consider his classical psychoanalytic essay on the *unheimlich* an early exegesis on the (un)homely *techne* of the domestic posthuman. The *Unheimlich*, usually translated into English as "uncanny," could also (as Freud himself points out) be translated as "unhomely"—a word we can take to mean *of the home* but not, in the connotation of the British notion of homely, cozy (e.g., comfortable, warm, relaxed). "The *Unheimlich*" is, in fact, a redescription of home's embedded forms of strangeness and its capacity, in Freud's words, in being so familiar as to "become increasingly ambivalent, until it finally merges with its antonym" (1919). This transformation of home places from utterly familiar into utterly strange happens when we look at them with a certain kind of purposely or accidentally alienated gaze. This gaze is figured in Freud's text by the metaphor of disembodied or gouged-out eyes in his recounting of "The Sandman" story. The gouged-out eyes could be said to figure a range of now-ordinary household technologies such as the camera and the television. They could also figure more broadly, presumably, the *techne* of disembodied, cutoff ears: sound media, including stereo systems and the telephone. And we could even see through them an evocation of the tender, if severed, hands of caregivers configured through blankets, playpens, toy boxes, highchairs, nanny-cams, tablets, and VCRs, and some of the same sound and visual technologies listed earlier when used by caregivers for the purpose of teaching or occupying children. Let's see what happens when we use the translation "unhomely" instead of "uncanny" for *unheimlich*, to recover the connotation repressed by the latter translation and so better capture the sense in Freud's essay not of otherworldly, gothic horror but of a home filled with strangeness when regarded by a particular kind of vision—in this text, the point of view of technology, or the point of view of the human fused to technology, for example, that of the posthuman.

Freud's "*Unheimlich*" was published in 1919 and is currently considered a seminal text in literary and film studies of gothic and horror genres; it is hardly a typical text in contemporary conversations about posthumanism or posthuman technogenesis. However, the standard English translation of the term as "uncanny" has been appropriated by contemporary robotics engineers to describe humans' discomfort with machines that look too much, but also not quite enough, like humans. The uncanny valley, as this concept is called, marks an experience of "intellectual uncertainty . . . as to whether something is animate or inanimate," such as when "the lifeless bears an excessive likeness to the living" (Freud, 1919; 140–1). Even in the original text, however, technology signifies as important to the genesis of the unhomely. The unhomely is associated with states of mind and movements that "arouse in the onlooker vague notions of automatic—mechanical—processes that may lie hidden behind the familiar image of a living person" (135), as in instances of extreme repetitions, doublings, and doubling-back—all functions that automated technologies facilitate and are fundamentally associated with as quintessential machine behaviors.

In "The *Unheimlich*," however, beyond standard mechanical technologies, quintessential domestic spaces such as windows, kitchen and dining tables, staircases, playrooms, and neighborhoods are all estranged by the introduction of technological imagery to them. There are the automatons that appear in homes and children's stories in the form of dolls, clones that are figured as doubles reflected in mirrors and windows, automatic or coincidental repetition as when one becomes lost in a neighborhood and keeps traveling in circles and so passing the same landmarks again and again, animism as when a table carved with crocodiles is imagined to come to life in the form of actual amphibious creatures crawling around in the living room, and prosthetics as in a fairy tale about a wife with a sausage nose (though this latter example is not considered unhomely but laughably outlandish by Freud). The technology that creates the shudder of unhomeliness is affiliated with not only very familiar domestic environments but also the kinds and styles of humans who ordinarily inhabit these environments. For instance, the dolls and doubles are the tiny humans, or children, who inhabit some houses and often look like doubles of their grown coinhabitants; repetition occurs through the creation of progeny and the way progeny become themselves first by repeating the behaviors and speech of their caregivers; animism is enacted by the enlivening of objects and pets into teachers and companions that occurs in many homes. Ordinary homes and their inhabitants bear extraordinarily technologically mediated characteristics. Freud traces the future of laboratory-made technologies like artificial intelligence, clones, algorithms, and the IoT as emerging from Victorian domestic structures, furniture, and people.

Freud attributes a capacity to see the continuity between these entities that are typically posed as oppositions to the adoption of an "infantile psychology." Though typically an infantile psychology is considered a developmental stage to be grown out of by noninfants in favor of the more rational and mature perspectives of an adult, infantile psychology is also treated as accessible to adults by *Gestalt* theorists, who idealize the embodied and exploratory qualities of infantile engagements through skin and touch, second personhood, and nonutilitarian thinking (e.g., infants are not yet so fully subjected to culturally constructed categories and mindsets). Mechanical properties like repetition (in the form of babbled words), automation (in the form of routinized care), animism (in the form of play), and doubling (in the form of caregiver mimicry) are all elements of the infantile psychological experience. We could extrapolate that a "posthuman" perspective is embedded in human development at its origins, not in its future, and is at the quintessence—not the antithesis—of humanity. Objects in the home that appeal to infantile psychology can be assimilated by their human users. As in the case of Rapaille's archetype-discovery story about Nestle, the relationship between technological innovation and infantile psychology is under-accounted for, and strong.

For Freud, unhomely *techne* are not extraordinary silicon entities but rather things like dolls, windows, stories, carpets, kitchens, mirrors, baby talk, family stories, and conversations. But following the logic that renders these domestic objects unhomely, unhomely *techne* can also easily be clothing, cosmetics, tchotchkes, pets, Roombas, televisions, kitchen tables, gardens, games, children's books, and movies. Unhomely *techne* bear in common their capacity thusly to turn home into a strange space, one filled with objects and entities through which we can access something superhuman in the sense of being both beyond and very human. Freud's attributes of unhomeliness—automation, animation, doubling, and repetition—are intrinsic properties of domestic artifacts and subjectivities that render these same artifacts and subjectivities extrinsic to themselves. Domestic posthumans don't look, sound, or feel the way we're accustomed to expect technological mediations to look, sound, or feel. As we begin to render our homes unhomely by looking at them through the lenses of mechanical and animal vision, we also begin to welcome new affects, experiences, and sensations into the posthuman imagination. As the range of affects and experiences and sensations expand, so too does the range of users who can be seen as past and prospective progenitors of transformation via human-nonhuman fusions. Adopting these other-eyes when we look around our homes is a first step in disrupting exclusionary technological and philosophical paradigms.

Notes

1   Not by Avital Ronell (1991), though, whose *Telephone Book: Technology, Schizophrenia, Electric Speech* sees plenty of meaning in all aspects of the material culture of telephony.

2   Herzog's account of the relationships and contrasts between facts, truth, meaning, and knowing is reminiscent of that of the American philosopher and statistician, Charles Peirce (1839–1914), for whom a founding principle was the belief that the world is filled with signs. See *Peirce on Signs: Writings on Semiotics by Charles Sanders Peirce* (1991), ed. James Hoopes.

3   Efforts to popularize the Singularity (Kurzweil 2006) and popular accounts of converging technologies' forecasted effects on the evolution of the human (Garreau 2005) could be seen as codifications of these technologies through popular myths and visions, as is consistent with Elaine Graham's (2002) account of how representations of the posthuman borrow from popular culture. Kurweil and Garreau employ overtly religious metaphors to describe their mythmaking efforts; as William Sims Bainbridge, a proponent of converging technologies and senior fellow of the Institute for Ethics and Emerging Technologies, puts it: "Humanity is crossing an abyss on a tightrope. Behind us is the old world of religious faith that compensated wretched but fertile people for the misery in their lives. On the other side, if we can only reach it, is a new land where we no longer have to live by illusions, where wisdom and procreation are compatible, where truth and life are one" (2007: 247). Braidotti's "four horsemen of the posthuman apocalypse" metaphor could also be read in this vein.

4   Thinking about the child that everyone has been (vs. the child that not everyone has) is a way to relocate children and childhood outside of the reproductive paradigm of family in which children are compulsory symbols of heteronormative power. Sheila Heti's (2018) account of motherhood as something that one can direct toward one's own (past) self or to one's ancestors (as when Heti writes about mothering her female ancestors by giving them another kind of life, one not used to bear children, that was never accessible to them in their own times) supports this alternative vision of children.

5 Apple is exceptionally good at leveraging myth in digital product launches. To wit *Time Magazine*'s article (Grossman 2005) on "Stevie's Little Wonder" (the new iPod), in which the photograph made the iPod look magical; the nomenclature of the tablet employed first by Apple and ultimately universally as a product category also evokes archetypal associations with religious artifacts.

6 The muddled history of defining technology in the philosophy of technology illustrates the extent to which what constitutes and does not constitute technology is a source of some confusion. While most definitions metaphysically welcome a variety of objects into the range of what is defined, practically speaking a very narrow range ends up within the consideration set. Katherine Hayles' work is a good example of the paradox; much of her work explicitly calls for analysis of a greater range of objects with less narrowly configured attributes in the field of posthuman studies. But few of her discussed examples actually enact that call. She sticks to analyzing video games, traffic algorithms, biostatistics, and so on, while envisioning the Universal Computer as the Motherboard of us all (Hayles 2005b: 3).

7 Myth, to recall the language of the previous chapter, is the superskin that enables bindings that are ontologically profound. It is an adhesive activated by sensations and emotions that lets us experience enmythed objects and events with our extended skin, as skin, to absorb them into skinship with us. Myth is the softwear that makes a posthuman tick (thump, throb, pulse—we need a better word for the way a softwear-powered posthuman signifies its aliveness, one that isn't tethered, as Mary Midgley points out, to the mechanical metaphor of a clock. More like the concert of heartbeats with the sounds of breath and swallowing).

8 Though both hooks and Young point to home as supporting human selfhood, both do so while disavowing simplistic constructions of unified subjectivity. In their work, home supports individual subjectivity but in ways that understand this as fluid, partial, and in relations of reciprocal support with others.

9 The television show *Pose* and movie *Paris Is Burning* offer good examples of the normative and preservative utilization of home and kinship structures in queer ballroom cultures. There, the archetype of the "house" is used by gay and trans people in New York as a space in which to foster misfits who leave natal families to come to the city and need shelter and a community. "Mothers" of ballroom houses are figures of any sex or gender who run houses and provide new kinship structures and a home life in addition to competing with dance.

10 See the Radiolab series on cassette tapes, including how they helped share stories prior to the internet and even were partly responsible for the birth of the internet ("Radiolab's New Series: 'Mixtape' | All of It" 2022).

Figure 7 Dolls, *Eliza's Peculiar Cabinet of Curiosities*, Folayemi Wilson.

Children live here, or once did, and where there's a child there's . . . What? A mother? A grandmother? Or a loss. This object tethers Eliza to her others and their stories, which are also her stories. Her teeming personhood is a cluttered second personhood. Even if Eliza's dolls stand in for children she never had, or children she lost, or children who were taken, or the child she used to be, there are other kinds of humans—Eliza's real or missing doubles—to consider when we contemplate her personhood. Eliza is not so much an entity as an orbit.

Chapter 6

Myths of Domestic Posthuman Artifacts

In the tradition of Roland Barthes' *Mythologies* (1972), what follows is a set of domestic posthuman artifacts in their enmythed states. An enmythed domestic posthuman artifact is richly storied and has passed through the eyes, ears, hands, and skin of children. It is numinous, in the sense of extending beyond mere facticity into an everyday-sublime realm where emotions and sensations deliver meaning. Such an artifact is perceived with not only the eyes but the skin through touch; its technomateriality is soft. A domestic posthuman artifact also helps humans in the creation of our second personhood, melding children and parents, merging partners, connecting friends, enabling care for self and others. Such artifacts foster conviviality (Illich, 1973; Escobar, 2018), slow things down, thrive in home places, and are often made by hand. Though they may appear in digital spaces or take on virtual forms, they thrive IRL, bring the feel of the real to the screen, and enact the implicit materiality of virtual/digital spaces. The artifacts are aesthetically intelligent and invite the heightened aesthetic intelligence of their users. Domestic posthuman artifacts are normative, which is to say that they possess an in-built capacity for adoption and assimilation. They are often small in size and simple in construction and may have existed in human culture for a very long time. They also have what Arturo Escobar describes as a "future with a future" (2018: 207), which is to say that their production and consumption have the capacity to continue to transform and augment humans in our relationships to both built and natural environments without taxing the capacity of these environments to thrive long term. None of the sample domestic posthuman artifacts examined here is considered unique or exemplary in the sense of being idealized examples. Rather, each gives a window into a genre of artifacts and a way of seeing them that may suggest other artifacts, reveal their myths, and imply design futures drafted out by other artifacts like them.

Sari

Sari, a 5000-year-old spun or woven swathe of fabric whose Sanskrit name means "strip of cloth," is an ancient Indian, Sri Lankan, Bangladeshi, Nepalese, or Pakistani wearable technology that is networked to humans not through wires or mechanical hinges but through weaving and draping. Draping means wrapping, tucking, folding, tying, and twisting to adhere fabric to a body and transform 2-D materials into 3-D, usually human, shapes. However, the 3-D-draped future of a sari on a body is already spun into its flat form on the loom, as skilled handweavers can control the density of patterns on the cloth to impact its hang and drape. No sewing, pinning, cutting, or soldering—no metal—is required to create a sari's 3-D shape. Through spinning, weaving, and draping, the properties of complex machinery to pivot, hinge, adhere, support are shown all to be an inborn feature of cloth. Sari is an alternative lesson in the origins and nature of technicity: What if our central metaphor for technology was not a machine but a textile? What if screens could do what a sari does? What if soldered things were sturdy and reusable as a sari in all its soft and fluid strength?

Some thirty regional areas in India alone produce saris in unique fabrics, colors, and patterns, and each also has its own style of draping to create a distinct silhouette. Mukulika Banerjee and Malika Verma Kashyap's digital archive, *The Sari Series* (2022), captures in two- to three-minute videos each over 80 distinct traditional sari draping styles practiced in different regions of India (according to Rita Kapur Chishti, a sari historian, there are over 100 potential drapes to capture). Worn by women of all ages and walks of life and for all kinds of occasions, sari holds capacities typically reserved for the virtual, like the ability to transcend socioeconomic status and complicate conventional identity markers or endlessly change forms, but enacts them with cloth instead of code. The sari is cosmopolitan in the sense of being able to deftly take on the spirit of a place but also move comfortably between many places (east/west, city/rural, home/street) without being tethered to any one place. The same might be said for a sari's relation to time, insofar as a modern and traditional sari can be wrapped identically and be as appropriate in the present as the past; likewise, activities, since a sari can be worn to sleep, do chores, work, shop, mother, marry, or attend a party. Each sari is a pluriverse, in Arturo Escobar's sense of a world containing many worlds of experiences, contexts, even bodies as it so deftly shrinks or grows to accommodate the fundamental instability of any human user's shape. Though a sari is intensely reflective of the customs, geographies, moods, stories, and rites of its making- and wearing-people, it is not considered disrespectful or culturally appropriative for Westerners to wear a sari, to combine aspects of saris with contemporary fashion trends, or to display or sew saris into other garments. It lends its form to other things; its myths do not fix its identity to one thing, place, time, or function. Saris are cosmopolitan-domestic agents that resolve the theoretical tension between those terms.

Saris are woven with the stories of their regions, as when Baluchari saris incorporate designs based on myths from the *Ramayama* and *Mahabharata* or when a Kanjeevaram sari weaver passes blessings to the wearer by incorporating the strength of an elephant, grace of a gazelle, or abundance of a grove of trees into a pattern. A sari whispers on the wearer; its sounds cannot be silenced when a sari is wrapped around a moving body. In Pooja Kaul's *Sundar Sari* (2019), a woman listens to the stories of her sari, told through memory, when pieces from her bridal trousseau rustle or come into contact with her skin.

A sari is women's wear hand woven on looms by men, and their trade, worth many millions of dollars, is also orchestrated by men in shops and markets. But according to Q's film *Sari Men* (2020), a man is changed by his relationship to a sari he makes or sells. He becomes liminal, even queer, in his absorption of elements of the sari. In his film, Q speculates that "the men who spend their lives within the folds of the sari somehow intrinsically understand the nuances of gender. Maybe the sari teaches them something. . . . Perhaps handling such tactile, living, breathing pieces of art makes these men fluid and subtly shifts their ideas of masculinity." At the end of *Sari Men*, an older man describes the glittering fanciness of an "all-over sari," entirely embroidered with sequins. Then another younger, slimmer man—perhaps his son—quietly pleats it into a set of baroque folds and wraps it round and round himself. He poses, his entire demeanor is possessed by an Indian construction of "feminine." "He" becomes "her," for a moment, but without sacrificing "him"-self (which is to say, he still appears masculine in this moment). The sari confers alternate engendering to the body and self that wears it.

Saris are superskins (Allerton, 2007) that bind a mother to her child as a set of second persons to each other. According to Deborah Lupton, soft material binding between infants and caregivers can become "an affectively-charged space" that exists as a kind of "skinship" forged through the cloth's absorption of "the smell or marks from the baby's body (traces of dribble, milky leakages, or tears, for example) if they are used over a period of time before being washed" (Lupton, 2013: 8–9). Saris are like sarongs, "with their ability to wrap, protect and hide parts of the body, have skin-like properties. They are like second skins because they are experienced as having a similar function as skin by wrapping and protecting the body, and become imbued with the substances of the body" (Lupton, 2013: 8–9). And as we see on askamma.org in the posts tagged "babywearing," fathers can wrap their children to their bodies, too. Sari lets a father be a mother, make a pouch, wear his infant on his body, feel his child as himself the way a mother does. Children wrapped onto the bodily surfaces of their families by saris move about the world, absorbing kinship customs, individual habits, the cultures of the home, and the life of the street as they enact the final stages of fetal development outside the womb, ensconced not only by the sari but all they can encounter in its safe-exposed circumference. A sari is an instrument of ectogenesis, an ancient reproductive technology for enabling babies to gestate outside a body, out in the world, enwombed in the sari, wrapped in the world.

Cat

"Oh cat, I'd say, or pray: be-ootiful cat! Delicious cat! Exquisite cat! Satiny cat! Cat like a soft owl, cat with paws like moths, jeweled cat, miraculous cat! Cat, cat, cat, cat" (Lessing, 1967, 2002: 71). This is the song that Doris Lessing sings to 'grey cat' in her book *On Cats* (1967, 2002), and though the words appear in print we know their sound: high, lilting, with a lingering through the vowels. They're sung quietly, up close, human nose to cat nose as the creature composes herself on a bedspread to receive her praise, or hovered over the top of a cat in the lap while caressing him. Cat purrs the answer, a long low base strum. Sometimes there are gurgles, clucks, trills, meows. The sounds of both partners in these two "companion species" (Haraway, 2003: 140) don't technically mean anything but nevertheless communicate: sensuous care, luxuriant affection, the deep enjoyments of close but purposeless attention. Humans sing this message with sounds and gestures, and cats copy it and sing it back. We like the sounds domestic cats make best because, essentially, they're ours (Nicastro, 2004; McComb et al., 2009). Everyone knows what everyone is thinking—but no one is "saying" anything. Our conversations with cats are "unthought" (Hayles, 2017). A capacity to communicate in this way enables "cosmopolitanism across animal species" (Willett, 2014: 94) in companion polyglots of sound, mood, gesture. Doris Lessing reads grey cat loud and clear, because "her food habits are an eloquent language" (47), and "the tip of cat's tail moved: not impatiently, but the visible expression of her thought: There's plenty of time" (143).

"What do you call a chip on a ponely?," my husband asks me. The answer is "chum." We call this our "Ghost" code: if one of us dies and returns as a ghost, the question and answer known only to the two of us will confirm each of our identities to the other. I'm not going to explain what the words in the question and response mean here, because publishing the secret code would defeat its private purpose! Suffice it to say that the terms all refer to our cat, Butters: these are "praise-names" (Lessing, 1967, 2002: 71) we've given his beloved parts as we rhapsodize, in "parentese" (Whang, 2022), his endlessly delightful body. There are the chip and the chum, but also his flippers, shark belly, tiger stripes, fat tail, and ringtail (he just has the one tail, but sometimes its names are different), dust ruffle, bat ears, bunny feet, crest, and so on. This list goes on, as long as our other list of his nicknames, which is a list that sixteen years into his life

Myths of Domestic Posthuman Artifacts

still keeps getting longer. My husband, a 200-pound straight cis man who calls himself "Butters' mommy" cackles with delight each time a new one occurs to one of us, using it again and again until it's a part of everyone's lexicon for good. Every new named part or nickname has an origin story. Butters' story is also our story: a thousand intimate moments, the excuse to rehearse them and call their feelings forward, the glue in our household's "(big), queer family" made up of trans(species)-kin (Haraway, 2003: 144).

The thing about pets is that they effortlessly and intuitively upend everything we ostensibly believe about the role played by language, intelligence, and consciousness in living the good life and having quality relationships.[1] What does it mean to be someone, know someone, without ever having a conversation with them? Unlike dogs, who at least pretend to understand, actually do learn some words in the form of commands and cues, and try to show some interest, cats don't do this, or feign it for our benefit, or otherwise try to please us. What does it mean to live intimately with but not need to please another person? Cats are doing something with us but it's not clear what. Adam Phillips (1996) asks, of humans, what could you do with a person besides get to know them? Cats, it would seem, know the answer.

Derrida, Deleuze and Guattari, and Cary Wolfe all advocate for the recapturing of the animal components of human being as a passageway (back) to posthumanity. For them, "becoming animal" means stepping outside of language and culture and becoming "pure affect animals," a circulation of impersonal feelings, disruption of signifying projects, abandonment of subjectivity, and unleashing of nonhuman sexuality (Willett, 2014). Donna Haraway observes the rejection in these authors of sentimental relationships between humans and their pets at home, their preference for the intensive energy of animal packs over individual creatures, their neglect of "tender pleasures," and the "playful, prosocial affects circulating among individuals and groups" (2003: 95) of humans and animals. "Becoming animal" in Derrida in particular and philosophy in general usually means becoming a wild pack animal. These philosophers: they are all "dog people." But "a hearth and a cat go together" (Lessing, 1967, 2002: 128), and while cats do not form packs or possess the coursing energy of synchronized packs they do gravitate toward units formed out of tenderness and charm: being petted, sleeping on laps, grooming and be groomed by you, and arranging themselves into compact cat-loaf shapes (the animal version of draping) against windows, carpets, and upholstery to show the gleaming colors of their fur and eyes. They will pile one on top of the other if you keep more than one; indeed, they will all pile on top of you if you lie down and stay still for them. Domestic animals' gentle arts of charm countervail wild animals' brutal ethics of survival with "the free giving of a grace, the spending of something given by nature in her role of spendthrift . . . something extra, superfluous, unnecessary, essentially a power thrown away" (Lessing, 1996, 2002: 116).

Cats, folding themselves into themselves like breathing origami, rub and wind around that spot where animals cross over into ornaments and are "animated, rather than eviscerated, by aesthetic congealment" (Cheng, 2018: 115). They are decoration, not as cruelty as the modernists constructed it (Kunin, 2010), but as the feminine embodiment of attention and care.

Anthropomorphism is the scourge of the philosophy of human-animal relations. Philosophers like to claim the otherness of animals and are excited by their wild, unknowable differences. But as Mary Midgely points out, "ruling that . . . all non-human life . . . must be so unlike us that none of it can be understood from a human standpoint at all" is "an arbitrary, groundless dogma" and "in the case of animals, evolution makes it most implausible" (128). Midgely refers to Darwin's assertions in *The Descent of Man* that humans and animals are not divided by differences of kind but rather by gradations and quantities of attributes like language, thought, aesthetics, spirituality, culture, and empathy. She further counters the idea that human language is invented only to be about humans, "to describe them and them alone" (1998: 124). Sri Lankan elephant trainers (*mahouts*) treat their elephants like human colleagues "whose moods must be understood and handled" (1998: 115). This approach is "an expensive and time-consuming way of getting work out of elephants" but one to which no more efficient alternative has yet been presented. And though *mahouts* may make many anthropomorphic errors about their elephant colleagues, if they do so "about (their) basic everyday feelings—about whether their elephant is pleased, annoyed, frightened, excited, tired, sore, suspicious or angry—they would not only be out of business, they would often simply be dead" (1998: 115). To make a mistake about a cat's feelings has different consequences. You might not end up dead if you make a mistake about the meaning of your cat's flick of the tail, food-ritual, or petting rites. But you might end up dead to him—a feeling that is surprisingly hurtful on the spectrum of interspecies wounds, and no less likely to end in desperately uttered and gestured prayers to be resuscitated by him.

#catsofinstagram trains us humans to get better at cats' language, and so be better practitioners of the interspecies care from which cats benefit. It features humans' recorded and shared observations of cats, usually in hyperfocused close-up and behaving in ways that approximate and mimic aspects of our own nature and behavior. By being cute, and like us, cats have moved online. They can take over our technology as a route to better taking over us, using humans' attraction to their familiar-strange behaviors to co-opt digital spaces in which we can look at them more closely, learn to identify with them more closely, and so take care of them more deftly. #catsofinstagram is cats' way of infecting humans with another life-extending virus in addition to toxoplasmosis, the risk-taking virus that people catch from cats to make them more likely to die in ways that will allow them to be eaten by cats. Cats are good at using viruses this way. In #catsofinstagram they help more than themselves. This virtual but cute, fluffy, introspective, social posthuman "artifact" is a live, nonhuman part of an environment that begs to be better cared for—a gateway drug to an environmentalism that extends principles of hospitality and care to nonhuman entities. Humans invented #catsofinstagram (right?) to help cats train us to "do unto (non-human) others as we would have done to us," because we are better able to see them as us even as (and perhaps because) their mimicries can't quite approximate us (remember the uncanny valley that we prefer our tech not to possess). As Doris Lessing puts it: "No, of course cats are not humans, humans are not cats; but all the same" (1967, 2002: 93).

Shit

I didn't know whether to call this section "shit," "gold," or "fashion," because the myths make that big a difference. We can start with the shit version of the story. Shit is not an artifact but a myth told by certain toilet designs and that does *not* lend itself to the creation of a domestic posthuman artifact. Shit is a waste myth, a condition upheld by aversion affects like shame and disgust that ensure we don't want to get anywhere near it once we've eliminated it. Etymologically, the verb form "shit" was devoid of vulgar connotation until around 1600 and simply meant to cut, split, or separate, all still useful connotations given humans' need (in order to survive) to separate shit not only from our bodies but, once expelled, from our food and water. In the West, shit is not just dirty but obscene; it's one of George Carlin's "seven dirty words that you can never say on television" (though I've said it at a few academic conferences and it's gone alright). Shit has to be hidden as quickly as possible and forgotten, separated not only literally from our bodies and nutrition but also from our consciousness, our concept of civilization, and even our understanding of humanity. To be unable to separate oneself from one's shit is considered dehumanizing; helping someone in this position is one of the primary ministries of caregiving, which makes shit a powerful second-person-maker.

Managing shit requires plenty of technology, however. Shit requires toilets, which require plumbing, which require sewers, which require sewage treatment plants and wastewater disposal methods, and which require chemical and mechanical drinking water treatments. And if any of this goes even a little bit wrong, the whole apparatus requires lots and lots of medicine. From one perspective, humans' development of massively scaled sanitation technologies is an undisputed triumph and, in its preventative health capabilities alone, a window to a global new humanity characterized by freedom from waterborne diseases, which are shit-borne diseases and the world's leading cause of death and disease (3.4 million annually according to a World Health Organization study in Berman, 2009). From another perspective, however, this technology and the myth that powers it poses a planetary danger. The danger is that the earth's soil needs fertilizer. Soil depletion and even extinction, which is a condition in which the organic matter in soil is stripped by farming and ultimately turns into sand, have been declared an imminent risk within the next sixty years by the UN's Food and Agricultural Organization ("Soil Erosion Must Be Stopped 'to Save Our Future,' Says UN Agriculture Agency" 2019). Soil is replenished by nutrients like potassium, nitrogen, and phosphorus. In a myth where humans produce fertilizer as a by-product of the natural processes of consumption and digestion and use toilets designed to connect stomachs to the earth, soil thrives and yields more nutrition. In a myth where we produce waste as a by-product of these same natural processes and use toilets designed to sever stomachs from the earth, soil becomes barren and constricts our nutrition. Our food stays disease-free but our soil becomes nutrient-low—and our water, designated to hold and hide waste in Western sanitation systems, is polluted. If shit is made out of a powerful myth that turns fertilizer into trash, we're shitting ourselves to extinction by doing a thing we cannot stop. Is there another story?

"Shit" is not natural, it's a myth. Teaching and learning about shit is a key care ritual in having and raising children. "Potty training," as some of those who use toilets call one component of shit acculturation and enmythment, is a mechanical process through which children learn to use the technology of the toilet, in part because they learn the myth that feces are not only dirty and uncomfortable but emotionally shameful to be near, sit in, sleep in, or need help separating oneself from. Western psychology equates the process of building this imaginary with its fundamental psychological structures; the birth of shit as shit is also the birth of self-imposed civilization through the super-ego. Shit shifts from being a part of us (to wit children who cry to flush their feces down a toilet) to the worst of us (to wit children who strip themselves naked to shit in order to keep their clothes from being contaminated while they use a toilet). But in order for it to do so we must become aware of shit as something separate from us. We learn the difference between it and us, accrued through rituals and stories, and eventually experienced viscerally, spontaneously. We learn this lesson thoroughly, usually by the time we're four or five years old. But since we have to learn it, there are other ways to see it.

Modern campaigns in Indian provinces like Odisha to eliminate the practice of open defecation, promote sanitation, and encourage peasants and the poor to use toilets succeed or fail on the basis of learning and spreading the shit myth (George, 2008). It may sound surprising to Western sensibilities to suggest that shit isn't shit without cultural help. But the story of Odisha's residents' resistance to toilets—and the province's ultimate attainment of open defecation free (ODF) designation in 2019—helps explain the concept. People there have had latrines built for them by government programs that subsidize or provide sanitation systems since the 1960s, so they are, at least in theory, plentiful and available.

Myths of Domestic Posthuman Artifacts

145

But many rural people in Odisha didn't care. "(They) had been defecating out of doors forever," and "didn't necessarily think there was anything wrong with it" (George, 2008). In fact, open defecation was believed by loyal twenty-first-century practitioners to be a better way than toilets of keeping elimination separate from people. Technically, they were right. Walking out to a distant field, far away from your family and neighbors, to shit in the bushes and leave it there is more geographically separate than walking into a room separated by a wall or blanket inside your home and leaving your shit in a tank. In the West, we accept this geographical proximity because it facilitates another distance, which is the important one between our shit and our feet, food, flies, water, and psyches. But it doesn't take too much of a leap of imagination to see why someone theorizing from a different lived experience would consider open defecation in the fresh air and solitude of nature to be cleaner, more private, and less intrusive than doing so in an indoor place inside their home or near it. And if the government-subsidized outhouse you've been given looks like a goat pen, grain storehouse, or kitchen—spaces that benefit from being near people—you might be forgiven for determining that you'd rather keep your goat, grain, or cooking supplies in it than shit in it. It just happens that the cleaner-seeming thing in that circumstance isn't more sanitary or more healthy when other nonhuman residents come into consideration: the bacterial and viral kind. When water sources and farmlands are nearby and children might find their way to that field to play, the cleaner-seeming option can be deadly. As we've been arguing all along, nonhuman residents of the bacterial and viral variety are, like those of the aforementioned feline variety, important considerations in home design.

In Odisha, a village development organization called Gram Vikas persuaded rural people convinced of the greater cleanliness and convenience of open defecation not only to use state-provided toilets but to want them enough to pay for even better ones themselves. They did this not through feats of engineering but by spreading the shit myth using representatives traveling to villages to meet with villagers. These representatives spread their myth in subtle ways by asking villagers to do myth-activating things like calculate the approximate quantity of feces openly defecated by the entirety of the village in units of truckloads; spend time lingering in the most popular shitting fields to require villagers to experience the sight and smell of shit in them; point out the proximity of farming, water, and playing children to these favored shitting spots; place fecal samples gathered from open defecation near food during meetings so that villagers could see flies moving back and forth between them; ask how much fecal matter villagers thought they might be inadvertently ingesting. The project was designed to trigger disgust and then shame by introducing villagers to the concept of shit, which is a fecal matter that has been powerfully negatively enmythed and made viscerally negatively numinous. Individuals who learned this myth went from being neutral about or opposed to indoor sanitation systems to radiant proponents of them, not only in their own homes but vocally in concourse with their neighbors. Gram Vikas' plan—at which they ultimately succeeded in Odisha—was to use the shit myth to help one province at a time become 100 percent ODF. It worked. While plentiful free toilets had never gone far, the shit myth transformed them into extraordinary domestic posthuman technologies, the impact of which is still in the nascent stages of global unfolding.

These toilets are nothing, however, compared to a differently enmythed, positively numinous elimination known in China not as shit but, in some circles, gold ("The Gold Standard" 2018). In this myth, toilets are differently designed tools from those used in India and the West; their particular design as artifacts as well as their unique design infrastructure facilitates the operationalization of shit as gold (and an extraordinary domestic posthuman artifact). Contemporary Chinese toilets have revitalized 4,000-year-old Chinese public sanitation methods that included ways not only to store human feces but also to collect it, sanitize its bacterial load, and redistribute it to nourish farm soil. The method was during centuries of successful practice in China called *fenbian*, a Mandarin word which translates: "urine and feces" (Barnes, 2023). English euphemism knows *fenbian* as night soil, which is urine and feces collected by porters from the pails and privies of towns and cities, transformed by composting into fertilizer, and sold to farmers to treat their crops. The night soil trade is a nomenclature embedded in a myth that so thoroughly transformed a plentiful waste product into market capital that the 1930s urban center for this trade, Shanghai, was dubbed "the Golden Wharf," for being the place where night soil was loaded onto barges and distributed to the provinces. The millennia-old capacity to see feces' downstream economic and utilitarian value has made China a fecal-filiac culture (George, 2008) and serves as a sharp contrasting example to the difference made by fecalphobic attitudes in both the West and India, where excrement might be dealt with in a sanitary manner but is not yielding large-scale economic growth or alleviating poverty.[2] These days in China the revitalized night soil trade is more likely to be referred to as a biogas boom. But biogas, like night soil, is shit by another name and story, and a case in which a rose by any other name is not a rose but something completely different.

Biogas is both an energy and fertilizer source, produced through the fermentation of organic materials like wood, vegetables, and excreta. The organic matter is collected in an oxygen-free "digester," in which microorganisms break down the material during a four-week-long process that kills pathogens and produces sugar, acids, and slurry. The sugar and acids become methane gas that can be used as fuel for cooking, lights, showers, and electricity; the slurry makes excellent, and sanitary, fertilizer. The benefits of the conversion in rural households are manifold. Farms that use biogas directly benefit from the availability of free fuel and fertilizers as well as reductions in smell, flies, chemicals (found in fertilizer and insecticides), and deforestation (for firewood and new farmlands due to soil erosion in existing farmlands). Indirectly, these households experience net financial gains because they don't have to pay for fuel, fertilizer, insecticides, and medicine to cure illnesses caused by waterborne diseases resulting from inadequate sanitation.

The Shaanxi Mothers Environmental Protection Volunteer Association, a subsidiary of the Chinese Women's Federation in Xi'an that works directly with provincial farming villages, has discovered a further indirect benefit of biogas. Dedicated to studying and alleviating the direct relationship between environmental crises and the poverty of women, the Shaanxi Mothers observed that women in their target villages were participating in deforestation and soil erosion tactics that perpetuated their poverty in addition to accelerating environmental crises. Clearing forests to make room for new fields after the old ones had been depleted and as a source of cooking and lamp fuel, women were also trapped in a time-consumption cycle that left no bandwidth for other activities that could alleviate their economic hardship. And though government-installed digesters were already available, many of the families who had them either failed to see the point of them or outright refused to use them. The Shaanxi Mothers thus embarked on an enmything campaign that helped women see not simply the direct aesthetic, health, and economic benefits of adopting biogas in their homes but also an indirect benefit: free time. Using biogas alleviated the burden of firewood collection, and cooking on biogas stoves shortened the cooking time of rice for the family from several hours to a few minutes. Spreading slurry on fields saved the soil but also saved women from using the time during which they weren't farming and caring for the family to clear new land. And here is where the Shaanxi Mothers stepped in again, this time not with biogas digesters, latrine buildings, and mythical scaffolding but with looms.

The Dong ethnic women in the village of Da Li are the makers of glossy indigo, a type of blue nankeen, China's indigenous textile that is woven, dyed, treated, and printed according to manifold techniques and patterns that vary by province around the country. Glossy indigo is a deep blue, almost purple, fabric that is handwoven from locally grown cotton on narrow wooden looms, dyed over a period of weeks in vats of locally farmed indigo leaves that are kept fermenting by the female inhabitants of every home, dried on hanging clotheslines in the sun, and then both beaten with sticks and treated with egg whites, ox blood, and other remedies until it reaches the desired depth of color, high glossy sheen, and stiff texture for which the fabric is known. The process can take as long as two years to complete and is synchronized with certain seasonal conditions to make sure that the dye takes or the gloss is right. Traditionally, women have used the laboriously created glossy indigo textiles to create ceremonial and everyday clothing, bedding, and other linens only for themselves and their immediate families; the intensive labor and time needed to make a single bolt of fabric has prohibited their making more than the minimum. In recent decades the craft, along with many heirloom practices in China, was in danger of disappearing entirely, in part because younger women throughout the provinces were moving away to work in factories and live in cities as their and their families' only means of economic mobility. This condition was, if not entirely created by soil extinction, dramatically exacerbated by it. Da Li is a tiered farming community built into the mountains in layers; as its soil was depleted by millennia of farming combined with the disappearance of *fenbian* in China beginning in the 1960s, villagers had to clear land farther and farther from their homes, spend more and more of their income on imported synthetic fertilizers, and travel greater distances to collect firewood as trees were cleared to farm. Much of this burden fell upon women, who in addition to participating in an ever-more-difficult agrarian lifestyle had to cook for themselves and their families without, or with minimal, electricity.

The installation of biogas digester toilets by the Shaanxi Mothers changed much of this. In the years since their intervention, rural farming communities like that in Da Li have revitalized local ancient textile weaving practices, and so generated what amounts in modernity to a women-centric artisanal economy in rare, 100 percent natural, zero-waste indigo glossy cloth textiles that gleam when presented at different angles to the light. Through a collaboration since 2016 between Da Li women, ATLAS Studio, and the Global Heritage Fund, a new cultural institution has been forged in and beyond Da Li that allows women to derive independent fiscal profit and mobility and enter the global economy using ancient modes of textile making. These modes of textile production model not only a means of fostering this specific textile but also one form of circular economy tethered to a new kind of night soil trade, the ancient value of *fenbian* in China, and what Arturo Escobar has called a future with a future for the fashion industry. And by turning shit not only into gold (which is easy) but style (which is nothing short of magical), the women of Da Li unveil the posthuman potentiality of differently enmythed excreta to create a soft, slow, beautiful future world.

Television

I'm not ashamed to admit that I learn from my TV. I'm not a child watching *The Electric Company* or even a teenager watching *Hallmark* and *National Geographic* specials after school. I'm a grown-up, watching Prime Time, ShowTime, HBO, Amazon, Hulu, Apple, Netflix, YouTube, Facebook Watch, and IGTV. And I'm not talking about learning facts—the lives of marmots; the history of the Civil War; the impact of the opioid epidemic; or how to count, read, and spell. I'm talking about learning how to be human in the era and place I've been given to do it in, especially since being a human is a thing that seems to keep changing in a world that less and less resembles the one the people who used to teach me things know how to use and thrive in. I'm talking about expanding not only my mind but my emotional landscape and depth. I'm talking about learning in a way that means growing and growing up, a thing it turns out an adult human can continue to do, especially with the help of TV.

Things I've learned recently from TV, a "transmodern teacher" (Hartley, 1999) that works across social and geographical boundaries to help humans assimilate emerging aspects of our worlds:

- What gender nonconforming is, how to say they/them instead of he or her, and why that matters ("Transparent," "Billions")

- How women can take on one another's shame and turn it into solidarity and ultimately pride ("Sex Education")

- That I need to question my desire to keep my work selves and my home selves safely separate ("Severance")

- What a land acknowledgment means and why it matters ("Yellowstone")

- How to integrate smartphones, tablets, and laptops into regular family life, not to escape from the people in it but to connect with them ("Modern Family")

- How people with bipolar disorder ("Homeland") and autism ("The Bridge") as well as a paraplegic and a little person ("Game of Thrones") bring their bodies uniquely to bear on solving hard problems

- What fat activism is, and kindness toward my own body ("Shrill")

- How to live with grief ("Fleabag," "The Leftovers")

- New ways to think about the hard parts of marriage ("Couples Therapy")

- Appreciation (and sometimes preference) for poor and working class cultural paradigms that thrive in the South Side of Chicago ("Shameless")

- About the insidiousness of patriarchy in conditions where it appears to have receded ("A Handmaid's Tale")

- About people, stories, and experiences from a vividly expressed point of view that isn't primarily White ("Insecure," "Empire," "The Chi," "The Wire," "Dear White People," "Black-ish," "Atlantic," "Reservation Dogs")

If this list sounds like a list of liberal social causes that's because it is one—because we are surrounded by and living through cultural transformations daily causing breaks with social traditions, and which modern humans often struggle to process and adapt to. The difference is that on television lessons in social change aren't a list of causes, rules of behavior, or metaphysical truths, they're a story. Television is drawn to social conflict because conflicts make good stories (McKee, 1997; Miller, 2017). Each TV story delves into conflict in a way that activates not only the mind but the heart and body of their audience. Knowing about patriarchy is one thing, but witnessing June's transformation, in "A Handmaid's Tale," into a loaner womb by a combination of legislation and social custom brings the concept to life in ways that come alive again while we're reading the news. This knowledge gets under the skin, stored in muscles, ready to recover when triggered by life. Mirror neurons ensure that humans are changed, and so our individual and collective futures are changed, by stories. They make us ready for experiences that we haven't had yet; allow us to profit from the real and imagined experiences of others; and ensure that when they do happen if they do happen our reactions will already have some physiological, cognitive, emotional, and cultural scaffolding (Gottschall, 2012). On television, counter-normative social practices aren't treated as radical, divergent, or disruptive but are knitted into existing concepts and structures by a preservative method akin to the visible mending, through techniques like darning and *sashiko*, of weathered fabrics by incorporating new ones in ways that strengthen and preserve the existing basic structure.

Though TV studies has taken on the mass media and individual storytelling component of specific television shows, television's banishment as a lowly domestic technology has caused its particular technicity to be ignored by critical posthumanism's accounts of emerging technologies with the power to change the very meaning of the human. Yet television is a machine for recounting stories that began to be implanted in our homes not quite a hundred years ago and that has managed to survive the digital revolution through transformation into a series of entertainment and social media apps. While it began as a storytelling box in the living room, it quickly moved into the bedroom, kitchen, and its own specially designated "TV Room." And then it started to climb onto us: desktops, then laptops, then onto smartphones and so into the palms of our hands, and then out of the home. TVs now roam wild in urban and suburban waiting rooms, offices, schools, trains, buses, parks, gas station pumps, and automobiles. The so-called "idiot box" has proved to be brilliantly adaptive, and following the law of the survival of the technological fittest it has outdone music, books, and film in its wily capacity to adjust to—nay, even absorb all other aspects of—digital and media culture. TV's negative enmythment as a low art form and destroyer of families and intelligence (Postman, 1985) hasn't stopped it from taking over and then transforming itself into high art. Emily Nussbaum's Pulitzer Prize (2016), the first to a TV critic, bore witness to the transfiguration of trash into treasure. The novel followed a similar trajectory but took longer (Watt, 1957).

Not that television's power lies in its ascent. On the contrary, John Hartley argues that television's power lies in its lowliness: if it "has a distinctive feature, it is that it is a 'dirty' category" (Hartley, 1992: 22). Dirty because it's not one media form, not one genre, not for one audience, not tethered to one place;

it's also disparaged and adulated, solitary and communal, public and private, enriching and trash, exciting and boring, terrible and transcendent. Like any good posthuman artifact, television is ontologically promiscuous.[3] It has that in common with life: "television . . . does nothing less than recreate the world of nature" (Hartley, 1992: 4). Not, as Hartley would have it, however, for our cynical "astonishment" and "(judgment)" (Hartley, 1992: 4), which assumes that the world of nature is inane. Television is a dirty pedagogue, to be sure—but also a caring one, in which its representations can be configured as a kind of love.[4]

How can teaching be dirty and promiscuous? Isn't teaching about transmitting good morals and values and cultivating better ways of thinking and doing things? Western myths about teaching are often relentlessly and rigidly wholesome. But as Maggie Nelson (2022) points out about certain constructions of care, which "can slip quickly into paternalism or control when it isn't experienced as care by its receiver (think of the last time someone did something you didn't want or like 'because they care about you')" (2022: 21), these demand our scrutiny. Is there a form of care that isn't synonymous with "politics, therapeutics, or direct service"? A form that disperses power and allows for differences of sensibility, experience, and desire between the caregiver and the cared for? Television's mode of transmodern teaching may offer it. Television's kind of caring is to take life in its wild array and, not so much tame it by shaping it in a particular way, as "churn" it "as your digestive system churns food" (Sillman, 2015: 22). This churning, "so earnest, so caring—with a smock, and our tongue between our teeth, paintbrush poised, trying so hard" (Sillman, 2015: 22) even when what's churned is "offensive or nasty" (Sillman, 2015: 47), is about calling the bits of lived experience most riddled with conflict and confusion out as the most worthy and gratifying to churn.

Allison Gopnik (2016), writing about parenting, similarly praises the concept of inviting "mess" (26) into the process and advocates for a version of care that is not about "working to achieve a particular outcome" or "a particular kind of person" (4). Her vision of a dirty parent, analogous to Hartley's dirty teacher, is startlingly eponymized as a grandmother, or more specifically, a *bubbe*. Grandmothers, Gopnik writes, have a "kind of distance" from parenting, one sufficient to permit exploration, and the *bubbe* of Gopnik's imagination is a grandmother-philosopher-scientist at Berkeley, "who runs a cognitive science laboratory and writes philosophy papers in between telling stories of the olden days and making blueberry pancakes" (8). Combining these perspectives forges a route, she claims, to understanding parenting in a way that takes us beyond parenting. Such, one might argue, is the role of the television, a dirty teacher and promiscuous (grand)parent intent on providing a form of care that doesn't yield particular kinds of people but churns growth and ongoing growing up, even in grown-ups.

Figure 8 Handwarmer, *Eliza's Peculiar Cabinet of Curiosities*, Folayemi Wilson.

The mechanical handwarmers of the past are beautiful functional objects that have fallen out of use and been forgotten, like all those serving pieces on "The Antique Road Show" that resurface looking not just alien but completely incomprehensible. We need a guide to tell us: this is an electric handwarmer! The distance between the uncanny and the everyday is not so far (though it may be long). Eliza's handwarmer: riddle solved. Eliza's hands: not just caring but cared for, kept warm, every part of her safe, touching and not working, picking up these objects as she roams about the world she is making.

Table

Some of my most vivid childhood memories are of being around the kitchen table, perhaps because so many family photos are from around the table. A pine, farmhouse drop leaf table that was long and thin, able to accommodate seven family members, and the occasional friends or relatives, in a small, tract home kitchen. Decades before Covid, it was protean—the site of regular family meals, but also the spot where we did our homework, laid out sewing patterns, played table games, completed jigsaw puzzles. It was also a regular site of squabbles and tension over haircuts, nail polish, bad behavior, and family jealousies. Already in 1825, Jean Anthelme Brillat-Savarin's masterpiece on food and gastronomy, *The Physiology of Taste: Meditations on Transcendental Gastronomy*, recognized the complex pleasures of the table: "There are often found collected around the same table, all the modifications of society which extreme sociability has introduced among us: love, friendship, business, speculation, power, ambition, and intrigue, all enhance conviviality. Thus it is that it produces fruits of all imaginable flavors." The kitchen table may be mundane, everyday, domestic, little noticed in posthumanism, and yet the site of fairly significant identity work in its own protean, promiscuous, posthuman way.

Furniture featured heavily in Mihalyi Csikszentmihalyi and Eugene Rochberg-Halton's survey of people's attitudes toward material objects. In their *The Meaning of Things: Domestic Symbols and the Self*, furniture was the most commonly cited cherished object in the home, important for its role in memories, associations, experiences, kin, and the self. Women especially commented on the importance of furniture in maintaining a network of social ties. Csikszentmihalyi and Rochberg-Halton report that when grandparents mentioned furniture, it was special as a sign of past events, of ties to family, and to other people (1981: 60–1). In "A Room of One's Own: Old Age, Extended Care, and Privacy," Iris Marion Young reflects on how ordinary acts of dwelling uncover "a material meaning of home as a necessary support for and enactment of personal identity" (2005: 155). She observes that her elderly father's easy chair, his chipped coffee mug, and his side table all play a material role in preserving and maintaining his identity. Hannah Arendt notes, "The things of the world have the function of stabilizing human life, and their objectivity lies in the fact that . . . men, their ever-changing nature notwithstanding, can retrieve their sameness, that is, their identity, by being related to the same chair and the same table" (Arendt, 1958: 137). While kitchen tables may be mundane, domestic artifacts, their stability and permanence, the sedimented meanings that come from dwelling with them for many years, sometimes for generations, enmyth them with a significance in the family's practices of relationality, second personhood, and forms of care.

As a material object, the kitchen table plays a role in fostering a particular dynamic: you are seated together, not separately on stools or on couches while watching television, you are facing one another, you have to sit down. Tables are often situated in a space, the kitchen or a dining room—now making a comeback in a post-Covid world—that separates itself from the rest of the home and helps to foster a sense of a shared project that is taking place around the table. And not that we should wax overly nostalgic or see through rose-tinted glasses. Kitchen tables may be the site of conflict as well as conviviality, where the family gathers to glare at each other, possibly hash out their differences. Our families are often the most inconvenient other people we ever meet (Berlant, 2022). Maybe the table is a patriarchal site where the father sits at the head and commands. In the table, form, function, and materiality are intimately connected. Importantly, the function is transparent as well: by virtue of our very bodies, we understand the nature of sitting and the arrangement of chairs around a table invites us to sit, and to sit together. How tables function is transparent, understandable, accessible—especially to the human form. Where our electronic devices are increasingly mysterious and hidden from us in terms of their innards, the kitchen table is transparent, solid. It persists. The table has no interiority hidden from view. It is fully and transparently on display, ready to be used. It invites engagement—focal engagement in Albert Borgmann's (1987) sense, sensorial engagement beyond the merely visual. Some people even set places for their pets at the dining table. In a 2021 survey of pet owners, nearly half of those polled (49 percent) let their pets sit at (or under) the dinner table so they can share meals with them, willing to overlook their pets' "dirty" ways so as to enjoy the pleasure of their company at meal time (Melore, 2021).

The protean kitchen table's power to mediate domesticity, relationality, and second personhood is on full display in Carrie Ann Weems' *The Kitchen Table Series, 1990* ("Carrie Mae Weems: *The Kitchen Table Series*," 1990), a groundbreaking and influential series of photographs in which the kitchen table takes center stage. In the series of twenty black and white photographs, the camera sits at one end of a table, as life unfolds at the opposite end. Sitting at or around the table, Weems, playing a character in a human drama, joins a shifting cast of other players, including possibly a boyfriend or lover, a daughter with whom she struggles, a group of friends with whom she commiserates, and finally, a single woman, staring defiantly at the camera, engaging with a pet bird, pleasuring herself, playing solitaire. All the while, the kitchen table persists in its solidity and permanence, rooting Weems' identity work in the tradition of Black women sitting around the table and sharing in acts of cultural production. As we noted in Chapter One, "Kitchen Table: Women of Color Press," founded by Barbara Smith and Audre Lorde, took its name, as Smith notes, as a nod to the historic and social roots of the kitchen as a central space—particularly for women.

> We chose our name because the kitchen is the center of the home, the place where women in particular work and communicate with each other. We also

wanted to convey the fact that we are a kitchen table, grassroots operation, begun and kept alive by women who cannot rely on inheritances or other benefits of class privilege to do the work we need to do (1).

Smith's recollections and preservative efforts publishing the work of women of color recall Katherine Hayles' own preservative efforts, discussed in Chapter One, while sitting at a kitchen table and reflecting on the work of Janet Freed to preserve the records of the Macy Conferences on cybernetics (Hayles, 1999: 80–3). The kitchen table serves as a site of both roots and resistance.

That pine, farmhouse table? My sister still has it. It's been refinished multiple times now and sits in her dining room, just off the kitchen.

Notes

1 Though designers who write about decentering the human (Wakkary, 2021: 26–8) include both furniture and pets in the category "nonhuman," we think it is important to distinguish between types of nonhumans that are objects and those that are animals. The category of nonhuman in discussions of both design and posthumanism is too mongrelized a concept to be quite right. Don't we have some reason to expect that how we relate to pets is qualitatively different from how we relate to things and designed objects? Lessing's endowment of animals with language illustrates one important difference, and the fact that we are more likely to talk to, name, and accommodate the distinctive character traits of a cat than a sari suggests that humans have an intuitive understanding of the distinction.

2 According to Nicole Barnes' (2023) account of the nightsoil trade in twentieth-century wartime China, the Chinese have been no less subjected than India to colonial sanitation encroachments, a process Ruth Rogaski (2004) has called "hygenic modernity" to express the centrality of hygiene and public health reform in China's encounter with imperialism and national formation. The night soil trade in China remained sufficiently associated with lucre in the mid-twentieth century to become a deeply contested site of colonial and then state power among the competing Nationalist and Communist parties, and Barnes even argues that the Communists' better manipulation of night soil power centers contributed significantly to their ascent. Ultimately, however, hygienic modernity led Chinese elites to manipulate national toilet habits in their aspiration toward recognition as a modern, sovereign state amid competing empires. As in India, "a concatenation of forces" pushed Chinese cities "away from night soil in the late 1970s and early 1980s." Vacuum-pump sanitation trucks, chemical fertilizers, and the household-responsibility system all converged to "sever the metabolic symbiosis between city and countryside. This triggered the ecological problems that still plague China, and the world, today [as] modern sanitation and flush toilets have saved us from many threats to our health but have introduced a new one" (2022: 27).

3 While the network era of the 1960s is often held up as the definitive model of television, media scholar William Uricchio argues that from the beginning television, as a concept and a technology, has enjoyed a remarkable conceptual flexibility and

intermedia character as it is positioned differently among related media, conceptual frames, and national developments. Television's "new media" convergence with the internet, streaming services, cell phones, and tablets, Uricchio argues, is simply a reflection of its historical flexibility (Uricchio, 2010).

4 Many people use television to combat loneliness, and studies suggest that at least on some levels, it works—and especially well for those who are experiencing financial hardships or are mentally or physically unwell ("Everyday Technology Fighting Loneliness" 2019).

Figure 9 C-3PO, *Eliza's Peculiar Cabinet of Curiosities*, Folayemi Wilson.

In her reflections on homemaking, Iris Marion Young notes that the things we surround ourselves with in our home have a sedimented history which tell the story of our lives (2005: 158). But some of those objects may look to the future as well and tell stories of things we imagine to come. C-3PO seems incongruous displayed in a nineteenth-century slave cabin, and yet one might imagine Eliza reaching out to future visions of posthumans, wondering about their humanity and what she might share with this technological marvel, what its place in the world was, and what her place might be in a world yet to come.

Conclusion

A Design Sampler for the Domestic Posthuman

There is a lesson to be learned in the gloves Helen Keller could have worn and those she chose to wear instead. Keller was the deaf and blind modernist writer, activist, and cultural icon who also partnered with MIT's Research Laboratory of Electronics and Norbert Weiner, the so-called father of cybernetics, in the design and testing of a cybernetic glove made to channel the sound of human voices into the wearer's hands and fingers. The hearing glove came of age in 1950 and was, in Weiner's words, "the first constructive application of cybernetics to human beings" (Mills, 2011; Nasser, 2014). Weiner's work was the cybernetic culmination of efforts dating back to the 1880s when Alexander Graham Bell made a "talking glove" for his deaf nephew and inaugurated a set of trials, sponsored by AT&T in the 1920s, to apply vibrotactile research to the construction of specialized hearing-apparel for the deaf. The glove functioned by capturing the vibrations of human voices within points on the gloves that were wired to the fingertips of the wearer. They were heralded as possessing the capacity to transform the lives of deaf people.

They didn't work. Keller's fingers couldn't decipher words from the vibrations—though she could "hear" the laughter of lab technicians in them every time she made a hilarious mistake. The project was retired within the year and, after three-quarters of a century's work, abandoned; though contemporary gloves do exist and can convert sign language into speech, they are designed to be used by the hearing. What Keller herself preferred, as a child, was the variation on Bell's nephew's gloves that she called "beautiful gloves to talk with" (Mills, 2011: 99): gloves operated by human touch as interlocutors pressed points on one another's hands. What Keller preferred as she matured was simply her naked "listening fingers" (Nasser, 2014), pressed as a receiver to a speaker's throat to capture not so much words as meaning-drenched sounds: the "soft slow speech" of Mark Twain reading his own prose, or "the humming" that "never stopped" made by news in a telephone wire.

Latif Nasser (2014) has attributed the gloves' failure to "the insurmountable hurdle" of "our own skin" encountering a limit in its own nature that would not yield, "despite cutting-edge technology" and "the sustained attention of some of the brightest minds in living memory" (Nasser, 2014). The gloves worked, Nasser concludes, but Keller's skin didn't. One might counter, however, that Keller's skin was working perfectly and that her own preferred means of communicating had accommodated to skin's inbuilt ways of receiving in a way the cybernetic gloves did not. It is, after all, a bit strange to determine that the flaw in cybernetic technology lies in the user's body being insufficiently customizable to it (though it happens all the time in all kinds of contexts within and beyond cybernetics, as anyone who's been mad at their body when their jeans don't fit can attest). Besides, Keller already had one cutting-edge technology at her disposal if she wanted it: the white cotton gloves that connected her hands to the hands of another. Nasser's inability to see them as such echoes Western civilization's wider inability to see cutting-edge technologies that don't conform to our narrowly construed myths about what constitutes a cutting-edge technology as such. This failure, which is an infrastructure failure in prevailing stories of technomateriality and technogenesis—an error in the prevailing technological imagination—doesn't just skew our understanding of what constitutes the history and present of technological development. It undermines our ability to design functional and desirable long-term futures.[1]

The Four *Bubbes* of the Domestic Posthuman

The domestic posthuman is a corrective philosophical category, carving out space for thinking about the posthuman through the inborn alterity of life stages and second personhood instead of only through digital and biomedical mediation and as a future evolutionary progression. It suggests a range of alternative technologies to contemplate and build upon beyond the usual suspects in mechanical engineering, computational science, pharmaceutical science, and genetics. It proposes new metaphors, materialities, places, and persons to think of when we consider the topic of technological development and who—and where—is driving it. And it redirects our attention to kitchen-table scientists and engineers who go by other names and work from within and around the home, itself reconfigured as a messy and lived-in counterpoint to technogenesis birthed in the sterility of the lab. These alternative figures weave, drape, talk, touch, and cuddle their way into futures with strong tethers both to the "future of the future"

Conclusion

and to the past. The past does not function in this model as a locus of nostalgia but creative inspiration, one modeled on human ectogenesis which allows for the growth of forms embedded in myth and culture. In technological innovation conventions taught by the disruptive energies of the aesthetic avant-garde (Perloff, 1986) and currently enthralled by the expansive, explosive energies of globalization, the idea of creativity through continuity and care is out of pace with the way contemporary Western civilization has approached notions of invention in art, industry, and the lab (Mies and Shiva, 1993). But that does not mean that continuity and care are inherently backward or sterile. We must train ourselves to look in new places, to new people, and use new myths to reinvest in the advancement of discoveries that may have been around for some time now.

The domestic posthuman aims to be a category brimming with all the exhilaration occasioned by gazing upon developments never seen before that hitherto has been reserved for technological developments of a very narrow kind. The very word "posthuman" suggests a form of lively and alluring alterity; as its philosophical mother, Donna Haraway (1991) understood when she applied the term cyborg to a woman, it is among the kinds of terms that estrange and elevate whom it is applied to. But the domestic posthuman also aims to be a category that respects the place-conscious, embodied, everyday creativity embedded in tradition, the under-resourced potentiality of the hands and skin, and the limitations of the human species to accept innovations that run counter to nature's slow and careful discernments about what works. We humans can handle a lot, but not everything; we can grow and grow up but not quickly. We have an inborn capaciousness, but we are not limitless. We might do well to attend to elements of our interesting, under-considered nature before plunging headlong into changing it. With these notions in mind, against or alongside Braidotti's "four horsemen of the posthuman apocalypse," an image with which we began, we might posit four *bubbes*, Allison Gopnik's philosophical-scientific Jewish grandmothers who have lived a little and have a little distance. The four *bubbes* of the domestic posthuman co-preside over the as-yet under-investigated potentialities within neglected but extraordinary aspects of *homo faber*, construed not as man the tool-grasper but as a human caregiver. These *bubbes* are:

- second personhood (e.g., relationships with carers during marginalized human life stages, which encompass infancy, childhood, adolescence, and old age);
- care (e.g., preservative, growth-minded love and attention directed toward others and received from others);
- softwear (e.g., the operations of skin and touch vs. brain and vision); and
- myth (e.g., the numinosity of objects, accrued through the experiences and spoken and unspoken story-encounters of children with them).

Importantly, the four *bubbes* of the domestic posthuman counter the four horsemen of the posthuman apocalypse in their approaches to making and thinking about technology, but they do not reject technology outright. Instead, they propose an alternative assemblage through which technogenesis can take place. Whereas the four horsemen usher innovations within what Achille Mbembe (2019) characterizes as the necropolitical extraction assemblage of global capitalism, neoliberalism, the military industrial complex, and digital technologies and do so in a register of disruptive and often literally destructive change, the *bubbes* expand and shift human-technology networks to include an assemblage comprised of caregivers, skin, soft objects, myths, stories, homemaking, and home places. The latter assemblage, which is fertile and generative—*vita* and *anima* against Mbembe's logic of extractive necrotics—has received little attention in critical posthumanism and yet may be more fundamental to the making of a stable posthuman future that humans can live with. The four *bubbes* seek to bequeath the domestic posthuman the opportunity to dwell, in the sense of remaining in place for a time, in a futured-future built to last (and that someone might want to last, and live in, in the first place). The *bubbes* foster the design of domestic posthumans modeled on the scale, pace, texture, and places of the kind of future-making that we all regularly encounter in our lives. It's called growing up—in this case, not as an individual organism but a species.

The domestic posthuman is not only a philosophical category but also a lived experience. As a practice, the domestic posthuman is thus informed by Black and feminist accounts of lived experience as countering metaphysical categories and assumptions with practices grounded in the everyday, ordinary, and sometimes messy lives of persons and life stages marginalized by Western philosophy. The domestic posthuman thus descends from the philosophical echelons inhabited by figures like Bennett (2010), Braidotti (2013), Clarke (2004), Hayles (1999), Verbeek (2005), or Wolfe to call for a design practice. Put differently, and taken out of the high, public register of design and into the lower, more homecentric one of craft: the domestic posthuman asks us to reconsider making. Making what? Making love, homes, lives, clothing, stories, friends, furniture, families. Unlike typical posthuman design frameworks, designing the domestic posthuman calls not only to scientists and engineers in their labs or bureaucrats in public office but to everyday designers working their crafts in and around their homes, living their lives in ways that we would all do well to see as creatively essential to the well-lived future of everyone.

Multum in Parvo

In *Massive Change*, a 2004 Vancouver Art Gallery exhibition and book, the preeminent Canadian changemaker Bruce Mau and his graduate students proposed a scale for designers to work in. It was to be extra-large and address the production of "super" things, such as the "superhard" materials (2004: 143) and "superstrong" synthetic fibers (2004: 145) being made by teams of "supersmart" multidisciplinary scientists. Consequently, supersizable technologies like transportation, information, buildings, synthetic materials, and global economic and digital systems all supplanted the narrow and effete consideration set of designers past, which included comparatively little things like books, clothes, wallpaper, textiles, furniture, pottery, and toys. Mau's alternate design scale shifted the work of his discipline away from the creative microsystems of ornament and style that preoccupied the major design movements of the nineteenth and twentieth centuries and toward a technology-centric, publicly oriented, institutionalized metadiscourse that allowed design to take on, in Mau's words, "the entire world" (2004: 69).

Massive Change testifies to the close contemporary alignment of a design-centric epistemology with technological development. The impact of their marriage is epitomized in the Silicon Valley motto, "move fast and break things." Mau's book begins with a recitation of broken things in which he sees the cradle of innovative design: "For most of us," his book begins, "design is invisible. Until it fails" (2004: 1). "Accidents, disasters, crises," he continues. "When systems fail we become temporarily conscious of the extraordinary force and power of design, and the effects that it generates. Every accident provides a moment of awareness of real life, what is actually happening, and our dependence on the underlying systems of design" (2004: 9). In Mau's configuration, to move fast and break things means intentionally to echo what happens when a plane crashes or a highway is damaged by an earthquake or a hog farm is flooded by a hurricane: these provide a "rupture, a shock to the system" (2004: 11) that "open[s things] up by breaking [them] down" (2004: 14). The complementing idea of velocity as creating the optimal conditions for breakage is captured in the adage, "haste makes waste." But since breakage is configured as a desirable condition, speed—or what Mau's Massive Change Network calls "acceleration," as in "accelerate massive, sustainable change"—is embraced.[2]

Implicit in the extra-large scale and super-fast pace of design's alignment with STEM are the sleek, smooth, hard, and virtual textures of silicon, metal, glass, plastic, plasma, and the digital world. So, in addition to prioritizing "huge problems" with "radical solutions" that foster the creation of "world changing companies," Google's so-called moonshot factory, a subsidiary called X, also prioritizes hardness. They call it doing "the hard work of finding the right questions" and follow a corporate directive to take on challenges described as "technologically hard" (Thompson, 2017). X's CEO, Astro Teller, is also explicit about the fact that he wants to explore huge, hard things at top speed, wearing roller skates around the office "98% of the time" in order to move faster, noting in one interview that X's so-called "Rapid Evaluation" process, through which employees decide what constitutes an X-worthy enterprise, is made

166   Designing the Domestic Posthuman

less to inspire quick productivity, since true innovation is recognized to be a "long journey," than to help the company fast-fail bad ideas at an accelerated rate. "The worst scenario for X," Teller explains, "is for . . . doomed projects to languish for years in purgatory, sucking up staff and resources." X employees get bonuses for shutting things down quickly, as when a project to turn seawater into fuel was progressing well from a technological perspective but considered economically infeasible because the price of gasoline had become too cheap for seawater fuel to compete with (at the writing of this sentence, in 2022, this logic exhibits a shortsightedness about the future that is both tragic and, in its failure of imagination regarding imminent possibilities, bizarre).

Those old concerns of bygone design days—concerns having to do with decorating and ornament, which is to say, with style—might not ought to be so readily discarded. In an earlier work than *Massive Change*, Mau lamented a future in which designers might be "doomed to a life of decorating and redecorating" (quoted in Levit and Levy, 2006: 91). Fortunately, he believed, there was an alternative and it was destined to be "hipper and more mainstream" than decoration (quoted in Levit and Levy, 2006: 92). However, one might wonder with Levit and Levy, Mau's eventual reviewers in *Harvard Design Magazine*, whether "worrying about merely decorating isn't a cover for worrying about what [decorating] really does, which is much more than decorating"—if also "much less than making the world (at least in the way Mau suggests)" (Levit and Levy, 2006: 88). What "[decorating] really does," they contend, is offer a mode of communication that runs counter to the scientific fashion, declining to "explain anything or help anyone" or make anyone "do [their] work better" (2006: 91) but rather producing "a language of forms through which one may have an intuition of the unrepresentable." One of the virtues of the ornamental aspects of presentation is to offer us "liberation from the underlying purposefulness that dedication to data can imply." Liberation, that is, from the notion that simply communicating more information or responding to information can solve problems that, "regardless of origin, are [assumed to be] solvable through some essentially technical feat." If changing the world is about "technical problems susceptible to technical solutions" (2006: 91), then other concerns and their expression don't matter. But as problem-solvers the world over all know, simply choosing the right model may not be enough; a "nexus of self-interests" (2006: 91), myths, and ontological underpinnings are always interceding.

Decoration, otherwise known as ornament, otherwise known as style, otherwise known a little less diminutively as aesthetics, otherwise known less diminutively but still dismissively in the contemporary academy as form—all address the subjective, intuitive, mythical, and ontological components of the world that keep it from being only a cluster of technical problems susceptible to technical solutions. Carl Jung called the string of mythical, ontological, and spiritual concerns that all tend to be compacted into form the numinosity of

Conclusion

167

the objects they encompass. Numinosity means a mystical, embodied, highly emotional, and even spiritual resonance. Without attention to the numinous elements of objects, we overlook a key domain for both failure and impact.

A great place to look to understand the countermand that a style-centric approach to design can offer is fashion. As Kassia St. Clair (2018) has argued, fashion's fundamental unit, the textile, is perhaps the original and most globally impactful technology in history and its elision from discussions of global technological progress is "inherently odd" (if not, given its status as a predominantly female and queer space, all that surprising). Notably, of all the massive design practices that Mau's enormous catalog encompasses—graphic design, industrial design, systems design, interactive media design, materials design, web design—the only one that does not make an appearance there or in any of his books is fashion design. Its exclusion from the fast, hard, huge project of "changing the world" is not coincidental. If world-changing is about problem-solving, fashion's "problem," at least as articulated by Vanessa Freidman's *New York Times* article on "Fashion's Woman Problem" in May 2018, is a "woman problem," which can be configured in a number of ways (Friedman, 2018). Let's start with the fact that 85 percent or more of the people graduating from fashion programs globally identify as women—a statistic that still excludes the plethora of women who are not college-educated but are working in textile mills and factories or doing piecemeal sewing from their homes worldwide, and of course, accounts only for the female-centricity of production in fashion. Such a feminine industry and womanish design practice is so hard to gel with Mau's own design discourse and vision that he completely excises it.

Fashion's woman problem, however, isn't just that it is a *mythically* queer, female space. Actually, in 2018, only 14 percent of major fashion brands were led by a female executive, and the current operation of global fashion brands is not a process that one today could call, in any symbolic, mythical, or metaphorical sense, either feminine or queer. In fact, over the last three decades, fashion has been transformed from a highly cyclical, which is to say seasonal, practice operating according to a pace determined by the annual movements of the weather (which is to say, with planetary slowness) into something more akin to computer networking. This has resulted in an entirely new entity, called "fast fashion," which has ravaged the globe in both human and environmental terms on a scale that some commentators consider second only to oil. Fast fashion reshapes fashion's fundamentally queer and feminine space into the image of its design and technology counterparts. It's an example of the effect getting faster, bigger, and harder can have on humans, nonhuman animals, and all our habitats.

But fashion originated and for most of the Anthropocene was practiced as a domestic art placing high value on the decorative and ornamental and thus not only technical utility but also mythical, intuitive, spiritual, and ontological values. Its domain of behaviors and objects are not so much ridiculed by figures like Mau and his collaborators as ignored, too essentially concerned with "decorating and redecorating" even to register in his manifesto on how the world of design could change the world. But fashion's emerging generation of practitioners are reacting by proposing a new pace, scale, texture, and place for fashion that other design practices could benefit from emulating.

Designing the domestic posthuman calls for—not a manifesto of design to counter Mau's, as this form seems better suited to massive design projects desiring to take on the world as a breakable object with which to do quick work. The domestic posthuman invites a design project more aimed at affecting the embodied materiality of humans and inspiring a relation to the world less about breaking and changing it than mending it. Thus, instead of a manifesto, we draw from the lexicon of textiles to offer a sampler, which in embroidery is a stitched display of options from which a designer can draw in future makings. Samplers may seem at first, from the high, hard, fast, large, and loud vantage of contemporary design to be an antiquated form practiced by grandmothers who don't know anything about the modern world. But consider the excitement that Black musicians have derived from the notion of sampling in creating rap and hip-hop in the early days of those forms. Perhaps inspired by the samplers of their quilting, embroidering grandmothers, these individuals did not so much oppose technology in some sort of Luddite rejection as adopt the rhythms, concepts, and energies of traditional embroidery and quilting to highlight the more ludic—which is to say, playful—elements of nascent sound technologies. Their grandmotherly attitude toward technology eschewed breaking for stitching, mending, quilting, and borrowing one's way into another thing altogether. Black rap and hip-hop musicians saw the technicity of embroidery and quilts and used it to repurpose computers to behave more like their grandmothers' needles and thread. This is an instructive positionality.

The following sampler of alternative approaches to design begins with elements of contemporary fashion studies' *bubbe*-inspired reaction against fast fashion by devising ways to shrink, slow, soften, and relocate it—for example, "decorating and redecorating," intentionally put back into design discourse. The principles can be applied beyond fashion to the construction of exhilarating but stable domestic posthuman dwelling.

"~~Make massive change~~"

Miniaturization

Miniaturization means rescaling units of impact from the massive to the micro and mini. Frances Ferguson's (2004) examination of Benthamite utilitarianism, a movement that could be seen as the origins of technocracy but in which Ferguson finds a useful model for rethinking scales of value, is instructive in this project. In Ferguson's account, microactions compounded over time and across collaborative communities change much but cost little and circumvent obstacles in ways that macroactions tend to aggravate. Also informative is Susan Stewart's (1984) comparative reading of the kind of mindsets and sensibilities that miniature versus gigantic technologies tend to create. For Stewart, whereas the gigantic is the scale of exteriority and the public sphere, the miniature is a scale to evoke and encourage interiority—a condition which technologies of the future might do well to aim to better enable.

~~"Move fast and break things"~~

Go slow and mend things

"Go slow and mend things" counters the slogan of Silicon Valley with a paraphrase of the Second World War home front slogan angled at conserving textiles through the efforts of civilians to "make do and mend." Go slow and mend, like make do and mend, is about an attitude toward waste management that sees trash not as waste but as the excess of utilitarian consumption and therefore as inherently ornamental and stylish. Go slow and mend means rethinking trash as style, applying mending techniques like darning and sashiko to worn materials to prolong their life, seeing the suggestion of new styles already implicit in fading ones, and learning the visual aesthetic of visible repair. Go slow and mend recognizes the storied quality of systems that exist, is curious about the myths impacted in them, and uses the numinosity of trash to upcycle it into more soulful new objects, events, and systems.

~~Design the World~~

Remember "homemade" and "handmade"

In evoking the -made (vs. designed), one might note both the disappearance and recent resurgence of craft in contemporary culture. Disappearance in the sense conjured by Ezio Manzini, who decries the "world of objects designed for rapid consumption, objects requiring a minimum of effort and attention to use them, but also objects that leave no lasting impression on our memories—a throw-away world that requires no effort but, at the same time, produces no real quality" (1995: 222). Failing to care for objects in the way that craft cares for them mirrors what Manzini sees as the dissolution of an "ecological sensibility" in which "caring for objects can be a way of caring for that larger object that is our planet" (1995: 239), and which humans—often frustratingly—must do in miniature, one made and used thing at a time. But making has also experienced a resurgence, as marked in the rise of craftivism (and craftivist manifestos) that try to reclaim approaches to construction in which the locus of origin and destination are considered and known ("Our Story," n.d.). In evoking not just the made but the homemade and notions of homemaking, one might note that three centuries of humanism have focused on the constructs of the public sphere and body politic and wonder what a homecentric approach to human-technology relations looks like. Homes contain a plethora of seemingly antiquated technologies that are still active sites of mediation but which have not been carefully examined in contemporary studies that tend to prioritize digital and computational systems as the reigning *techne* of the Anthropocene. Importantly, homemade things and the process of homemaking tend to privilege the human hand and touch (homemade is often synonymous with handmade). Technology with better haptic resonance poses an interesting question and problem, as does thinking about how the conventional prioritization of the functions of the human head over the hand in laboratory AI construction has sent it in a direction set to lead both machines and our sense of human intelligence in directions we may not want to espouse in the future.

~~Solve "technologically hard problems" with software and hardware~~

Invest in softwear design

Hardware and software are the commonplace technomaterialities of the Anthropocene. We need a new one, better able to accommodate the insight of Russell Belk, that "digital possessions as well as most digital devices lack the soft tactile characteristics of clothing and furniture that make it possible to almost literally embed our essence in such possessions" (Belk, 2006, 2013). Softwear is literally and figuratively soft, available to touch and perception through the skin and skin ego, enmythed, and numinous.

~~Labs, offices, institutions~~

Learn the languages of home places and third places

In "Designing Technology for Domestic Spaces: A Kitchen Manifesto," Intel's Genevieve Bell and the MIT Media Lab's Joseph Kaye's contextualization of their essay's emergence is as important as the article's argument. As they wrote in a footnote in an early draft of their essay, their paper's idea was born out of "a hyperbolic conversation" and a "flurry of emails." The first draft was written over two nights, fueled by Vietnamese coffee, in the midst of a hot Boston summer; the second "composed at a series of cafe tables in and around Dublin" and "in the hop-rich scent of the old Guinness Brewery" (2002). Bell and Kaye call attention to the scenes of their essay's making because they hope it can serve as a model for future collaborations between Intel and the MIT Media Lab, and more broadly between industry and research institutions. But it can also serve as an important watermark of how and where ideas are born, often after work and outside the lab, in the cafes, bars, coffee shops, community centers, restaurants, and other hangouts that are neither work nor home but which spatialize opportunities for stepping out of both one's work-life and home-life to rest from them with forms of thinking and conversing we might consider important elements of adult play. Oldenburg calls these "third places," which are "distinctive informal gathering places . . . [that] represent fundamental institutions of mediation between the individual and the larger society" (Oldenburg, 1989: xxviii) and also articulate relationships between home and the rest of the world. These places are the heart of a community's social vitality, the grassroots of democracy, and the cradle of good ideas. Their languages encompass hyperbole, jokes, stories, memories, and feelings—all dialects learned around some version of kitchen table and a shared meal in childhood and carried into adulthood as a way of grounding oneself in social networks and systems.

~~Design Thinking~~

Listening to Granny

On Sunday mornings, my husband makes breakfast. Last week, he made eggs and sausage and then, out of the blue, decided to make sausage gravy. Do you know how to do that? I asked. Sort of, he said. Granny used to do it. Channeling childhood memories of gravy made by Granny Blanche, who would, if she were alive, be 103 years old, he made the gravy. It was delicious. But was it hers? I wanted to know. Pretty close, he said. Thus a 56-year-old man who lives in Chicago, works in cyber security, and just happens to love to cook like Granny Blanche became—last Sunday and on countless other occasions—a conduit to a generation of farmers who lived in and around Ramseur, North Carolina in the early twentieth century. Turns out their way of cooking—rejected by our parents' generation—is back in style.

And then there is another scene: me, on the phone with my mother, my sister, my aunt. I'm in Chicago and they're all in Florida, but we're collectively trying to recreate the recipe of one Josephine Alice Kring (d. 1995), my New England-born Italian grandmother who married a civil servant from Indiana and with whom she moved, in her midlife, to Hawaii. There, she made dishes fusing her native Italian cooking styles to the Japanese, Pacific, Filipino, and Chinese recipes she encountered there and whose food she loved, and I'm still on a quest to recreate her chicken long rice, a classic Hawaiian dish that is delicious in its own right but that my grandmother made transcendent by reinventing it in some mysterious, recipeless fashion that all of us who tasted it decades ago longs for but none of us has had again since she last made it. No one collected the recipe. Why, since we loved it? Well, hadn't she done it wrong anyway, mixing Italian with Hawaiian-Chinese culinary styles like some . . . housewife? Turns out, culinary fusion is a thing now too.

Gayatri Spivak (2013) writes about "learning to learn from below," referring to a system of education that begins not with conventional gatekeepers and knowledge-holders but with those typically seen as the ones who need to be taught and who in fact have things to teach. This kind of reorganized knowledge transmission can happen across cultures and social class. But it can also happen across generations, especially across generational pauses in which, having followed the logic of adolescence into adulthood one rebels against one's parents' way of doing things and returns to the everyday lives of one's grandparents not with nostalgia but a sense of genuine curiosity and discovery.

A core mode of transmission in learning to learn from below is listening to forms of stories exchanged at bedtime or over meals, around the table. Children absorb these as adults offer them, as anchors to place and family. They are often wrapped in their soft objects, which might include their pajamas, blankets, stuffed animals, and dolls—or simply the soft presence of another person. These stabilizing rituals, which hinge on repetitions amplified to a degree that can be frustrating for caregivers, facilitate the passage of innovations through the intergenerational laboratories of home kitchens and bedrooms. When the sun goes down, Allison Gopnik writes, and the busyness of daytime living pauses, is when the elders start to talk. And what they say is often a story about the family, its personalized (one might say, humanized) variations on the histories it has lived through, an animated version of certain objects in the home with all their rich patinas. Learning to learn from below means thinking about how children interact with design and borrowing that radical mindset. It also means repositioning grandmothers as exciting, nonconformist posthuman figures, allowing us to rediscover our posthuman future where we might least expect to find it.

Notes

1   Keller's two sets of gloves, juxtaposed against her home-grown method of reading lips and other hands with her own hands, parallels more contemporary incursions of cybernetics into deaf culture via the technology of cochlear implants. The latter variation has been more openly contentious, however. See Robert Sparrow's (2005) "Defending Deaf Culture: The Case of Cochlear Implants."
2   Mau's call for acceleration aligns him with Deleuze and Guattari, who issue a call to purveyors of global capitalism and neoliberalism "not to withdraw from the process, but to go further, to 'accelerate the process'" because "the truth is that we haven't

seen anything yet." Accelerationism more broadly construed is a movement whose position is that "technology, particularly computer technology, and capitalism, particularly the most aggressive, global variety, should be massively sped up and intensified—either because this is the best way forward for humanity, or because there is no alternative. Accelerationists favour automation. They favour the further merging of the digital and the human. They often favour the deregulation of business, and drastically scaled-back government. They believe that people should stop deluding themselves that economic and technological progress can be controlled. They often believe that social and political upheaval has a value in itself" (Beckett, 2017).

Figure 10 Quilt, *Eliza's Peculiar Cabinet of Curiosities*, Folayemi Wilson.

In a domestic posthuman smart home aliveness is the most important thing. Such a home might best be conceived as the cabinet of our curiosities and understood through the metaphor of quickness—not in the Silicon Valley sense of fast (think fast fashion or fast food) but rather in the sense, as they say in the Yorkshire dialect, of "wick." In Eliza's wick/quick home, there are no dead things. Even the plant and animal specimens signal the presence of her live mind.

Wick homes thrive through actual and metaphorical quilting, a process of suturing fragments of things together to create the eventual warm ensconcement of a blanket. Quilted blankets provide a homeopathic version of Didier Anzieu's envelopment therapy, which fortifies the ego by fortifying the skin. Quilts are crafted by grandmothers who see new uses in old materials and pass them along to children and children's children to keep track of. Quilts are made not only to ensconce but to decorate, importing the riot of colors, patterns, and textures found in nature into human domestic interiors. Whereas critics have seen decoration as cruelty (Kunin 2010: 87), grandmothers see it as quick-care. Quiltmaking is wickmaking through the alchemy of trash collecting, waste-mending, and mythmaking—often literally accompanied by the motions of moving hands in combination with the sounds of storytelling voices.

Eliza's scraps of quilted fabric, however, don't evoke the fine artistic objects now collected in museums and sold for thousands. She's saved a bedraggled corner, more like the remains of some child's soft support system that someone who loved that child couldn't bear to get rid of. In some sense that "someone" is Folayemi Wilson, loving Eliza and her bedraggled but no less important life-support system consisting of Star Wars figurines, a couple of dolls, boxing gloves, a hand-warming instrument, buttons, botanicals, the shards of a blanket, and whatever else the two of them can find to hold, lift, mark, mend, protect, ornament, and warm her.

References

Adam, Alison. (1998), *Artificial Knowing: Gender and the Thinking Machine*, London: Routledge.

Allerton, Catherine. (2007), "The Secret Life of Sarongs: Manggarai Textiles as Super-Skins," *Journal of Material Culture*, 12 (1): 22–46.

Alpert, Jane. (1973), "Mother Right: A New Feminist Theory," *Off our Backs*, 3 (8): 22–8.

"An Internet of Soft Things" (n.d.), Available online: https://aninternetofsoftthings.com/ (accessed September 18, 2022).

"Anderson Cooper on Diane Arbus" (2015), *Harper's Bazaar*, February 19. Available online: https://www.harpersbazaar.com/culture/features/a10029/anderson-cooper -0315/ (accessed September 19, 2022).

Anzieu, Didier. (2016), *The Skin Ego*, trans. Naomi Segal, London: Routledge.

Apps for Autism. (2012), *60 Minutes* [Television Show], S44E43, Aired July 15, 2012.

Arendt, Hannah. (1958), *The Human Condition*, 2nd edn, Chicago: University of Chicago Press.

Ariès, Phillippe. (1960, 1965), *Centuries of Childhood: A Social History of Family Life*, trans. Robert Baldick, New York: Vintage.

Asma, Stephen and Rami Gabriel. (2019), *The Emotional Mind: The Affective Roots of Culture and Cognition*, Cambridge, MA: Harvard University Press.

Badmington, Neil. (2003), "Theorizing Posthumanism," *Cultural Critique*, 53 (53): 10–27.

Baier, Annette. (1985), *Postures of the Mind*, Minneapolis: University of Minnesota Press.

Baier, Annette. (1991), "A Naturalist View of Persons," *Proceedings and Addresses of the American Philosophical Association*, 65 (3): 5–17.

Bailey, Spencer. (2022), "Google Design Guru Ivy Ross on Why Everything is Pattern and Vibration," *Time Sensitive*. Available online: https://timesensitive.fm/episode/google -design-ivy-ross-pattern-vibration/ (accessed October 2, 2022).

Bainbridge, William Sims. (2007), *Across the Secular Abyss: From Faith to Wisdom*, Lanham: Lexington Books.

Balsamo, Anne. (2011), *Designing Culture: The Technological Imagination at Work*, Durham: Duke University Press.

Barber, Elizabeth Wayland. (1993), *Prehistoric Textiles: The Development of Cloth in the Neolithic and Bronze Ages with Special Reference to the Aegean*, Princeton: Princeton University Press.

Barlow, John Perry. (1996), "A Declaration of the Independence of Cyberspace," *Electronic Frontier Foundation*, February 8. Available online: https://www.eff.org/ cyberspace-independence (accessed September 10, 2022).

Barnes, Nicole Elizabeth. (2023), "The Many Values of Night Soil in Wartime China," *Past and Present*, 259 (1): 194–228.

Barthes, Roland. (1972), *Mythologies*, New York: Hill and Wang.

Bauman, Zygmunt. (2000), *Liquid Modernity*, Cambridge: Polity.

Beatie, Thomas. (2008), "Labor of Love," *The Advocate*, 14 March. Available online: https://www.advocate.com/news/2008/03/14/labor-love (accessed September 10, 2022).

Beckett, Andy. (2017), "Accelerationism: How a Fringe Philosophy Predicted the Future We Live In," *The Guardian*, 11 May. Available online: https://www.theguardian.com/world/2017/may/11/accelerationism-how-a-fringe-philosophy-predicted-the-future-we-live-in (accessed September 15, 2022).

Belk, Russell. (1988), "Possessions and the Extended Self," *Journal of Consumer Research*, 15 (2): 139–68.

Belk, Russel. (2006), "Remembrances of Things Past: Silent Voices in Collections," in Karin Ekstrom and Helene Brembeck (eds.), *European Ad Vances in Consumer Research*, 392–97, Valdosa, GA: Association for Consumer Research.

Belk, Russell. (2013), "The Extended Self in a Digital World," *Journal of Consumer Research*, 40 (3): 477–500.

Bell, Genevieve and Joseph Kaye. (2002), "Designing Technology for Domestic Spaces: A Kitchen Manifesto," *Gastronomica*, 2 (2): 46–62. An earlier draft of this essay is accessible at: https://alumni.media.mit.edu/~jofish/writing/gastronomica24.pdf (accessed September 16, 2022).

Benjamin, Walter. (1936/1968), "The Work of Art in the Age of Mechanical Reproduction," in Hannah Arendt (ed.), Harry Zohn (trans.), *Illuminations*, 59–67, San Diego, CA: Harcourt, Brace & World.

Bennett, Jane. (2010), *Vibrant Matter: A Political Ecology of Things*, Durham: Duke University Press.

Berlant, Laura. (2016), "The Commons: Infrastructures for Troubling Times*," *Environment and Planning D: Society and Space*, 34 (3): 393–419.

Berlant, Laura. (2022), *On the Inconvenience of Other People*, Durham: Duke University Press.

Berman, Jessica. (2009), "WHO: Waterborne Disease Is World's Leading Killer," *VOA*, October 29. Available online: https://www.voanews.com/a/a-13-2005-03-17-voa34-67381152/274768.html (accessed October 1, 2022).

Berrol, Cynthia F. (2006), "Neuroscience Meets Dance/Movement Therapy: Mirror Neurons, the Therapeutic Process and Empathy," *The Arts in Psychotherapy*, 33 (4): 302–15.

Bolter, Jay David. (1984), *Turing's Man: Western Culture in the Computer Age*, Chapel Hill: The University of North Carolina Press.

Borgmann, Albert. (1987), *Technology and the Character of Contemporary Life: A Philosophical Inquiry*, Chicago: The University of Chicago Press.

Bowles, N. (2018), "A Dark Consensus About Screens and Kids Begins to Emerge in Silicon Valley," *The New York Times*, October 29, Section B1. Available online: https://www.nytimes.com/2018/10/26/style/phones-children-silicon-valley.html (accessed October 1, 2022).

Braidotti, Rosi. (2013), *The Posthuman*, Cambridge: Polity Press.

Braidotti, Rosi. (2016), "Posthuman Feminist Theory," in Lisa Disch and Mary Hawkseworth (eds.), *The Oxford Handbook of Feminist Theory*, 673–98, Cambridge: Oxford University Press.

Braidotti, Rosi. (2019), "A Theoretical Framework for the Posthumanities," *Theory, Culture and Society*, 36 (6): 31–61.

Brillat-Savarin, Jean Anthelme. (2011), *The Physiology of Taste: Meditations on Transcendental Gastronomy*, trans. M. F. K. Fisher, New York: Vintage.

References

Brown, Judith. (2009), *Glamour in Six Dimensions: Modernism and the Radiance of For*, Ithaca: Cornell University Press.

Brown, Pauline. (2019), *Aesthetic Intelligence: How to Boost It and Use It in Business and Beyond*, New York: Harper Collins.

"Caprica (TV Series 2009–2010) — IMDb" (n.d.), Www.imdb.com. Available online: https://www.imdb.com/title/tt0799862/ (accessed April 30, 2023).

CaringBridge. "Personal Health Journals for Recovery, Cancer & More | *CaringBridge*," n.d. https://www.caringbridge.org/ (Accessed 18 April 2023).

"Carrie Mae Weems: The Kitchen Table Series, 1990" (n.d.), Available online: http://carriemaeweems.net/galleries/kitchen-table.html (accessed June 1, 2022).

Cascone, Sarah. (2017), "Revisiting Diane Arbus's Most Famous Photo on Her 94th Birthday," *Artnet News*, March 14. Available online: https://news.artnet.com/market/diane-arbus-birthday-890000 (accessed September 10, 2022).

Casella, Eleanor and Karina Croucher. (2011), "Beyond Human: The Materiality of Personhood," *Feminist Theory*, 12 (2): 209–17.

Cassirer, Ernst. (1944), *An Essay on Man*, New Haven: Yale University Press.

"Cats of Instagram" (n.d.), Available online: https://catsofinstagram.com/ (Accessed September 15, 2022).

Chamberlain, David. (1998), "Babies Don't Feel Pain," in Robbie Davis-Floyd and Joseph Dumit (eds.), *Cyborg Babies*, 168–89, New York: Routledge.

Cheng, Anne Anlin. (2018), "Ornamentalism: A Feminist Theory for the Yellow Woman," *Critical Inquiry*, 44 (3): 415–46.

Clark, Andy. (2004), *Natural Born Cyborgs: Minds, Technologies, and the Future of Human Intelligence*, Cambridge: Oxford University Press.

Code, Lorraine. (1991), *What Can She Know? Feminist Theory and the Construction of Knowledge*, Ithaca: Cornell University Press.

Coeckelbergh, Mark. (2011), "Human Development or Human Enhancement? A Methodological Reflection on Capabilities and the Evaluation of Information Technologies," *Ethics and Information Technology*, 13: 81–92.

Coeckelbergh, Mark. (2012), "How I Learned to Love the Robot': Capabilities, Information Technologies, and Elderly Care," in Ilse Oosterlaken and Jeroen van den Hoven (eds.), *The Capability Approach, Technology and Design*, 77–86, New York: Springer.

Collins, Patricia Hill. (1991), *Black Feminist Thought*, New York: Routledge.

Corbett, Sarah. (2017), *How to Be a Craftivist*, New York: Penguin.

Cornell, Drucilla and Kenneth Michael Panfilio. (2010), *Symbolic Forms for a New Humanity: Cultural and Racial Reconfigurations of Critical Theory*, New York: Fordham University Press.

Costanza-Chock, Sasha. (2020), *Design Justice: Community-Led Practices to Build the Worlds We Need*, Cambridge: The MIT Press.

Craftivist Collective. (n.d.), Available online: https://craftivist-collective.com/ (Accessed April 16, 2023).

Craig, Megan. (2015), "Play, Laugh, Love: Cynthia Willett's Challenge to Philosophy," *philoSOPHIA*, 5 (2): 59–69.

Csikszentmihalyi, Mihalyi and Eugene Rochberg-Halton. (1981), *The Meaning of Things: Domestic Symbols and the Self*, Cambridge: Cambridge University Press.

Damasio, Antonio. (1999), *The Feeling of What Happens: Body and Emotion in the Making of Consciousness*, New York: Harcourt Brace.

DeCook, Julia R. (2021), "A [White] Cyborg's Manifesto: The Overwhelmingly Western Ideology Driving Technofeminist Theory," *Media, Culture & Society*, 43 (6): 1158–67.

References

DeFalco, Amelia. (2018), "Beyond Prosthetic Memory: Posthumanism, Embodiment, and Caregiving Robots," *Age, Culture, Humanities: An Interdisciplinary Journal*, 3: 1–31.

DeFalco, Amelia. (2020), "Towards a Theory of Posthuman Care," *Body & Society*, 26 (3): 31–60.

Derrida, Jacques. (1978), "The Ends of Man," in Alan Bass (trans.), *Margins of Philosophy*, 109–36, Chicago: University of Chicago Press.

"Design Justice 101 with Sasha Costanza-Chock," *The Radical AI Podcast*. Available online: https://www.radicalai.org/design-justice (Accessed April 16, 2023).

"Diane Arbus" (n.d.), *Louisiana Museum of Modern Art*. Available online: https://louisiana.dk/en/exhibition/diane-arbus/ (accessed September 15, 2022).

Dickinson, Elizabeth Evitts. (2019), "Beauty and the Brain," *Johns Hopkins Magazine*, September 16. Available online: https://hub.jhu.edu/magazine/2019/fall/neuro aesthetics-suchi-reddy-ivy-ross-susan-magsamen/ (accessed September 10, 2022).

Donald, Merlin. (2001), *A Mind So Rare: The Evolution of Human Consciousness*, New York: W. W. Norton and Company.

Doty, Alexander. (1993), *Making Things Perfectly Queer: Interpreting Mass Culture*, Minneapolis: University of Minnesota Press.

Dreilinger, Danielle. (2021), *The Secret History of Home Economics: How Trailblazing Women Harnessed the Power of Home and Changed the Way We Live*, New York: Norton.

Ellul, Jacques (1983), "The Search for Ethics in a Technicist Society," trans. D. Gillot and C. Mitcham. *Research in Philosophy and Technology*, 9 (16).

Empatica. (n.d.), "Empatica | Medical Devices, AI and Algorithms for Remote Patient Monitoring." Available online: https://www.empatica.com/ (Accessed April 23, 2023).

Escobar, Arturo. (2018), *Designs for the Pluriverse: Radical Interdependence, Autonomy, and the Making of Worlds*, Durham: Duke University Press.

"Everyday Technology Fighting Loneliness" (2019), *Wavelength*. Available online: https://wavelength.org.uk/wp-content/uploads/2019/06/WaveLength-Everyday-technology-fighting-loneliness.pdf (accessed October 1, 2022).

Fallman, Daniel. (2010), "A Different Way of Seeing: Albert Borgmann's Philosophy of Technology and Human–computer Interaction," *AI & Society*, 25: 53–60.

Ferguson, Frances. (2004), *Pornography, the Theory: What Utilitarianism Did to Action*, Chicago: University of Chicago Press.

Fernandez, Karen and John Lastovicka. (2011), "Making Magic: Fetishes in Contemporary Consumption," *Journal of Consumer Research*, 38 (August): 278–99.

Ferrando, Francesca. (2019), *Philosophical Posthumanism*, London: Bloomsbury Academic.

Field, Tiffany. (2014), *Touch*, 2nd ed, Cambridge: The MIT Press.

Firestone, Shulamith. (1970), *The Dialectic of Sex*, New York: Quill.

Flax, Jane. (1990), *Thinking Fragments*, Berkeley: The University of California Press.

Flax, Jane. (1993), *Disputed Subjects*, London: Routledge.

Forlano, Lauro. (2017), "Posthumanism and Design," *She Ji: The Journal of Design, Economics, and Innovation*, 3 (1): 16–29.

Foucault, Michel. (1973), *The Order of Things*, New York: Vintage.

Freud, Sigmund. (1919), *The Uncanny*. Available online: https://web.mit.edu/allanmc/www/freud1.pdf (accessed October 2, 2022).

Friedman, Vanessa. (2018), "Fashion's Woman Problem," *The New York Times*, May 20. Section ST: 2. Available online: https://www.nytimes.com/2018/05/20/fashion/glass-runway-no-female-ceos.html (accessed October 1, 2022).

References

Fry, Tony. (2012), *Human by Design*, London: Berg.

Fry, Tony. (2020), *Defuturing: A New Design Philosophy*, London: Bloomsbury.

Galt, Rosalind. (2011), *Pretty: Film and the Decorative Image*, New York: Columbia University Press.

Gane, Nicholas. (2006a), "Posthuman," *Theory, Culture & Society*, 23 (2–3): 431–4.

Gane, Nicholas. (2006b), "When we have Never been Human, What is to be Done?: Interview with Donna Haraway," *Theory, Culture & Society*, 23 (7–8): 135–58.

Garland-Thomson, Rosemarie. (2011), "Misfits," *Hypatia*, 26 (3): 591–609.

Garreau, Joel. (2005), *Radical Evolution: The Promise and Peril of Enhancing our Minds, our Bodies-- And What it Means to be Human*, New York: Doubleday.

Geertz, Clifford. (1973), *The Interpretation of Cultures*, New York: Basic Books.

Gehlen, Arnold. (1988), *Man: His Nature and Place in the World*, trans. Clare McMillan and Karl Pillemer, New York: Columbia University Press.

George, Rose. (2008), *The Big Necessity: The Unmentionable World of Human Waste and Why It Matters*, New York: Metropolitan Books.

Gibson, Margaret. (2014), "Introduction: Queering Motherhood in Narrative, Theory, and the Everyday," in Margaret Gibson (ed.), *Queering Motherhood: Narrative and Theoretical Perspectives*, 1–26, Bradford: Demeter Press.

"The Gold Standard" (2018), *Goldstandard.org*. Available online: https://www.goldstandard.org/ (accessed October 1, 2022).

Gopnik, Alison. (2009), *The Philosophical Baby*, New York: Farrar, Straus and Giroux.

Gopnik, Alison. (2016), *The Gardner and the Carpenter*, New York: Farrar, Straus, and Giroux.

Gopnik, Alison. (2017), "Making AI More Human," *Scientific American*, June: 62–5.

Gopnik, Alison. (2020a), "Childhood as a Solution to Explore–exploit Tensions," *Philosophical Transactions of the Royal Society*, 375 (1803): 1–10.

Gopnik, Alison. (2020b), "Vulnerable yet Vital," *Aeon*. Available online: https://aeon.co/essays/why-childhood-and-old-age-are-key-to-our-human-capacities (accessed September 16, 2022).

Gottschall, Jonathan. (2012), *The Storytelling Animal: How Stories Make Us Human*, New York: Houghton Mifflin Harcourt.

Graham, Elaine. (2002), *Representations of the Post/Human: Monsters, Aliens and Others in Popular Culture*, News Brunswick: Rutgers University Press.

Grene, Marjorie. (1974), *The Understanding of Nature*, Dordrecht: D. Reidel Publishing Company.

Grene, Marjorie. (1995), *A Philosophical Testament*, Peru: Open Court.

Grene, Marjorie and N. Eldridge. (1992), *Interactions*, New York: Columbia University Press.

Grossman, Lev. (2005), "Stevie's Little Wonder," *Time Magazine*, September 12.

Guglielmo, Amy, Jacqueline Tourville, and Giselle Potter. (2018), *How to Build a Hug: Temple Grandin and Her Amazing Squeeze Machine*, New York: Atheneum Books.

Gunnarsson, Lena. (2013), "The Naturalistic Turn in Feminist Theory: A Marxist-Realist Contribution," *Feminist Theory*, 14 (1): 3–19.

Hansen, Mark. (2006), "Media Theory," *Theory, Culture and Society*, l23 (2–3): 297–306.

Haraway, Donna. (1991), *Simians, Cyborgs, and Women*, New York: Routledge.

Haraway, Donna. (2003), *The Companion Species Manifesto: Dogs, People, and Significant Otherness*, Chicago: University of Chicago Press.

Haraway, Donna. (2008b), *When Species Meet*, Minneapolis: University of Minnesota Press.

Hartley, John. (1992), *Tele-ology: Studies in Television*, London: Routledge.

Hartley, John. (1999), *Uses of Television*, London: Routledge.

Hassan, Ihab. (1977), "Prometheus as Performer: Toward a Posthumanist Culture?" *The Georgia Review*, 31 (4): 830–50.

Hawkes, Kristen. (2004), "The Grandmother Effect," *Nature (London)*, 428 (6979): 128–9.

Hawkes, Kristen. (2020), "Cognitive Consequences of Our Grandmothering Life History: Cultural Learning Begins in Infancy," *Philosophical Transactions of the Royal Society*, 375 (1803): 1–9.

Hawkes, Kristen and James Coxworth. (2013), "Grandmothers and the Evolution of Human Longevity: A Review of Findings and Future Directions Evolutionary Anthropology," *Evolutionary Anthropology* 22: 294–302.

Hawkes, Kristen and Richard Paine, eds. (2006), *The Evolution of Human Life History*, Santa Fe: School for Advanced Research Press.

Hayles, N. Katherine. (1999), *How We Became Posthuman*, Chicago: University of Chicago Press.

Hayles, N. Katherine. (2005a), "Computing the Human," *Theory, Culture & Society*, 22 (1): 131–51.

Hayles, N. Katherine. (2005b), *My Mother Was a Computer*, Chicago: University of Chicago Press, 2005.

Hayles, N. Katherine. (2010), "Wrestling with Transhumanism," in G. R. Hansell and W. Grassie (eds.), *Transhumanism and Its Critics*, 215–26, Philadelphia: Metanexus Institute.

Hayles, N. Katherine. (2012), *How We Think: Digital Media and Contemporary Technogenesis*, Chicago: University of Chicago Press.

Hayles, N. Katherine. (2017), *Unthought: The Power of the Cognitive Nonconscious*, Chicago: University of Chicago Press.

Herr, Hugh. (2018), "How We'll Become Cyborgs and Extend Human Potential," *TED Video*, 15:03. Available online: https://www.ted.com/talks/hugh_herr_how_we_ll _become_cyborgs_and_extend_human_potential.

Herzog, Werner and Moira Weigel. (2010), "On the Absolute, the Sublime, and Ecstatic Truth," *Arion: A Journal of Humanities and the Classics*, 17 (3): 1–12.

Heti, Sheila. (2018), *Motherhood: A Novel*, New York: Henry Holt and Company.

Hodges, Andrew. (2014), *Alan Turing: The Enigma: The Book that Inspired the Film the Imitation Game*, Updated ed, Princeton: Princeton University Press.

Homann, K. B. (2010), "Embodied Concepts of Neurobiology in Dance/Movement Therapy Practice," *American Journal of Dance Therapy*, 32: 80–99.

hooks, bell. (2014), *Yearning: Race, Gender, and Cultural Politics*, New York: Routledge.

Hrdy, Sarah Blaffer. (2009), *Mothers and Others*, Cambridge: Harvard University Press.

Hughes, J. (1988), "The Philosopher's Child," in M. Griffiths and M. Whitford (eds.), *Feminist Perspectives in Philosophy*, 72–89, London: Palgrave Macmillan.

Hutson, Matthew. (2018), "How Researchers are Teaching AI to Learn Like a Child," *Science*, May 24. Available online: https://www.science.org/content/article/how -researchers-are-teaching-ai-learn-child (accessed October 1, 2022).

Ihde, Don. (2003), "Beyond the Skin-bag," *Nature*, 424: 615.

Illich, Ivan. (1973), *Tools for Conviviality*, New York: Harper Row.

Issenman, Betty. (1997), *Sinews of Survival: The Living Legacy of Inuit Clothing*, Vancouver: UBC Press.

Jacob, François. (1977), "Evolution and Tinkering," *Science*, 196 (4295): 1161–6.

Jantzen, Grace. (2004), *Foundations of Violence*, London: Routledge.

References

Jasanoff, Sheila. (2015), "Future Imperfect: Science, Technology, and the Imaginations of Modernity," in S. Jasanoff and Sang-Hyun Kim (eds.), *Dreamscapes of Modernity*, 1–33, Chicago: University of Chicago Press.

Jung, Carl. (1964), *Man and His Symbols*, New York: Doubleday.

Kaul, Pooja. (2019), *Sundar Sari*, (online video) 12:47. Available online: https://youtu.be/R4zDwxGwPq4 (accessed October 8, 2019).

Kunin, Aaron. (2010), "Decoration, Modernism, Cruelty," *Modernism/modernity*, 17 (1): 87–107.

Kurzweil, Ray. (2006), *The Singularity is Near: When Humans Transcend Biology*, New York: Penguin Books.

Lassègue, J. (1996), *What Kind of Turing Test Did Turing Have in Mind?* Available online: https://www.researchgate.net/publication/265007809_What_Kind_of_Turing_Test_Did_Turing_Have_in_Mind (accessed September 23, 2022).

Lassègue, J. (2009), "Doing Justice to the Imitation Game," in R. Epstein, G. Roberts, and G. Beber (eds.), *Parsing the Turing Test*, 151–72, Dordrecht: Springer.

Latour, Bruno. (1993), *We have Never Been Modern*, trans. Catherine Porter, Cambridge, MA: Harvard University Press.

Latour, Bruno. (1996), *Aramis, or the Love of Technology*, trans. Catherine Porter, Cambridge, MA: Harvard University Press.

Le Doeuff, Michele. (2002, 2003), *Philosophical Imaginary*, London: Bloomsbury.

Lee, Nick. (2008), "Awake, Asleep, Adult, Child: An A-Humanist Account of Persons," *Body & Society*, 14 (4): 57–74.

Lemke, Sieglinde. (1998), *Primitivist Modernism: Black Culture and the Origins of Transatlantic Modernism*, Oxford: Oxford University Press.

Lemmens, Pieter. (2017), "Thinking Through Media. Stieglerian Remarks on a Possible Postphenomenology of Media," in Y. Van Den Eede, S. Irwin O'Neill, and G. Wellner (eds.), *Postphenomenology and Media*, 185–206, Lanham: Lexington Books.

Lessing, Doris. (2002), *On Cats*, London: Flamingo.

Levit, Robert and Evonne Levy. (2006), "Design Will Save the World!," *Harvard Design Magazine*, 24: 86–92.

Lewis, Katherine Reynolds. (2016), "Abandon Parenting, And Just Be a Parent," *The Atlantic*, September 23. Available online: https://www.theatlantic.com/family/archive/2016/09/abandon-parenting-and-just-be-a-parent/501236/ (accessed October 1, 2022).

"Li Edelkoort and Google Explore How Digital Devices Can Be More Sensorial" (2018), *Dezeen*, April 13. Available online: https://www.dezeen.com/2018/04/13/li-edelkoort-google-softwear-exhibition-milan-design-week/ (accessed October 1, 2022).

Lindemann, Hilde. (2014), *Holding and Letting Go: The Social Practice of Personal Identities*, Cambridge: Oxford University Press.

Lloyd, Genevieve. (2000), "No One's Land: Australia and the Philosophical Imagination," *Hypatia*, 15 (2): 26–39.

Lorde, Audre. (1988), *A Burst of Light: Essays*, Ann Arbor: Firebrand Books.

Lupton, Deborah. (2013), "Infants And/As Objects," August 16. Available online: https://www.academia.edu/4257406/Infants_and_as_objects (accessed August 10, 2022).

Malafouris, Lambros. (2016), *How Things Shape the Mind*, Cambridge: The MIT Press.

Mandemaker, Lisa. (2022), "Artificial Womb." Available online: https://www.lisamandemaker.com/work-1/artificial-womb (accessed September 16, 2022).

Manzini, Ezio. (1995), "Prometheus of the Everyday: The Ecology of the Artificial and the Designer's Responsibility," in R. Buchanan and V. Margolin (eds.), *Discovering Design: Explorations in Design Studies*, 219–44, Chicago: University of Chicago Press.

Manzini, Ezio. (2015), *Design, When Everybody Designs*, Cambridge: The MIT Press.

Mau, Bruce Mau. (2004), *Massive Change*, New York: Phaidon Press.

Mbembe, Achille. (2019), *Necropolitics*, Durham: Duke University Press.

McComb, Karen, Anna M. Taylor, Christian Wilson, and Benjamin D. Charlton. (2009), "The Cry Embedded Within the Pur," *Current Biology*, 19 (13): R507–R508.

McGee, Julie. (2016), "Afterword: Radical Connoisseurship," in *Eliza's Peculiar Cabinet of Curiosities*, Exhibition Catalog. Milwaukee: Lynden Sculpture Garden.

McKee, Robert. (1998), *Story: Substance, Structure, Style and the Principles of Screenwriting*, New York: ReganBooks.

MealTrain.com (official site) - Organize Meal Support in Minutes. (n.d.), "MealTrain.Com (Official Site) - Organize Meal Support in Minutes." Available online: https://www.mealtrain.com/ (accessed April 23, 2023).

Melore, Chris. (2021), "Pet Priorities: 1 in 5 Share Meals with Their Furry Friends -- 6 Percent Bathe with Their Pets! Study Finds," *StudyFinds*, November 8. Available online: https://studyfinds.org/share-meals-bathe-with-pets/ (accessed October 1, 2022).

Menakem, Resmaa. (2017), *My Grandmother's Hands: Racialized Trauma and the Pathway to Healing our Hearts and Bodies*, Las Vegas: Central Recovery Press.

Meyrowitz, Joshua. (1985), *No Sense of Place*, Cambridge: Oxford University Press.

Miah, A. (2008), "A Critical History of Posthumanism," in B. Gordijn and R. Chadwick (eds.), *Medical Enhancement and Posthumanity*, 71–94, Berlin: Springer.

Midgley, Mary. (1985), *Evolution as Religion*, London: Routledge.

Midgley, Mary. (1992), *Science as Salvation: A Modern Myth and Its Meaning*, London: Routledge.

Midgley, Mary. (1994), *The Ethical Primate*, London: Routledge.

Midgley, Mary. (1996), *Utopias, Dolphins, and Computers: Problems of Philosophical Plumbing*, London: Routledge.

Midgley, Mary. (1998), *Animals and Why They Matter*, Athens: University of Georgia Press.

Midgley, Mary. (2001), *Science and Poetry*, London: Routledge.

Midgley, Mary. (2003), *The Myths We Live By*, London: Routledge.

Midgey, Mary. (2018), *What is Philosophy For?*, London: Bloomsbury Academic.

Mies, Maria and Vandana Shiva. (1993), *Ecofeminism*, London: Zed Books.

Miller, Donald. (2017), *Building a Story Brand: Clarify Your Message So Customers Will Listen*, New York: HarperCollins Leadership.

Mills, Mara. (2011), "On Disability and Cybernetics: Helen Keller, Norbert Wiener, and the Hearing Glove," *Differences*, 22 (2–3): 74–111.

Moravec, Hans. (1988), *Mind Children*, Cambridge, MA: Harvard University Press.

Moravec, Hans. (2013), "Pigs in Cyberspace," in Max More and Natasha Vita-More (eds.), *The Transhumanist Reader*, 177–81, Malden: John Wiley & Sons.

Mudde, Anne. (2022), "Crafting Relations and Feminist Practices of Care," *Journal of Global Ethics*, 18 (1): 64–81.

Mullins, Aimee. (2009), "My 12 Pairs of Legs," *TED Video*, 12:36. Available online: https://www.ted.com/talks/aimee_mullins_my_12_pairs_of_legs.

Nasser, Latif. (2014), "Helen Keller and the Glove That Couldn't Hear," *The Atlantic*, September 19. Available online: https://www.theatlantic.com/technology/archive/2014/09/helen-keller-and-the-hearing-glove/380336/ (accessed September 10, 2022).

Nayar, Pramod. (2014), *Posthumanism*, Cambridge: Polity Press.

References

Nelson, Maggie. (2022), *On Freedom: Four Songs of Care and Constraint*, Minneapolis: Gray Wolf Press.

Nicastro, N. (2004), "Perceptual and Acoustic Evidence for Species-Level Differences in Meow Vocalizations by Domestic Cats (Felis catus) and African Wild Cats (Felis Silvestris Lybica)," *J Comp Psychol*, 118 (3): 287–96.

Oldenburg, Ray. (1989), *The Great Good Place*, Boston: Da Capo Press.

Orrmalm, Alex. (2020), "Culture by Babies: Imagining Everyday Material Culture Through Babies' Engagements with Sock," *Childhood*, 27 (1): 93–105.

Ortner, Sherry. (1996), *Making Gender*, Boston: Beacon Press.

"Our Story" (n.d.), *Craftivist Collective*. Available online: https://craftivist-collective.com/our-story/ (accessed September 1, 2022).

Pacey, Arnold. (1983), *The Culture of Technology*, Cambridge: The MIT Press.

Pallasmaa, Juhani. (2007), *The Eyes of the Skin: Architecture and the Senses*, London: John-Wiley and Sons.

Park, Shelley. (2013), *Mothering Queerly, Queering Motherhood: Resisting Monomaternalism in Adoptive, Lesbian, Blended, and Polygamous Families*, Albany: SUNY Press.

Peirce, Charles Sanders. (1991), *Peirce on Signs: Writings on Semiotic by Charles Sanders Peirce*, ed. James Hoopes, Durham: University of North Carolina Press.

Perloff, Marjorie. (1986), *The Futurist Moment: Avant-garde, Avant Guerre, and the Language of Rupture*, Chicago: The University of Chicago Press.

Philips, Adam. (1996), *On Flirtation: Psychoanalytic Essays on the Uncommitted Life*, Cambridge, MA: Harvard University Press.

Pickering, Andrew. (2010), *The Cybernetic Brain*, Chicago: University of Chicago Press.

Piercy, Marge. (1991), *He, She and It*, New York: Ballantine Books.

Plant, Sadie. (1997), *Zeros and Ones: Digital Women and the New Technoculture*, New York: Doubleday.

Portmann, Adolf. (1990), *A Zoologist Looks at Humankind*, trans. Judith Schaeffer, New York: Columbia University Press.

Posnock, Ross. (2018), "Ross Posnock — 'Trust in One's Nakedness' James Baldwin's Sophistication," *Boundary 2*, December 7. Available online: https://www.boundary2.org/2018/12/ross-posnock-trust-in-ones-nakedness-james-baldwins-sophistication/.

Poster, Mark. (2006), *Information Please: Culture and Politics in the Age of Digital Machines*, Durham: Duke University Press.

Postman, Neil. (1985), *Amusing Ourselves to Death*, New York: Random House Books.

Prensky, Marc. (2001), "Digital Natives, Digital Immigrants," *On the Horizon*, MCB University Press, 9 (5).

Q. (2020), *Sari Men* (online video), 10:10. Available online: https://youtu.be/PNPbo94-tzs (accessed October 1, 2022).

"Radiolab's New Series: 'Mixtape' | All of It" (2022), *WNYC*. Available online: https://www.wnyc.org/story/new-radiolab-series-mixtape/ (accessed September 29, 2022).

Rapaille, Clotaire. (2007), *The Culture Code: An Ingenious Way to Understand Why People Around the World Buy and Live as They Do*, New York: Broadway Books.

Reddy, Vasudevi. (2008), *How Infants Know Minds*, Cambridge, MA: Harvard University Press.

Reed, Lori. (2000), "Domesticating the Personal Computer: The Mainstreaming of a New Technology and the Cultural Management of a Widespread Technophobia, 1964–," *Critical Studies in Media Communication*, 17 (2): 159–85.

Reid, Colbey Emmerson and Dennis M. Weiss. (2024), "Alternative Domiciles for the Domestic Posthuman," *Posthuman Architectures: Theories, Designs, Technologies and Futures*, Ed. Mark Garcia, 94 (1).

Rheingold, Howard. (1993), *The Virtual Community*, Reading: Addison Wesley Publishing Co.

Rich, Adrienne. (1979), "Motherhood: The Contemporary Emergency and Quantum Leap," in *On Lies, Secrets, and Silence: Selected Prose 1966–1978*, 259–73, New York: W. W. Norton.

Rittel, Horst and Melvin M. Webber. (1973), "Dilemmas in a General Theory of Planning," *Policy Sciences*, 4 (2): 155–69.

Roco, Mihail C. and William Sims Bainbridge, eds. (2002), *Converging Technologies for Improving Human Performance*, Dordrecht: Kluwer.

Rogaski, Ruth. (2004), *Hygienic Modernity: Meanings of Health and Disease in Treaty-Port China*, Berkeley, esp. 13.7.

Ronell, Avital. (1991), *The Telephone Book: Technology, Schizophrenia, Electric Speech*, Lincoln: Nebraska Press.

The Sari Series. (2022), "Border&Fall." Available online: https://thesariseries.com/ (accessed September 15, 2022).

Schwartz, Oscar. (2019), "Untold History of AI: Invisible Women Programmed America's First Electronic Computer," *IEEE Spectrum*, March 25. Available online: https://spectrum.ieee.org/untold-history-of-ai-invisible-woman-programmed-americas-first-electronic-computer.

Sharon, Tamar. (2012), "A Cartography of the Posthuman: Humanist, Non-Humanist and Mediated Perspectives on Emerging Biotechnologies," *Krisis*, 2: 4–19.

Sharon, Tamar. (2014), *Human Nature in an Age of Biotechnology: The Case for Mediated Posthumanism*, Dordrecht: Springer.

Sillman, Amy. (2015), "Shit Happens," *Frieze*, 10 November. Available online: https://www.frieze.com/article/shit-happens (accessed September 10, 2022).

Small, Meredith. (1998), *Our Babies, Ourselves*, New York: Anchor Books.

Smith, Barbara. (1989), "A Press of Our Own Kitchen Table: Women of Color Press," *Frontiers: A Journal of Women Studies*, 10 (3): 11–13.

Smith, Roberta. (2020), "The Radical Quilting of Rosie Lee Tompkins," *The New York Times*, June 26, Sec: Arts. Available online: https://www.nytimes.com/interactive /2020/06/26/arts/design/rosie-lee-tompkins-quilts.html (accessed October 1, 2022).

Smith, Virginia. (2007), *Clean: A History of Personal Hygiene and Purity*, Cambridge: Oxford University Press.

"Soil Erosion Must Be Stopped "to Save Our Future Says UN Agriculture Agency" (2019), *UN News*, December 5. Available online: https://news.un.org/en/story/2019/12 /1052831 (accessed September 1, 2022).

Solomon, Andrew. (2012), *Far from the Tree: Parents, Children and the Search for Identity*, New York: Scribner.

Soper, Kate. (2009), "Unnatural Times? The Social Imaginary and the Future of Nature," *The Sociological Review*, 57 (2): 222–35.

Soper, Kate. (2012), "The Humanism in Posthumanism," *Comparative Critical Studies*, 9 (3): 365–78.

Sparrow, Robert. (2005), "Defending Deaf Culture: The Case of Cochlear Implants," *The Journal of Political Philosophy*, 13 (2): 135–52.

Spigel, Lynn. (2001), *Welcome to the Dreamhouse*, Durham: Duke University Press.

Spigel, Lynn. (2005), "Designing the Smart House: Posthuman Domesticity and Conspicuous Production," *European Journal of Cultural Studies*, 8 (4): 403–26.

References

Spivak, Gayatri Chakravorty. (2013), *An Aesthetic Education in the Era of Globalization*, Cambridge, MA: Harvard University Press.

St. Clair, Kassia. (2018), *The Golden Thread: How Fabric Changed History*, London: John Murray.

Sterrett, S. G. (2012), "Bringing Up Turing's 'Child-Machine'," in S. B. Cooper, A. Dawar, and B. Löwe (eds.), *How the World Computes*, 703–13, CiE 2012. Lecture Notes in Computer Science, Vol. 7318. Berlin, Heidelberg: Springer.

Stewart, Susan. (1984), *On Longing: Narratives of the Miniature, the Gigantic, the Souvenir, the Collection*, Baltimore: Johns Hopkins University Press.

Stiegler, Bernard. (1998), *Technics and Time*, trans. Richard Beardsworth and George Collins, Stanford: Stanford University Press.

Stone, Alison. (2019), *Being Born: Birth and Philosophy*, New York: Oxford University Press.

Stone, Allucquere Rosanne. (1995), *The War of Desire and Technology at the Close of the Mechanical Age*, Cambridge: The MIT Press.

Tanner, Nancy Makepiece. (1981), *On Becoming Human*, Cambridge: Cambridge University Press.

Thompson, Derek. (2017), "Google X and the Science of Radical Creativity," *The Atlantic*, November. Available online: https://www.theatlantic.com/magazine/archive/2017/11/x-google-moonshot-factory/540648/ (accessed October 1, 2022).

Trevathan, Wenda. (2011), *Human Birth: An Evolutionary Perspective*, New York: Routledge.

Tuan, Yi-Fu. (1980), "The Significance of the Artifact," *Geographical Review*, 70 (4), 462–72.

Turing, Alan. (1950), "Computing Machinery and Intelligence," *Mind*, 59: 433–60.

Turkle, Stone. (1995), *Life on the Screen: Identity in the Age of the Internet*, New York: Simon and Schuster.

Twenge, Jean M. (2017), "Has the Smartphone Destroyed a Generation?" *The Atlantic*, September. Available online: https://www.theatlantic.com/magazine/archive/2017/09/has-the-smartphone-destroyed-a-generation/534198/ (accessed October 1, 2022).

Uricchio, William. (2010), "TV as Time Machine: Television's Changing Heterochronic Regimes and the Production of History," in Jostein Gripsrud (ed.), *Relocating Television*, 27–40, London: Routledge.

US Weekly Staff. (2022), "Famous Celebrity Pregnancies: Baby Bump Hall of Fame," *US Weekly*, June 6. Available online: https://www.usmagazine.com/celebrity-moms/pictures/bump-hall-of-fame-200989/ (accessed October 1, 2022).

Vaccari, Andrés. (2002), "What is technology? Unravelling a great idea," presented at Annual National Conference of the Cultural Studies Association of Australia, Melbourne, Australia, December, 2002.

Vaccari, Andrés. (2012), "Dissolving Nature: How Descartes Made Us Posthuman," *Techno*, 16 (2): 138–186.

van der Kolk, Bessel. (2015), *The Body Keeps the Score: Brain, Mind and Body in the Healing of Trauma*, New York: Penguin.

Verbeek, Peter-Paul. (2005), *What Things Do: Philosophical Reflections on Technology, Agency, and Design*, University Park: Pennsylvania State University Press.

Wakkary, Ron. (2021), *Things We Could Design: For More Than Human-Centered Worlds*, Cambridge: The MIT Press.

Watson, Julie. (2020), *Lo-TEK : design by radical indigenism*, Cologne: Taschen.

Watt, Ian. (1957), *The Rise of the Novel*, London: Chatto & Windus.

Weems, Carrie Mae. (1990), The Kitchen Table Series. Photographs. Available online: https://carriemaeweems.net/galleries/kitchen-table.html (Accessed April 18, 2023).

Weheliye, Alexander. (2015), *Habeas Viscus*, Durham: Duke University Press.

Weiss, Dennis. (2019), "On the Subject of Technology," *Azimuth*, 7 (14): 27–40.

Weiss, Dennis. (2023), "Natality and the Posthuman Condition," *Film and Philosophy*, 27: 29–46.

Whang, Oliver. (2022), "'Parentese' Is Truly a Lingua Franca, Global Study Finds," *The New York Times*, July 24, Sec.: Science. Available online: https://www.nytimes.com/2022/07/24/science/parentese-babies-global-language.html (accessed September 10, 2022).

Wiessner, Polly W. (2014), "Embers of Society: Firelight Talk Among the Ju/'hoansi Bushmen," *Proceedings of the National Academy of Sciences – PNAS*, 111 (39): 14027–35.

Willett, Cynthia. (1995), *Maternal Ethics and Other Slave Moralities*, New York: Routledge.

Willett, Cynthia. (2001), *The Soul of Justice*, Ithaca: Cornell University Press.

Willett, Cynthia. (2014), *Interspecies Ethics*, New York: Columbia University Press.

Winner, Langdon. (1986), *The Whale and the Reactor: A Search for Limits in an Age of High Technology*, Chicago: University of Chicago Press.

Wolfe, Cary. (2010), *What is Posthumanism?* Minneapolis: University of Minnesota Press.

Young, Iris Marion. (2005), *On Female Body Experience: 'Throwing Like a Girl' and Other Essays*, Cambridge: Oxford University Press.

Zihlman, A. L. and D. R. Bolter. (2004), "Mammalian and Primate Roots of Human Sociality," in R. W. Sussman and A. R. Chapman (eds.), *The Origins and Nature of Sociality*, 23–52, London: Routledge.

Index

Note: Page numbers followed with "n" refer to endnotes.

acceleration   165, 172 n.2
adolescence   48, 54, 65, 79, 80, 172
aesthetic intelligence (AI)   93, 101–2, 137
AI. *See* artificial intelligence (AI)
allogrooming   106–8
Alpert, Jane   73–4
animism   129–30
annuraaq. See inuit raincoats
anthropocentrism   26, 46–7, 65
anthropomorphism   10, 26, 37, 142
Anzieu, Didier   93, 102–4, 107
Arbus, Diane   71, 72, 77–9
archetypes   111, 123, 124, 130
Arendt, Hannah   154
artificial intelligence (AI)   4, 31, 96, 130
artificial womb   73–5
"the arts of personhood", Baier, Annette   4, 6, 51, 54–7, 60
Asma, Stephen   103
automatons   129–31

baby   50, 74, 77–8, 82, 84, 104–5, 139
Baby (first electronic stored-program computer)   19–23, 25, 32
   birth of   19–20, 35, 38 n.2
   growth of   24, 32, 33
   technogenesis of   28
baby bumps of Instagram   7, 74
Badmington, Neil   25, 26, 34, 37, 66 n.2, 83
Baier, Annette   49
   personhood   41, 50, 51, 54, 56
   "the arts of personhood"   4, 6, 51, 54–7, 60

Banerjee, Mukulika   138
Barlow, John Perry   79
Beattie, Thomas   74–5, 85
becoming animal   72, 141
becoming human   72
Belk, Russell   99, 106, 170
Bell, Genevieve   170–1
Benjamin, Walter   99
Bennett, Jane   10
Berlant, Lauren   8, 120
biogas   146–8
   digester toilets   148
biosocial eros   51, 61, 65
birth
   of Baby (first electronic stored-program computer)   19, 20, 35, 38 n.2
   of human   24, 48–50
   of posthuman   19–20, 23, 28, 32, 48–50
Bolter, Deborah   50, 51, 80, 115 n.2
Bolter, Jay David   31, 33
Bowles, Nellie   79
Braidotti, Rosi   10, 30–2, 60, 72, 93, 108, 123, 163
Breuer, Josef   104
Brillat-Savarin, Jean Anthelme   154
Brown, Pauline   93, 102
Bruner, Jerome   57

capabilities   45, 46
care   46–7, 50, 60–2, 151, 163
   child   54, 56–8, 60, 80
      by grandmothers   84–5
   elder   45–6, 61, 63
   impact of technology on   45, 60

and nurturance 54, 60
of television 151
caregiver-child relations 59
caregivers 10, 49–51, 55, 57, 58, 164
caregiving 34, 55, 84
childhood and 80
robots 45–8, 60–2
women and 34
care of bodily surfaces (COBS)
studies 107
Cartesian self 81, 83
Cassirer, Ernst 111–13
cat 7, 140–3
#catsofinstagram 142–3
Cavarero, Adriana 48
Chamberlain, David 78
child 35, 43, 50–1, 54, 57, 61, 65,
78–81
brain 21, 25
nurturer and 57
play 65, 79, 80
child-caregiver relations 54, 56
childhood 50, 51, 54–6, 65, 66 n.4,
79–80
and caregiving 80
innovation 80
child-machines, Turing, Alan 21, 35
children 4, 6, 25–8, 33–7, 43–4,
51–7, 65, 123–5, 128–30,
131 n.4, 137, 139, 172
and adults 53, 55
grandmothers' care for 84
human-machine relations 60
potty training 144
robotic care 60
storytelling for 57
teaching the 54
and technology 59, 79–80
China
indigenous textile 147
night soil trade 146, 148, 156 n.2
toilets in 146, 148
Clark, Andy 101, 164
clone technology 124
cloth/clothing 95, 97, 99, 104–6
sari 138–40
Code, Lorraine 3, 53
Coeckelbergh, Mark 45–7, 60–3
coevolution 22, 24

Collina Strada's masks 109–10
Collins, Patricia Hill 50
companion species 72, 140
computer 26–8, 31–4
"Computing Machinery and Intelligence"
(Turing) 20, 39 n.10
contemporary emergency 5, 36, 64
Corbett, Sarah 82, 83
cosmopolitan homes 126
Costanza-Chock, Sasha 11 n.2,
38 n.2, 95
craftivism 82, 169
craftwork 82–3
Craig, Megan 61
critical posthumanism 8, 32, 44–8,
52, 53, 58, 60–2, 64–5,
66 n.2, 150, 164
Csikszentmihalyi, Mihalyi 154
culture codes 123
cutting-edge technology 162
cybernetic glove 161–2, 172 n.1
cybernetics 2, 22, 23, 25, 27, 32,
36, 84
wombs 73–4
cyberspace 22
cyborg 32, 39 n.13, 62, 71–5, 84–6,
96, 163

death of Man 23–6, 28, 33
decentered self 73, 81, 82
DeCook, Julia 32
decorating and redecorating 166, 168
DeFalco, Amelia 46–7, 60–3
deficit model of infancy 78, 87 n.1
Deleuze, Gilles 7, 141, 172 n.2
Derrida, Jacques 7, 19, 23, 25, 26, 141
designer baby 78
"Designing Technology for Domestic
Spaces: A Kitchen Manifesto"
(Bell and Kaye) 170–1
digital natives 79, 81
disabled 85–7
domestic labor 36, 55
domestic posthuman 2–4, 34–6, 45,
48, 52–5, 58, 60, 64–5, 73,
75, 81, 86–7, 93, 108, 113,
124, 127, 131
artifact 137, 143, 146
biosocial eros 65

design 168
fashion 114
four bubbes 162–4
homemade 126
imaginative vision for human-
technology relations 64
skin and touch 93
technologies 110
technomateriality 93, 96–7, 100
unhomely *techne* 121, 128
Doty, Alexander 72
draping 138
Dreilinger, Danielle 77

ecstatic truth 122
elder care 45–6, 61, 63
Eliza's Peculiar Cabinet of Curiosities
(Wilson) 41
embroidery 168
Escobar, Arturo 5–7, 66 n.6, 110,
137, 138, 148
extended skins 106, 132 n.7
extractive necrotics 164

facts 121–2
Fallman, Daniel 87 n.5
fashion 109, 114, 167–8
face masks 109–10
fast fashion 167, 168
fenbian 146, 148
Ferguson, Frances 168–9
Firestone, Shulamith 73–4
Flax, Jane 34, 49, 50, 66 n.7, 82
Foucault, Michel 19, 22–4
four bubbes 10, 162–4
four horsemen of the posthuman
apocalypse (Braidotti) 10, 93,
121, 123, 131 n.3, 163, 164
Freed, Janet 36, 156
Freud, Sigmund 104, 121, 128, 130
Unheimlich 128–31
frivolous bodily decorators 114
Fry, Tony 5–7, 39 n.9, 110
furniture 99, 154, 156 n.1

Gabriel, Rami 103
Galt, Rosalind 114
Gane, Nicholas 37
Garland-Thomson, Rosemarie 86

Gehlen, Arnold 77
Gibson, Margaret 7
glossy indigo textiles 147–8
goddess 74
Google 97
Google Search
humanism 23
posthumanism 23–4
Google X 165–6
Gopnik, Alison 50, 55, 56, 65, 80, 84,
85, 104, 124, 151, 163, 172
go slow and mend things 169
Graham, Elaine 19–20, 23, 25,
66 n.2, 131 n.3
Graham Bell, Alexander 161
Gram Vikas, Odisha 144–5
Granada, Luis de 78
grandmother(s) 4, 5, 8, 10, 64, 83–5,
151, 163, 168, 171–2
Grene, Marjorie 49, 81, 111
grooming 106–8
growth and development 49–52, 60,
61, 72
Guattari, Félix 141, 172 n.2
Gunnarsson, Lena 58
gynophobia 36

handmade 108, 110, 169–70
Haraway, Donna 32, 37–8 n.1,
39 n.13, 52, 66 n.2, 72, 74,
141, 163
cyborg 37 n.1, 39 n.13, 74
Hartley, John 150, 151
Hassan, Ihab 31
Hawkes, Kristen 84–5
Hayles, Katherine 25, 27, 33, 35–6,
56–7, 66 n.2, 85, 132 n.6,
156, 164
origins of the human 32
posthuman 19–23, 26, 31, 35
HCI. *See* human-computer interaction
(HCI)
Held, Virginia 49
Herr, Hugh 85–6
Herzog, Werner 121–2, 131 n.2
Hodges, Alan 20
home 9, 27, 36, 39, 54–5, 58–60,
66 n.6, 106, 125–9, 131, 170
cosmopolitan 126

family values   125
  house and   54
  myths of   125, 126
  numbers or configurations of
      people   126, 127
  place   1, 10, 124–6, 129, 137,
      164, 170
  as preservative space   126
  richly numinous space   127
  technology in   60
  unhomely   131
  women's work in   5, 36, 64
homemade   121, 124–6, 169–70
homemaking   10, 54, 66 n.6, 164,
    170
hooks, bell   55, 126, 132 n.8
How We Became Posthuman (1999,
    Hayles)   19–22, 26, 31, 35
Hrdy, Sarah Blaffer   78, 84–5
Hughes, Bree   79
Hughes, Judith   72
human
  abilities   55
  -animal relations   141, 142
  birth of   24, 48–50
  life history   48, 49, 51, 55, 60, 62,
      72, 73, 80
  and machine   34, 46–7, 61
  origins   7, 8, 19, 22, 25, 28–30,
      32, 34, 39 n.12
  premature birth   49
  -robot relations   47
  as symbolizing creatures   112, 113
  -synth relations   46
  -technology relations   7, 8, 27, 34,
      44–6, 60, 62, 71, 170
    imaginative vision for   64
    myth in   109–11
"the human"   24, 53, 72
human-computer interaction
    (HCI)   87 n.5
humanity, and technology   30, 33
human-machine
  boundary   47, 48, 58
  relations   60
human remains   37
Humans (drama)   44–8
  Joe Hawkins (character) in   43, 44,
      59, 62, 63

  Laura Hawkins (character) in   43,
      59, 62, 63
  Renie Hawkins (character) in   44–6,
      48, 58–60, 65
  Sophie Hawkins (character) in
      43–8, 58–65

infantile psychology   130
infants   4, 5, 28, 34, 49, 50, 53, 55,
    57, 59–61, 77, 78, 80, 104–5
  -caregiver relationship   51, 55–7,
      61, 139
  grandmothers and   84–5
  parents care   78
  preterm   74
  soft objects of   57–8, 67 n.8
  storytelling to   57
Internet of (Soft)Things   98
inuit raincoats   94, 115 n.1

Jantzen, Grace   64
Joe Hawkins (character in *Humans*
      drama)   43, 44, 59, 62, 63
Jung, Carl   104, 111–13, 122, 166
  myths   111–12
  numinosity   112–13
Juvenile Synthetic Overidentification
      Disorder (JSOD)   43, 44, 48,
      59, 63

Kashyap, Malika Verma   138
Kaul, Pooja   139
Kaye, Joseph   170–1
Keller, Helen   161–2, 172 n.1
kitchen tables   35–7, 39 n.14, 127,
      154–6, 171
The Kitchen Table Series, 1990
      (Weems)   37, 39 n.14, 154–5
Kittay, Eva   86

Latour, Bruno   7, 32, 111
Laura Hawkins (character in *Humans*
      drama)   43, 59, 62, 63
learning to learn from below   172
Lessing, Doris   140, 143, 156 n.1
Lindemann, Hilde   56, 82, 86
Lorde, Audre   114, 156
Lupton, Deborah   57, 78, 104, 139
Lyotard, Jean-Francois   25, 26

Index

machine 25–7, 31, 33
  child- 21, 35
  human and 34, 46–7, 61
  myth 110
Mandemaker, Lisa 74
mängelwesen, baby as 77–8
Manovich, Lev 56
Manzini, Ezio 6, 169
Massive Change (Mau) 164–7
material culture 57
matter 113
Mau, Bruce 164–8, 172 n.2
Mbembe, Achille 4, 164
meanings 121–2
Meyrowitz, Joshua 127
Midgley, Mary 8, 31, 49, 54, 75, 78,
    82, 94, 99, 132 n.7, 142
  imaginative visions 28–31
  myths 28–31, 33
mind children 24, 25
  Moravec, Hans 21–2, 35
miniaturization 168–9
misfit 86–7
misogynist mythology 114
modern sari 138
Montagu, Ashley 61
Moravec, Hans, mind children 21–2,
    35
mother 5, 6, 25–6, 49–51, 64, 65
  milk 57
  storytelling 57
motherhood 7, 36, 74, 75
mothering 5, 7, 35, 36, 50, 64, 84
move fast and break things 165
Mudde, Anne 82, 83
Mullins, Aimee 85–6
mythogenetics 25, 28–34
myths 8–10, 35, 73, 108–13, 122,
    124, 132 n.7, 163–4
  birth of the posthuman as 28
  cat 140–3
  as form of storytelling 111
  goddess and cyborg 74–5
  of home 125, 126
  in human-technology
      relations 109–11
  imaginative vision as 29–31
  Jung, Carl 111–12
  machine 110

Midgley, Mary 28–31, 33
  of posthuman technogenesis 31
  sari 138–40
  shit 143–8
  storytelling 111, 113
  of technogenesis 64
  technology 94
  television 148–51

N97 mask 108, 109
Nasser, Latif 162
natality 48–9, 52, 59, 62, 64, 65, 72,
    73
Nayar, Pramod 32, 47, 72
Nelson, Maggie 151
Nestle 123, 130
night soil trade 146, 148, 156 n.2
nonhuman 52, 54, 72, 156 n.1
numinosity 112–13, 121–5, 128, 166–7
Nussbaum, Emily 150
Nussbaum, Martha 45

ODF. *See* open defecation free (ODF)
Odisha (India), open defecation
    in 144–5
Oldenburg, Ray 171
open defecation 144–5
open defecation free (ODF) 144, 146
Orrmalm, Alex 104, 105
Ortner, Sherry 30
Other AI 93, 101–2
othermothering 6, 50, 58, 64, 65

pack therapy 103–4
Pallasmaa, Juhani 66 n.6, 95, 110
Park, Shelley 85
Parker, Rozsika 82
pathetic anthropomorphic figure 26
pélage 106–7
personal protective equipment
    (PPE) 108, 109
personhood 4, 48, 49, 58, 60, 62,
    73, 82, 87
  Baier, Annette 41, 50, 51, 54, 56
  psychoanalytic theory 102
  second 7–9, 41, 56, 60, 72–3, 75,
    78, 81–3, 85–7, 93, 102, 108,
    119–20, 125, 130, 137, 139,
    155, 162–3

pets 4, 128, 141, 156 n.1. *See also* cat
Philips, Adam 141
Piercy, Marge 84
Portmann, Adolf 49
Posnock, Ross 102
Poster, Mark 81
posthuman 2–4
  birth of 19–20, 23, 28, 32, 48–50
  cybernetics 22, 36
  design 4
  domestic (*see* domestic posthuman)
  Graham, Elaine 19–20, 23
  Hayles, Katherine 19–23, 26, 31, 35
  imaginative vision 28–30, 33, 64
  mythogenetics 25, 28–34
  origin stories of 7, 8, 19, 22, 25, 28–30, 32, 34, 39 n.12
  technogenesis 19–24, 32, 33, 60, 129
    myth of 31
  and technology 32–4, 47
  value of the concept of 37
posthumanism 3, 4, 7, 28, 31–3, 35, 38 nn.1–2, 52–3, 57, 65, 66 n.2, 72–3, 110
  Badmington, Neil 25–6, 34, 37, 83
  case of Sophie in *Humans* (drama) 43–8, 58–65
  critical 8, 32, 44–8, 52, 53, 58, 60–2, 64–6, 66 n.2, 150, 164
  critique of 57
  and design theory 110
  Google Search 23–4
  Hayles, Katherine 19–23
  as imaginative visions 30
  radical 66 n.2
  second persons 7–9, 73, 75, 81, 85–7, 93, 120
  theorizing the 25–7, 34, 37, 83
  Western philosophy 34
  Wolfe, Cary 19, 23–4
posthumanist gesture 23, 26
postmenopausal women 84
PPE. *See* personal protective equipment (PPE)
premature
  babies 74
  birth 49

preservative homemaking 54
prosthetic coevolution 24
prosthetics 85–6, 124
psychoanalytic theory 102

quantum leap 1
  of imagination 36, 64

radical posthumanism 66 n.2
Rapaille, Clotaire 123–4, 130
Real Humans 46, 47, 60
Reddy, Vasudevi 104
Renie (character in *Humans* drama) 44–6, 48, 58–60, 65
Representations of the Post/Human (2002, Graham) 19, 20
reproduction 73, 74
Rich, Adrienne 5–6, 35–6, 64, 65
  contemporary emergency 5, 36, 64
  quantum leap of imagination 5, 36, 64
Robot and Frank 46–7, 60–1
robots
  caregiving 46–8, 60–2
  embodiment and touch 61
  gendered and racialized 60
  sociable 60, 63
Rochberg-Halton, Eugene 154
Ross, Ivy 93, 97–8

St. Clair, Kassia 94–5, 167
sari 138–40
second personhood 7–9, 41, 56, 60, 72, 73, 75, 78, 81–3, 85–7, 93, 102, 108, 119, 120, 125, 130, 137, 139, 155, 162, 163
self 81–3, 102
  decentered 73, 81, 82
sense 102–3
Shaanxi Mothers 147–8
shit
  biogas 146–8
  Chinese toilets 146
  as gold 146
  management 143
  myth of 143–8
  open defecation 144–5
  sanitation 144–7

Index

teaching and learning   144
toilets   144–6, 148
skin   10, 50, 61, 93–4, 101–3, 105–6,
      130, 132 n.7, 164, 170
   extended   106, 132 n.7
   and mind   102
skin clothing systems   94
skin ego   93, 100–7, 170
skinship   57, 104, 105, 128, 132 n.7,
      139
Small, Meredith   50
Smith, Barbara   37, 155
Smith, Virginia   107
sociable robots   60, 63
social grooming. *See* allogrooming
sociality   50–1, 56–7, 65
soft objects   9, 10, 67 n.8, 97, 98,
      164
   of infants   57–8
soft tactile   99, 170
softwear   7, 93, 96–100, 105, 106,
      113, 128, 163, 170
Solomon, Andrew   125
Soper, Kate   62
Sophie Hawkins (character in *Humans*
      drama)   43–8, 58–65
Spigel, Lynn   54
Spivak, Gayatri   172
Stewart, Susan   169
Stiegler, Bernard   24, 32, 34, 39 n.9
Stone, Alison   48, 49, 51–2, 59,
      105
storytelling   56–7, 94, 95, 107
   myth as form of   111, 113
superskins   104, 105, 132 n.7
   saris as   139
symbols   112, 113
synths   43–4, 46, 47, 58–60, 62, 63

tactile sociality   50, 51, 56, 57, 65
Tanner, Nancy Makepeace   50, 51
technogenesis   48, 60, 73, 75,
      129
   of Baby (first electronic stored-
      program computer)   28
   posthuman   19–24, 32, 33
     myth of   31
technological mediations   4, 52,
      66 n.3

technology   22–4, 26, 27, 31, 34, 37,
      45–8, 52, 59, 62, 64
   change   46
   children and   59, 79–80
   in home   60
   humanity and   30, 33
   impact on care   45, 60
   myths   94
   posthuman and   32–4, 47
technomateriality   93, 96–7, 100
technoscience   8, 20, 32, 34, 39 n.13
television   7, 148–51, 156 n.3
   as caring   151
   dirty pedagogue   150–1
   as transmodern teacher   150–1
Teller, Astro   165–6
textiles   95, 97, 98
   indigo glossy cloth   147–8
theory of everything   75
third places   171
toilets   7, 144–6, 148
toothcomb   107
touch   50–1, 57, 61–2, 93, 100–1,
      103–4, 110, 112, 113, 130.
      See also skin
   infant and caregiver   61
   robots   61, 64
traditional sari   138
transgressing boundaries   58
transmothering   50, 126
Trevathan, Wenda   50
truth   121–2
Turing, Alan   20–1, 39 n.10
   child-machines   21, 35
Turing Test   21, 39 n.10
Twenge, Jean   79

Understanding Nature (Grene)   49
Unheimlich (uncanny, Freud)   129–31
unhomely   121, 128–31

Verbeek, Peter-Paul   164
vocal grooming   106, 107

Wakkary, Ron   6, 7, 11 n.1, 110
Watson, Julia   94
Weems, Carrie Mae   37, 39 n.14, 155
Weheliye, Alexander   53
Weiner, Norbert   161

What Is Posthumanism? (2010, Wolfe) 19, 23–4
Wiessner, Polly 56
Willett, Cynthia 25, 49, 52, 54, 56, 57, 59, 61
 genealogy of the person 50–1
Wilson, Folayemi 41, 67
Winner, Langdon 124
Wolfe 66 n.2, 108, 141, 164
Wolfe, Cary 25, 26, 28
 posthumanism 19, 23–4
womb 73–5, 105
 cybernetic 73–4

women 5, 27, 28, 33–5, 37, 43, 49, 50
 and caregiving 34
 fashion 167
 infantile experience 34
 kitchen as a central space for 155
 work in home 5, 36, 64

Young, Iris Marion 36, 54, 113, 126, 132 n.8, 154

Zihlman, Adrienne 50, 51, 80